THE 111 TRAITS OF A STRONG CHRISTIAN

BY

TIM HICKS © 2016

THE 111 TRAITS OF A STRONG CHRISTIAN

TABLE OF CONTENTS

#110 Seeks to make the most out of every day by being active... pg. 399

#111 Refuses to play the role of cripple... pg. 404

* Take note that among the traits, the common themes will be Reverence, Faith, Courage, Sincerity, Assertiveness, Sacrifice, Joy, and Diligence.

ACKNOWLEDGEMENTS

My sincerest gratitude goes out to Kristi Lehman for all of her time and effort spent on reviewing my manuscript and editing it for coherence, logic, biblical accuracy, spelling, punctuation, syntax and the like. Her Christ-like diligence and commitment to quality have been a tremendous help in bringing this project to fruition. Also, my thanks go out to Brad Knight for his time and effort spent on integrating the elements for the covers and for other computer-related input that he supplied. A big thanks goes to Moriah Tyler, the highly talented artist who painted the picture for the front cover which speaks volumes about Christian strength. Special thanks goes to Rebecca Lenig-Ramirez for helping me with formatting my manuscript on the computer. And, last but not least, a big shout out to all those people who've chosen to be my enemies in life. If it weren't for you, I wouldn't have had such a great prompting to become strong and subsequently to write this book.

*Note that all Scriptures mentioned herein come from the King James version of the Bible.

GLORY TO GOD!

INTRODUCTION: MY TESTIMONY

So, where do I begin? The origins of this book go back to Christ and the times of the Bible writers. Even many childhood experiences of mine have contributed to the writing of this book, some of which I will share throughout. However, there was one crisis in particular that took place in 2004 that set into motion many personal ups and downs that would eventually prompt me to write this.

Back in May of 2004 I had graduated with my Bachelor's degree in Spanish from Towson University in Towson, Maryland. Upon graduation I began looking for jobs in Maryland in which I could use my Spanish degree. I didn't really find any positions that I liked. So, I began to look for jobs teaching English in Costa Rica, the country I had fallen in love with in 2002 during a week-long visit there. I stumbled upon a volunteer position teaching English in Monteverde, a small village in Costa Rica. I figured at least it'd be a way to get my foot in the door for something paid down the road. The volunteer position would start in February 2005. Around September 2004 I volunteered to be a bus chaperone with the bus ministry operated by Church of the Open Door in Westminster, Maryland where I had attended for about 8 years.

On Sunday, October 17, 2004 my life

changed forever. As I was riding in my seat on the church bus along with kids being returned home after church, one of the kids, a tiny 14-year-old boy named Joshua, looked at me and said, "I'm going to sue you for everything you got!" I figured he was upset because one of the kids whose behavior I had corrected was his little sister. I remained quiet the rest of the way home and chose not to ride the church bus anymore after that.

A few weeks had gone by and I received a phone call from a detective Brown with the Carroll County Sheriff's office. He said he wanted me to come in to discuss an incident on the church bus. Knowing that I had done nothing wrong, I agreed to meet with him. During the interview, he asked me if I had threatened Joshua on the bus that day. I, being honest, said no. He told me that the charge of second degree assault was being brought against me because I had (allegedly) roughed Joshua up physically and (allegedly) threatened to bring harm to his family. Detective Brown never considered the possibility that Joshua was lying nor did he mention anything about Joshua's threat to sue me. He ignorantly and automatically believed that Joshua was telling the whole truth. I was arrested and later released that same day on my own recognizance. I was ordered by the court not to leave the state and to appear for trial in April 2005.

I appeared for trial with my attorney who had told me that we were going before a judge

Hughes, who purportedly saw things for what they were. At trial my attorney suggested to me that I not testify on my own behalf because he thought I wouldn't make a good witness (due to my nervousness, I suppose). I took his advice and didn't testify. So, I sat and listened to the testimonies of the plaintiff, Joshua, and his sister. As I had predicted, their testimonies contradicted each other. For example, the one said that I had grabbed Joshua in the chest area and roughed him up as I shouted a threat to him, whereas the other one said that I grabbed his shoulder and roughed him up while whispering a threat to him. They ended up contradicting each other on about 6 different details altogether. My attorney and I both thought that the judge would pick up on these inconsistencies and thus realize that they were lying. I mean, logically, they can't both be telling the truth if they are continuously contradicting each other. It was a no-brainer, I thought. The judge went to his chambers for a few minutes and then returned with his decision. He seemed to waiver back and forth between both sides but ended up pronouncing me guilty. If I hadn't been so apathetic at the time, I probably would've shouted, "You idiot!"

Two months later at sentencing, I was given a 1-year suspended sentence, three years of probation, anger management classes, a psychological evaluation, and a bill for court costs. I attended the anger management classes while seeing psychologist a Dr. Raznick weekly and reporting for monthly probation. After about ten months, the classes were completed and I was about to go back before the same judge, with a letter from the psychologist (that he charged me fifty dollars for) stating that I was well enough psychologically to accept a teaching position which I had been offered via the sister of a Mexican friend of mine. Surprisingly the judge agreed to let me go to take the position, provided that I still report for probation by mail monthly.

I arrived in Guadalajara, Jalisco during holy week in April 2006. A young lady named Talia Peña, whom I had met about a week earlier on a dating site, agreed to pick me up from the airport. We met and she dropped me off at my motel so I could relax and get ready for dinner later on with her. Shortly after I got into the motel room, I turned on a T.V. An episode of the Six Million Dollar Man was on. This just happened to be my most favorite show from childhood even though I had only vague memories of it. I didn't realize it at that moment, but I think that me seeing that show on the T.V., was God's way of saying to me, "It's time to rebuild." Although I didn't believe it then, I needed to be rebuilt emotionally speaking. Talia and I had dinner and she drove me about an hour the next morning to a little town called Jocotepec.

Once in "Joco," I met a lady friend of my aunt who quickly pointed to a touristy place down the road where I ended up living for two of my three months there. Talia went on her way and I only saw her one more time after that at a swimming pool. The school that had hired me had closed up, so I ended up living as a tourist instead of as a teacher. I began to make some friends around town and joined Baudelio's Gym, which was run by local competitive bodybuilder Baudelio Figueroa. While at the gym, Baudelio took me under his wing and gave me a lot of life advice, some of which was biblical. At the gym I felt at home, like I belonged. There was a calling there. I could feel it but couldn't quite see it yet.

When I wasn't in the gym I hung out with Veronica Ochoa, a good friend I had met on my first day in town there. I began to see through her, and some others, that it's possible to live humbly and be content. Half of her home did not have a roof on it, but somehow she and her family found contentment in the little that they had.

I soon found a local Christian church and started attending services there. One night at church during a character-building seminar, I was watching a video of a preacher who said that God allows us to go through storms and trials in order to build our character. I thought the guy was nuts. I didn't realize at the time that God wants us to grow continually in character and thereby increase our emotional strength. I ended up teaching, alongside the pastor there, a soul-winning course that I had translated into Spanish, to interested members of the church. Unbeknownst to me at the time, by teaching people to win souls to Christ, I was actually beginning to put into practice the I-got-you-covered attitude, which later would be revealed to me as one of the traits of a strong Christian.

I returned home after my three months were up and, in 2007, prepared for a trip to Santo Domingo, the capital of the Dominican Republic, to coach baseball to youths there. I was already quite fluent in Spanish at the time, but wanted to work on my Spanish baseball vocabulary. So, I translated every baseball term I could from English to Spanish. I ended up with eighteen pages of terms which I practiced with vigorously so I could use them in conversation while coaching baseball. As it turned out, the kids there were using the English baseball terms regularly, so I didn't really need to know the Spanish terms to communicate with them. It had seemed as if I had labored in vain, but, looking back, I was perfecting my diligence, which would be one of the three main themes of my ministry years later. I'd come to realize eventually that God doesn't do anything half-heartedly, nor should we.

As June of 2008 finally rolled around, my probation was ending and I chose to go to Costa Rica, finally, as a volunteer to build homes for the underprivileged. I originally was placed with a family of five who ran a produce business out of their home. Soon I discovered that the family had some serious communication defects. Lots of yelling and screaming, avoiding conversation with others as much as possible, and so on.

After about 2 months of getting the cold shoulder, I asked to be placed with another family, one who would fulfill my need for conversation and make me feel like I mattered. I got what I asked for. I was placed with a family that regularly conversed with me in an intelligent manner, one with whom I could practice my vocabulary that I was learning, one that made me feel like I was welcome there.

During the day when I was building homes, God would show me another way of living. He was showing me, once again, that I could live humbly and be content, although I still had an attitude of ingratitude from my time in the U.S. Eventually I came to realize that I could live with less, and God taught me how to do so. I became appreciative of the blessings that had been bestowed upon me. I began to read biographies of sports stars for I was fascinated by some of the obstacles that they had overcome. Little by little, God was rebuilding me, and I was overcoming dangerous mindsets that had become traps for me. At the end of my three months there I returned home to the U.S. and worked in the supermarket stocking groceries for several more years, while improving upon my health, strength, and diligence.

In 2012 I was working diligently as a frozen food leader at a supermarket. Certain lazy individuals did not like this, for it went against their spirit of laziness. A certain manager was told about my diligence, but in a negative way, by the lazy people. I was seen as a threat to their way of life, so this particular manager decided to verbally threaten, on the phone, to fire me if I continued to be diligent. It was ridiculous and my head was spinning, for I could not make sense of it. I left this manager a note saying that I would not tolerate his threat and would use the weapons of love and forgiveness to fight this battle. I further was seen as a threat due to my mention of "weapons" and was subsequently fired. I was not worried and knew that God would provide another job for me in due time. When not looking for work, I would spend my days at the park hearing from God. One day He spoke volumes to me. Actually in one twenty-four-hour period at the park, He revealed to me the 111 traits of a strong Christian. I wrote them down hurriedly. Naturally I wanted to translate them into Spanish; so I did. I soon realized the significance of the number 111. A few days before I was fired from my job, I had a prophecy spoken over me by the prophetess Lisa Hicks at a church service. She said I would be seeing three of the same number soon and regularly. I did begin to see three of the same number whenever I looked at the clock. Then I counted the number of traits and found it to be 111. I began to study the traits and put them into practice in my daily life.

A couple of years went by and I returned to Costa Rica for a teaching job. I spent about 2 weeks teaching in a small private school different subjects such as English to children. The job did not work out and I began spending time with some strong Christians through a mutual friend that I had gotten reacquainted with after I had arrived in the country. I felt led to make an impact on the people, to give them something. God led me to share with each Christian leader I knew there a copy of the 111 traits of a strong Christian. I also soon felt led to write this book and to teach some of the traits to a group of homeless people in a local eatery run by a woman named Doña Olga. I ended up teaching six mini-sermons, if you will, to the homeless men and women in this eatery. I then knew that this would be my calling – missionary in Costa Rica, teaching and living out there the 111 traits, exemplifying the God-honoring habits of Health, Strength, and Diligence in order to build up the Costa Ricans so they too can become strong, God-honoring Christians.

So, what is a strong Christian exactly? It's someone who chooses to do what Christ would do in a given situation, as opposed to what the world would typically do. The strong Christian will often stand alone, not follow the crowd, and focus on what pleases God instead of seeking that which man will applaud. In a society where we are brought up to seek to impress man, it is often difficult for one to avoid pleasing man, to please God instead. It's not a matter of knowing better; it's a matter of which spirit you choose to please at a given moment, a spirit of the flesh or the Holy Spirit. You too can become a strong Christian (or stronger) if you so choose. The key word is "choose." Will you choose to do what Christ would do, or will you succumb to the weakness of giving in to the flesh? Follow me and I will show you how you can utilize your God-supplied strength to do what Jesus would do.

Chapter 1

A strong Christian emphasizes the need to associate with the wise

A wise man is strong; yea, a man of knowledge increaseth strength. - Proverbs 24:5

Proverbs 24:6 says, "For by wise counsel, thou shalt make thy war: and in multitude of counselors there is safety." It is by wise choices that our strength is displayed. So, how does one go about acquiring the prerequisite of wisdom? Well, God is more than willing to gift us with wisdom. He mainly shows us wisdom first by leading us to His word in the Bible. If our hearts are ready to receive it, He will put before our spiritual eyes the truth in whatever wisdom is relevant in a given moment. This is when we are alone. God also puts wise people in our lives to help us along.

If I stop to think about it, I can recall hundreds of instances in my life when I was given wise counsel and, as a result, I ended up in safety after doing or saying something because I heeded the counsel. Similarly, I can recall hundreds of instances when I associated with and listened to foolish people and subsequently ended up in trouble. I learned from an early age that it is better to walk alone than to be in bad company. I would go for a while as a loner and then be drawn to someone, thinking so and so probably isn't too bad. I didn't take into account that so and so was probably struggling with his/her own demons. I didn't compare them to Jesus. One such instance was the high-speed police chase I ended up in at the age of sixteen.

One night in the summer of 1993, a co-worker invited me on a little joyride in his grandfather's car, one of those big boats from the 70's. Naively I agreed, thinking it might be fun. We set out sneakily at 2 a.m. and pushed the car down the street from his house, so as not to wake his aunt to the sound of the roaring engine. He started the car, we both got in, and he drove to another area about 20 minutes away. We agreed that I would have a little fun by driving as well, so I hopped into the driver's seat and drove for about 5 minutes to a gas station. We then switched again and he began driving back home while swerving along the roadway for fun. Naturally a cop saw us and attempted to pull us over. My co-worker got the bright idea that eluding him and escaping would be the best way to handle the situation. So, he attempted to do just that and thus the high-speed chase began, which would soon involve about 10 cop cars, give or take. After about 10 minutes or so of 100-mile-per-hour driving, he ended up crashing the car into an embankment at about 30-miles-per-hour. We were subsequently arrested and I quickly began to see the foolishness of my decision to go along with someone who clearly had no intention of utilizing wisdom in his lifestyle choices.

Then, one day as I sat staring at a figure of Jesus Christ on my living room shelf, God taught me a simple lesson: "The more people look like my son Jesus, the less you need to be concerned. The less they look like Him, the more you need to be concerned." In other words, I should be comparing the traits of the people I associate with with those of Jesus. Do they exhibit the fruits of the Spirit? Do they behave like Jesus did? Would they? Are they loving and compassionate towards their fellow man? Do they have your/my best interest at heart? Do they have unselfish motives when dealing with people? The more no answers you get to these questions, the more you need to consider not associating with them.

It is because of my troubles, deceptions, and disappointments etc. with people that I often approach people, asking them questions and telling them truth with childlike sincerity. I want to know early on if the person I'm meeting can handle the truth, and if so, how much truth. Jesus was full of truth and could always be trusted. Therefore, the more truth your associates/friends etc. can handle, the better off you are with them. The more they can't handle the truth, the more you should distance yourself from them. The egotistical-minded person who can handle little truth is not the sort of toxicity you need in your life, for there is no weakness in truth handling (acceptance). The more truth you can handle (accept), the stronger you will become. Therefore, surround yourself with other strong truth-handlers that can build you up and counsel you with strength-enhancing wisdom.

Proverbs 24:12 says, "Be not thou envious against evil men, neither desire to be with them. For their hearts studieth destruction, and their lips talk of mischief."

Chapter 2

A strong Christian recognizes that all strength
ultimately comes from God

The Lord will give strength unto his people; the
Lord will bless his people with peace. - Psalm
29:11

One of the hardest things for man to admit is
that his strength comes from God. Both his
physical and his emotional strength are God-
given. Oftentimes man is duped into thinking, in
reference to his emotional strength, that his
arrogance is his strength; it is not. There is
strength and then there is attitude, also known as
arrogance.

To the untrained eye they might look the
same, but they are not. Strength says I can do all
things through Christ which strengthens me.
Attitude says I can do anything I feel like under
my own power. Strength says I've been hurt, but
I don't seek to hurt others. Attitude says nobody
can hurt me because I'm too tough to get hurt.
Strength says I'm willing to do it God's way.
Attitude says I will do it man's way for he
knows best.

Strength is fueled by the Holy Spirit whereas
attitude is fueled by ego. The arrogant long for
their own glory, and thus can't attribute their
perceived strength to God. Anything ego deems
oneself to be creator. This is foolishness, for all

of us did not originate on our own, but through God's creative hands. All creation originates with Him. All of our earthly projects that we like to take credit for...the credit is due to Him.

I remember in the seventh grade I had had a dispute with the school librarian. I don't even recall what the dispute was about, but I remember feeling slighted. As a result, I ended up writing a rap song (which I had never done before) in order to show her that I couldn't be hurt. The fact was I was hurt, and I sought to get an attitude, which was my defense mechanism. The rhythm of rap music serves this purpose - expressing or exhibiting arrogance so that the intended audience will think that the rapper can't be hurt. But the fact that I wanted to express my inability to be hurt, actually revealed the fact that I, indeed, had been hurt. Instead of being strong and telling the truth that I had been hurt, I decided to get an attitude. The world had taught me that this was strength; it was not.

Looking back years later, I realize that I had been running on ego-driven arrogance. I was not utilizing strength and therefore could not attribute such to God. Remember this - there is no arrogance in strength. There is only God-inspired courage. The more you attribute your strength to God, the stronger you will become.

Proverbs 8:13,14 say, "The fear of the Lord is to hate evil: pride, and arrogancy, and the evil way, and the froward mouth do I hate. Counsel is mine, and sound wisdom: I am understanding;

I have strength."

Chapter 3

A strong Christian seeks to exemplify the fruits of the Spirit in his/her daily walk

But the fruit of the Spirit is love, joy, peace, long-suffering, gentleness, goodness, faith, meekness, temperance: against such there is no law. - Galatians 5:22,23

Just as we awaken each day with the option to choose either wisdom or foolishness, we also choose daily to exemplify either the fruits of the Spirit or the works of the flesh. Only Jesus was able to walk this Earth and not succumb to the works of the flesh. So, in our sin-natured bodies, we have to realize that it's not a matter of knowing which one is better. It'll ultimately come down to which one you decide to succumb to. The weak will choose the works of the flesh, whereas the strong will choose the fruits of the Spirit. Oftentimes we say we know better but choose worse. Why? Because we tend to do whatever feels best as opposed to doing what we know is best.

A strong Christian will choose to exemplify the fruits because the Holy Spirit lets him/her know that doing so requires strength. Any old weakling can easily succumb to the works of the flesh, but as Christians we are to stay away from them. The more you can stay away from them and exemplify the fruits, the stronger you are. This daily choice between the two is mainly what sets apart the weak from the strong. The weak will often give in to peer pressure and instant gratification, foolishly believing they are doing what is most beneficial to them. The strong tend to foresee the end thereof in succumbing to those things and how it is foolish to exhibit the works of the flesh.

The works of the flesh work against the fruits of the Spirit. For every work of the flesh, there is a fruit of the Spirit that can defeat it. For example, love defeats hatred. Some fruits will be easier to exhibit than others, based on our desires. I personally have struggled with patience throughout my life. I've always been a very fast-paced person, seeking instant gratification. I have come a long way in this area. With God's help, I have moderated my pace. A lot has to do with my priorities and my trust in God. The more I got my priorities lined up with God's, the more patient I learned to be with His other children. God had taught me that there is strength in patience. Any old weakling can go around being impatient, but it takes strength to restrain oneself, knowing that God has empowered you to use patience with those who need it.

So, one's strength will typically be shown when he/she does the opposite of what the majority would do. The majority will seek to please the flesh; the minority will seek to please the Spirit. How strong will you choose to be in your daily walk when given the choice between the works and the fruits?

Galatians 5:24,25 say, "And they that are Christ's have crucified the flesh with the affections and lusts. If we live in the Spirit, let us also walk in the Spirit."

Chapter 4

A strong Christian respects God's creations as such and seeks to preserve life rather than to destroy it

Thou shalt not kill. - Exodus 20:13

As unfortunate as it may be, a few times in life we may find ourselves causing harm to another living creature in order to protect ourselves from harm. This should be the exception, the only time we bring harm to another. As one of God's many creations we are to seek keeping creations alive. This is why God entrusted Adam, the first man, with looking after God's animals.

Sometimes it may be necessary to end the life of a clean creature, and that it is ok to eat, such as fish that have fins and scales. Such creatures are for our food. The good Lord gave us certain creatures to be eaten. So, it's ok to end their life if they are to be eaten. When it comes to men, however, we are not to act as weaklings, giving into the work of the flesh by murdering.

Often times Satan, in his trickery, will convince one who is bent on murder, that he/she is trapped and that murder is the key to freeing oneself. The murderer has not been convinced of the aforementioned Christian trait. He/she does not possess, nor desires to exhibit, the fruits of the Spirit. His/her ego is too strong-willed to acquiesce before the potential murder victim. The murderer, when he/she murders, is saying to God, "I don't desire to honor you. I don't desire to fulfill my purpose." This is a weak mindset, one which you don't have to possess. You can choose to walk with the mindset of a strong Christian.

I remember when I was six-years-old I was accosted by a boy a year younger than me. I was just minding my own business, playing as one does at that age. There was a brief physical attack, but I was not seriously injured. I remember throughout the years, right up until graduation, him messing with me from time to time with the intent to harm me. I could discern that he had demons inside of him and had no regard for the life of another. I could tell he was the type who would kill another human being in cold blood. Years later, when I was about thirty or so, I read in the local newspaper that this boy, as a man, had shot two men over drugs in the back parking lot of a convenience store in my home town. Eventually he was arrested and put on trial for murder. Had he chosen to respect God's creations by seeking to preserve life rather than to destroy it, his life might have turned out differently. He had foolishly chosen not to walk as a strong Christian, ignoring God's word.

The strong Christian, while respecting God's creations as such and seeking to preserve life, says to God, "You knew what you were doing when You created life." The strong Christian, while realizing that all creation has its purpose, lends a helping hand. Anything we do to promote the furtherance of the life of God's creations, the more we honor God. The more honor we bring to God, the stronger we become. Remember the weak seek to dishonor Him. Therefore, it is our duty as strong Christians to abstain from weakness by taking care of His purpose-filled creations.

Ephesians 4:32 says, "And be ye kind one to another, tenderhearted, forgiving one another, even as God for Christ's sake hath forgiven you."

Chapter 5

A strong Christian recognizes that God and the Bible are the final authority in his/her life

For the word of God is quick, and powerful, and sharper than any two-edged sword, piercing even to the dividing asunder of soul and spirit, and of the joints and marrow, and is a discerner of the thoughts and intents of the heart. – Hebrews 4:12

As young people trying to fit in and find our place in this world, we have a tendency to seek out that one person, or sometimes group of people, that has "the answers." When we don't have a mentor or someone to look up to, we tend to seek out those who seemingly have been equipped with "the superior human mindset." This mindset doesn't exist in anyone but Jesus Christ. We can learn this mindset by studying the Bible, especially the New Testament parts that deal with Christ's life. Christ is the only one whose mindset we should seek to have. All others fall short.

Since God is the only one ultimately authorized to judge us, it is to His authority that we should submit. Oftentimes we erroneously go about seeking the approval of so-called authority figures who think they've been equipped with the superior human mindset. They may indeed appear to have temporary authority over you in a given situation, but ultimately it's to God's authority that you must answer. It is to biblical standards to which we will be held accountable regarding our actions.

The weak will give in to peer pressure and will convince themselves that man is the final authority on human conduct. The strong shall be set apart by their unwillingness to be coerced into conforming to any type of anti-biblical acquiescence. In other words, they act decisively according to God's authority as told in the Bible. They do what Jesus would do. Oftentimes people, with feigned inquisitiveness, would ask Jesus trick questions to see if He would reply in such a way that would implicate himself as willing to deviate from His Father's authority. Jesus was never willing to do so. Even today such questions are asked of us, to see if we will put man's authority above God's. As strong Christians we are not to succumb. This, I admit, will be more difficult than other strong Christian traits to exhibit, but it can be done. For many they will find themselves justifying the possible relinquishment of certain dreams, goals, and freedoms as they contemplate which authority to submit to. Remember, you can be that strong Christian who takes a stand, serving as an example for others. Also, remembering that your fellow man has not been equipped with the superior human mindset will make it easier to walk this trait out. The question is: who are you trying to please, God or man?

Proverbs 16:25 says, "There is a way that seemeth right unto a man, but the end thereof are the ways of death."

Chapter 6

A strong Christian takes seriously the stewardship of all of God's resources

And God said, Let us make man in our image, after our likeness: and let them have dominion over the fish of the sea, and over the fowl of the air, and over the cattle, and over all the earth, and over every creeping thing that creepeth upon the earth. - Genesis 1:26

God put man in charge of His resources while on Earth, but oftentimes I will see man wasting these resources. People will use produce to have food fights. Poor people will be exploited for the greed of the wealthy. Money will be used to satisfy lustful desires. The Sun's energy will be neglected, as well as that of the wind and water. Our own bodies, will be neglected for the sake of pleasing the flesh, when we could be utilizing them for good. The list goes on and on regarding man's wastefulness. The attitude of carelessness is not what God intended for us.

God intended for us to administer the resources that He supplied in a way that would be beneficial to mankind, so that nothing would go to waste. Even the excrement of animals can be used for fertilizer. One has to think that something is seriously wrong with man's priorities when there are nations who seek to deprive the poor and give excessively to the rich. When God created man, He supplied him with plenty of resources: fruits and vegetables for food; animals for labor, transport, and food; water and milk for drinking; bees for honey; the Sun for light and energy etc. When we are not good serious stewards of these resources, we are being wasteful, and Earth's inhabitants suffer as a result.

People will go hungry and become ill. Electric bills will soar. Man will develop a disdain for his fellow man's well-being. These resources are provided for man's well-being, not for his greed and neglect. Let's not forget the Bible as one of God's resources. The great book is replete with information, wisdom, and tools to help maximize our effectiveness here on Earth. We read how Jesus made sure everyone had enough to eat. Jesus never wasted God's resources. He sought to be a good steward for mankind's benefit. Since God will supply all of our needs, it is of utmost importance that we administer the resources we have, not worrying about tomorrow, for God will provide without fail.

Unlike the greedy thief who says that God will not supply, we are to trust in His provision, and be constantly on the lookout for opportunities to be good stewards so that man benefits and God gets the glory. The weak won't take seriously stewardship for they do not value their relationship with God enough to do so. The strong, however, choose to follow Jesus's example by not following the crowd, by utilizing God-supplied resources for the benefit of Earth's inhabitants. The more seriously you take this stewardship thing, the stronger you are and the stronger your commitment to your relationship with God will be.

Genesis 1:28 says, "And God blessed them, and God said unto them, Be fruitful, and multiply, and replenish the earth, and subdue it: and have dominion over the fish of the sea, and over the fowl of the air, and over every living thing that moveth upon the earth."

Chapter 7

A strong Christian appreciates openly the nature that God created

And they were both naked, the man and his wife, and were not ashamed. - Genesis 2:25

When one is a good steward of God's resources, it is probably because one has come to appreciate the nature that God created. There is an attitude of gratitude that we should all possess in regard to God's creations, as we recognize that everything in nature has its purpose in this world. Oftentimes we dislike or have disdain for the very things that God created, which is to say that God created something useless; it's not true. We are not to take for granted the things in nature that God provided. All things have been created to fit into His divine plan for this world. Many times I hear people complain of the rain, the snow, the cold, the heat, the humidity, and so on. I myself have been one of the complainers. Once I came to realize that a) God doesn't make mistakes and b) everything has its purpose, I started appreciating what God created. The more I saw how everything He created was good, the more I realized how much He knew what He was doing when He created it all.

The things in nature that we don't appreciate oftentimes seem to trouble us or cause us discomfort. For example, when I worked at a grocery store, I was suddenly thrust into a position working frozen foods full-time. I was not looking forward to this since I had a disdain for the extreme cold because it made me uncomfortable, especially in the hands. But over time I came to appreciate the extreme cold. I realized that it helped to keep many foods for people to eat later. I realized it helped to even out my body temperature as I worked arduously, sweating to keep the freezer organized. As God had me in this role of frozen food leader, He essentially was making me stronger. I came to withstand temperatures and conditions that I previously had been uncomfortable with. I was leaving weakness and ingratitude and entering into a mindset of strength and self-confidence. My diligence and patience were increasing as well. I could see how my increased handling of the very things I didn't appreciate before was making me stronger. It wasn't so much a matter of ability as it was a matter of a changed mindset. I came to become comfortable with the thing that I had not appreciated before. I was in a new comfort zone and felt overjoyed knowing that God had brought me there for my betterment.

I find it rather disheartening when I hear people say that they hate the rain or the snow. Since God created these things, and all things that He created were good, we are being ungrateful or unappreciative when we say such things. The people who don't appreciate the things in nature choose to remain in weakness. The strong Christian appreciates openly these things, choosing to recognize that God created such things not only for a purpose, but also to challenge us to grow in character. The more we choose to appreciate God's natural creations, the stronger we become. The more we appreciate nature, the more likely we are to worship God, for we see that His mighty hand was at work creating those things. I find it to be much more peaceful when I'm out in nature, in the woods, surrounded only by God-made things, away from man-made things. When we focus on man-made things, we tend to look to man for answers. When we focus on God-made things, we tend to see the care and love that He made those things with, thinking about us as He did so.

When I see women in their natural state, they look best. It's not that some women don't look prettier fixed up. It's that there is an unpretentiousness that is appealing and attractive. When people avoid the natural look, it's their way of saying, "I choose to deviate from the way God created me to be." I know from experience that that is a dangerous mindset, one which can cause a lot of headaches and undue stress. Happy is he who appreciates the nature that God created and subsequently gives Him thanks for it. In return God will bless him/her who does give thanks. It's part of how a mutual relationship with God works. The more you choose to appreciate openly (as opposed to being ungrateful) the nature that God created, the more pleased He is with you and the stronger you will become, knowing God created such things for your growth, not to annoy you.

Chapter 8

A strong Christian realizes his/her time is too precious to waste on worldly judgment

Grudge not one against another, brethren, lest ye be condemned: behold, the judge standeth before the door. - James 5:9

You might be wondering what worldly judgment is. Worldly judgment is using one's own standards, as opposed to biblical standards, to judge one's fellow man. We know we are judging someone when we hold someone else's perceived wrong against the person, usually in the form of a grudge. Let's say, for example, I see a man enter my church building wearing tattered rags which are dirty. I see he wants to enter the sanctuary for the Sunday service. If I look down on him and silently accuse him of knowing better, because I think that he should be dressed in his "Sunday best" so as to impress people or God, then I am using my own standard to judge him, for there is no biblical dress code. God is more concerned with the inside of a person than He is with the outside.

For about 10 years I went to a certain church where this sort of judgment was rampant. I would constantly hear the pastor criticize people and certain denominations for their standards. There was even a certain deacon who criticized me for the amount of money I gave to the church, as well as the kind of clothing I wore there. I asked him what the biblical dress code standard was. He told me he'd have a verse about it the next time we met. Next time came. And the time after that. And the time after that. He never could tell me the verse wherein it speaks of the "biblical dress code." It's because there is no biblical dress code. He even criticized Christian rock music. I asked him what kind of music was truly Christian worship music. He said "The kind they play at our church," meaning only old-time hymn type music. Again he had no verse to back up what he was saying. A part of me began, for a while, to adopt this sort of judgmental mentality. Even though I saw the hypocrisy of it all, I learned to be a performer, that is, to act Christian on Sunday but to let loose the rest of the week, for I saw this sort of behavior in the people I went to church with.

I went around for years with that mentality that I should have one foot in the world, and the other in God's kingdom. Since I saw worldly judgment coming from the pastoral team and all other church leadership, I felt justified in my approach of going around judging people based on my own standards. It was a certain haughtiness although I didn't realize it at the time. I was walking around in weakness, too chicken to give up worldly judgment. I struggled for a long time with this type of judgment and I sought for God to set me straight about it, for I knew I didn't have a healthy mindset. Then, one day, God revealed to me some things, via a radio sermon by Dr. Tony Evans, about worldly judgment. God revealed that we aren't to use worldly judgment on others (or ourselves, for that matter). Rather we are to use discernment to avoid what is foolish and to seek that which is wise.

The weak foolishly go around wasting their time by using worldly judgment on others for two main reasons: 1) so they can feel superior; 2) because they feel they were called to judge others in this way. First of all, we weren't called to feel superior to our fellow man. Secondly, we weren't called to use worldly judgment on them. Once you realize you weren't called by God almighty to do these two things, then you should start to focus on spending your time understanding others' perceived mistakes, shortcomings, errors, sins, wrongdoings and the like. Once you have understood that we all make mistakes and that our imperfect nature causes us to slip up, you open the door for compassion. Once you have compassion in your heart, then you just may realize how good it feels to build others up. The more you do this, the more you will distance yourself from that unhealthy mindset of worldly judgment. The more you distance yourself from that mindset, the stronger you will become. Remember, the weak think that if they don't judge in this way, then they are not harnessing a potential tool to make themselves feel superior. A strong Christian, however, realizes there is no strength in using worldly judgment on people, for his/her time is too precious to waste on those things that could only serve to puff up our ego.

I Samuel 16:7 says, "But the LORD said unto Samuel, Look not on his countenance, or on the height of his stature; because I have refused him: for the LORD seeth not as man seeth; for man looketh on the outward appearance, but the LORD looketh on the heart."

Chapter 9

A strong Christian sets out to treat all of God's creation with dignity and humanity without being a respecter of persons

Then Peter opened his mouth, and said, Of a truth I perceive that God is no respecter of persons: - Acts 10:34

I know from personal experience how it feels not to be treated with dignity and humanity. Often times, so we can feel smart or powerful, we categorize people and treat them according to what category they best seem to fit into. We come up with category titles such as homeless, aristocratic, and middle class and tend to assign a certain worthiness to each person based on his/her title. God doesn't need to separate people into classes, for we are all the same in His eyes. That's what being no respecter of persons means. We aren't to treat people better or worse because of some perceived category we might think they fit into.

It is often those who are perceived as being in the "lowest" class that are treated the worst in a society. There is a high correlation between our perception of others' identity and the way we tend to treat them. For example, if we think that someone is royalty, we tend to treat him/her quite well; a young lad courting a young lady, for instance. If we think that people are human garbage, we tend to treat them accordingly. Satan wants us to categorize people in this way so that we end up easily being able to justify not treating certain people with dignity and humanity; in other words, with honor and worthiness. God did not create certain people to be treated poorly. More times than not, people actually end up playing the role of someone who doesn't feel worthy or honorable because the belief that he/she is so has been drilled into his/her head repeatedly for years. Without even realizing that Satan is persuading them, many people will sinfully look down on others in an undignified way and treat them inhumanely. It boils down to man's ego and his sinful desire to feel superior to his fellow man. Once again we aren't called to feel superior to our fellow man.

It might just occur to you that if you treat people like they are worthy of honor and dignity, they might end up believing they are so. Jesus did not discriminate; he talked with people of all walks of life. His treatment of people did not depend on their perceived position in society. He didn't feel the need to puff up his ego by talking down to someone. He simply and plainly told the truth to all without being a respecter of persons. He treated everyone with dignity and humanity regardless of how sinful they might have appeared in the eyes of the world.

Many times I have been discriminated against in my life. I didn't need to ask for the discrimination. It was others' perception of my identity and their ego that caused them to treat me without dignity and humanity. I remember in

2008 when I was living in Costa Rica. I found out through a roommate that the rest of the English-speaking volunteers (about 10 people) that were there were planning a trip to a resort town the same day. I said that I wanted to go. I met up with them but could tell right away through vibes, bodily language, and tone of voice that I was not welcomed by certain "cool" people. I knew in my mind that I didn't fit into their perceived idea of coolness, but I didn't care; I wanted to go anyway. When we were in the resort town, I noticed that every time the "cool" people wanted a picture taken, I was the one who was asked to take the picture. I'm sure they thought they were pulling the wool over my eyes, but they weren't. They simply figured that if I were the one taking the picture, then I couldn't appear in it, thereby "eliminating" all their fears of having to remember me when they looked at the pictures in the future. Having been on the receiving end of such treatment, I desire even further to avoid treating others in this way. It is through such experiences, that God allows, that our character grows, or can grow. Oftentimes God permits us to experience others in this way in order to show us how not to be.

Remember, a strong Christian doesn't discriminate based on some perceived category that the weaklings in the world would have others fit into. A strong Christian sets out to treat others with the same dignity and humanity that Christ showed towards people. To do otherwise is usually an indication that there is a heart problem fueled by one's ego. We don't have to follow the same pattern as the weak, thinking we are too cool to treat others like they are beneath us. The more you can treat others in a Christ-like way, the stronger you will become.

James 2:9 says," But if ye have respect to persons, ye commit sin, and are convinced of the law as transgressors."

Chapter 10

A strong Christian takes care of number one in order to take care of number two

Slothfulness casteth into a deep sleep; and an idle soul shall suffer hunger. - Proverbs 19:15

I remember some time ago seeing a documentary about a 900-pound woman who died at age 29 from obvious weight-related causes. Her children, thin and relatively healthy, were left motherless. Children need their mother. That got me thinking about my own mother who died at age 49 from the effects of the slothful lifestyle. From 10 years of age and onward, I was without a mother at home. It would be about another 12 years until her death, but her absence made an impact on my development, for I lacked that nurturing parent that helps a child to grow up healthily. Fortunately, I had a revelation during her time in the hospital that made a positive impact on my life.

In 1987 my mom walked out on me, my dad, and my siblings. She kept in contact, but was not there to play her motherly role. Truthfully I was glad she was gone because she was a smoker; and I hated smokers. On the other hand, I was longing for a mom, as well as a non-dysfunctional family. I did without the best I could, and even tried, albeit rather unsuccessfully, to cling onto certain women my dad was dating after my mom's departure. With my dad working 2 or 3 jobs to keep the house running, I pretty much ended up raising myself. I did alright and even made some occasional blunders along the way, but it never was the way it should have been without a mom present.

Fast forward to 1996. I remember my mom, who had received a full set of dentures the year before at age 45, went into the hospital for a quintuple bypass operation. She had spent the previous 35 years of her life as a smoker, a junk food addict, and living the slothful lifestyle in a dirty apartment alongside her new husband. It was sad for me to have seen her demise, from a weekly Sunday school teacher in the late 70's to her utter neglect of her temple. God gave her another chance. She stopped smoking for a while, but her husband continued to smoke. I was 19 at the time and grudgingly bought a pack of cigarettes for her husband when she asked me to, as she rode around the grocery store in a motorized shopping cart, too weak (or unwilling) to push her own cart. God, through a local church, had provided her with a new apartment and all that she needed to get back on her feet again. She was unwilling to make enough of a change in lifestyle to make significant progress.

It had been 3 years since her operation when Christmas of 1999 came. Against the advice of many family members present at our Christmas gathering, she began smoking again. That was the last time I saw her alive. Two weeks later, due to her health problems caused by sloth and gluttony, she passed away in her sleep. I had lost the one person who had given birth to me. She had not taken care of number one, so she couldn't take care of number two, which was me. I had learned some of her gluttonous, slothful ways as a child, and it has been somewhat of a struggle to shake off those bad habits throughout the years.

The revelation I had during one of her stints in the hospital in the late 90's happened while I was in the waiting room. I had been into weight training and fit living for some years up to that point, but it was when I was watching a Kiana Tom exercise program on a TV that it really hit me. The Holy Spirit spoke to me while I was watching it and said, "Fitness and health are the answer." What He meant was that sloth and gluttony were not the traits that I, Tim Hicks, should be living out. When Jesus walked the Earth, He took care of himself in a healthy way, so that He could be there for others who needed Him. Sick people aren't known for being there for others in times of need; healthy people are. We must learn to resist the fleshly ways of this world and take care of number one if we are to be there for number two, whomever that may be. The strong will resist the temptation to give into slothfulness. The more you abhor slothfulness and the detriment thereof, the stronger you will become.

Proverbs 22:6 says, "Train up a child in the way he should go: and when he is old, he will not depart from it."

Chapter 11

A strong Christian realizes that all life has its purpose

And God said, Behold, I have given you, every herb bearing seed, which is upon the face of all the earth, and every tree, in the which is the fruit of a tree yielding seed ; to you it shall be for meat. - Genesis 1:29

I remember at age 15 receiving the revelation that all life has its purpose. As a child I had questioned the existence of God. Then, one day, I saw that someone must have created everything around us. I began to see that nothing was created accidentally. I saw that each thing in nature had its purpose. People, for example, are created for honoring God with our lives, with our conduct. Dogs are created to provide companionship to the lonely and to teach us humans about true friendship. Trees are created for shade, shelter, and many other things. Scavengers are created to be nature's garbage disposals in the air, in the water, and on land. Goats provide milk for our nourishment. Bees provide honey for the same reason. Plants provide medicine for our well-being. The Sun provides light and energy. The mountains provide an opportunity for us to exercise. The snow provides a break from summer and a chance for us to get stronger by enduring and handling cold temperatures. The list goes on and on.

I find it to be rather sad that many people think tobacco is to be chewed or smoked; it isn't. It should go without saying that tobacco consumption leads only to unhealth and disease, physical and mental. There are no health benefits to smoking tobacco; in it, there is only utter disdain for God's will for us to honor Him by taking care of our temples. The weak will often use things in nature for purposes they are not meant to serve. They will eat junk food of any type and grow ill. They will drink and get drunk, thereby killing brain cells. They will get black lung disease by working in the coal mine instead of harnessing the energy provided by the wind, Sun, and water, not to mention their own food. Man will create all sorts of technological gadgets to get out of performing labor instead of using the God-given things in nature to get something done. The weak often choose to ignore the purposes that God intended for all life, in order to do things man's way. Man often thinks that he can one-up God by creating something with a purpose so as not to "succumb" to the purported "weakness" or "dullness" in God's creations.

A strong Christian, however, sees the foolishness in man's thinking and the wisdom in God's creative hands. The strong Christian realizes that if he/she does things according to the purposes intended by God for the life He created, things will go much more smoothly for him/her. For example, when a man and a woman copulate, a baby can soon be born. When homosexuals do their thing, a baby can't be born. Therefore, men and women weren't meant for homosexual behavior, for it serves no godly purpose. Certain diseases exist because of man's sin. Oftentimes those who are sexually improper get infected with such diseases because they neglected to realize the real purposes of the things in nature. When man plants seeds in the ground, food grows up for him to eat. When he takes care of his animals, they grow healthy enough to provide milk, eggs, and honey for him, all of which give him health. When he cares for his horses, they can provide transportation for him. When cares for his oxen, they can provide muscle on the farm.

This isn't rocket science, at least not to me it isn't. It works rather simply: use the things in nature for the purpose God designed them for and God will bless you for it. This is because God looks at your intentions. He knows what purpose you assign to the things in life. By taking this into account and using life for its designated purposes, you are honoring God and thus being strong in your Christian walk. The more you do this, the stronger you are.

Genesis 1:30 says, "And to every beast of the earth, and to every fowl of the air, and to everything that creepeth upon the earth, wherein there is life, I have given every green herb for meat: and it was so."

Chapter 12

A strong Christian assesses the past, not to criticize negatively, but only to see how things should be done in the future

...saith the LORD: for I will forgive their iniquity, and I will remember their sin no more. - Jeremiah 31:34

There is a fruitlessness in dwelling regretfully on past mistakes that we should aim to avoid. Oftentimes we think, "So and so should have known better," as if we all came into this world "knowing better." It'd be quite fruitful for us to reflect and confess our past mistakes and then move on quickly as opposed to living in regret. Regretters tend to be perfectionists who waste their time trying to reach an unrealistic standard or expectation. I am one of them.

I've noticed in my own life that the more I get away from the worldly judgment mindset, the less I tend to remember the past mistakes of others. It is because of this lack of dwelling that I know I'm not focused on judging others for their past mistakes. Instead, when I do recall a mistake, I make a fervent effort to avoid it and to do things in a good way. All too often those who mistakenly believe they were called to judge others based on others' past mistakes, are still stuck in that judgmental mindset. We see this play out a lot in the political arena. What do candidates do? They dig up all the dirt they can on their opponents and try to convince potential voters that they should tie the other candidates' past mistakes to their current identity. Muckraker politics is what it's called. It's a trick of Satan. Our identities, in actuality, are not tied to our past mistakes. Your identity and the traits you display are two different things. If we follow the mindset of the muckrakers, then EVERYBODY can be identified as a dirty politician, for all have fallen short of the sinless glory of God.

I could do some dirt digging of my own and then easily turn the tables on you by convincing people that the mistakes of your yesterday are who you are today. Now how would that feel? Not good, I bet. But, it would be fair! Oftentimes I have thought, "If I had only done things differently, I would not be in my current mess". It's alright to think this momentarily, but we don't want to dwell on this type of thought so that it eats away at us. I've even gone so far as visiting "safe sites" -- places where I felt safe just before I fell into some tragedy or crisis. I'd go there as a way of "traveling back in time." I felt that if I could re-create a safe scenario that existed before my fall, then I could somehow take a different path that would lead to a safe present-day existence. Our pasts exist so we can learn from them, so they can be used for testimonies, so we can see how to do things in the future. Our pasts can't be changed unfortunately. It's nice to think, sometimes, that they can!

So, it's important to use our discernment so as not to fall into the traps that might bring us regret. It's important to use those past experiences of ours and of others to avoid making foolish mistakes in the future. It's for our betterment. It's to show others a righteous way of living. It shows others that we are overcomers and that we seek to live wisely.

Psalm 37:3 says, "Trust in the Lord, and do good; so shalt thou dwell in the land, and verily thou shalt be fed."

Chapter 13

A strong Christian puts godliness before the
standards of men

*If any of you lack wisdom, let him ask of God,
that giveth to all men liberally, and upbraideth
not; and it shall be given him. - James 1:5*

Oftentimes as young people we lack answers,
So, what do we tend to do? All too often we
ignorantly seek out man's way of doing
something. We first create an idol, that is to say,
someone who seemingly has "the answers."
That one person whose philosophy will lead us
down the road to righteousness. Once we view
that person as having the answers, we tend to
blindly accept anything that comes out of
his/her mouth. I can think of a million examples
of men and women who, in human history, were
philosophers, scholars, professors, leaders,
dictators and so forth who had followers. The
followers oftentimes were people who chose to
follow the teachings and the standards of the
men and women they were following as
opposed to the teachings and standards of Jesus
Christ.

I can remember as a young person, being a
bit misguided in some areas, in search of a
mentor. We live in a "monkey see, monkey do"
society; we often imitate the behavior we see. I
grew up watching shows about strong men: The
Incredible Hulk (Lou Ferrigno), He-Man, The
Six Million Dollar Man etc. I was fascinated by

strength, which is what led to my early participation in weightlifting and bodybuilding. I was enticed to live a healthy life by the shows, movies, and characters I saw. Some of this is good, insofar as the philosophies and traits I follow are godly. We have to be careful, though, not to fall into that trap of idolizing someone and then blindly following their standards, however evil or ungodly they may be. Been there, done that.

It takes strength to put godly standards before the standards of men. Men will devise all sorts of macho standards for other men to try to measure up to. This behavior is rooted in man's ego; it should be avoided. For example, a top pro-bodybuilder will come out with a workout video or book to get you to do things his/her way, as opposed to a godly way. Oftentimes man will try to one-up God in the nutrition field by coming out with a "superior" line of nutritional products to get you healthy. I've got news for you: you can't one-up God. This one-upmanship bit against God is one of Satan's oldest tricks. He will get you to follow some financial guru, some overpriced psychologist, some overpriced personal trainer, some egotistical sociopath who is willing to trick you into thinking they have "the answers."

It says it simply in James 1:5. All we have to do is ask God for wisdom and He will gladly give it to us. He wants us to have it and to use it daily. Proverbs is my favorite book in all of the Bible because of all the tidbits of valuable wisdom it contains that I can and have used to do things wisely and avoid foolishness. When you are dealing with someone who may seemingly think he/she has the answers, ask yourself if it seems likely that he/she prayed to God recently for wisdom. Look at how they have been living. Do a little digging. Do they appear to be living according to godly standards or do they seem like they are following some man-made way of life?

Remember, the weak will weakly succumb to man's way, foolishly thinking that man knows best. The strong are wise and realize that God knows best. The strong will learn to think for themselves and not follow the crowd, avoiding idolizing man, and following the standards of Jesus.

Colossians 3:5 says," Mortify therefore your members which are upon the earth; fornication, uncleanness, inordinate affection, evil concupiscence, and covetousness, which is idolatry:"

Chapter 14

A strong Christian seeks the company of the meek and humble

The meek also shall increase their joy in the LORD, and the poor among men shall rejoice in the Holy One of Israel. - Isaiah 29:19

One of my favorite parts about being humble is the joy it brings. Humble can be defined as "having or showing a consciousness of one's defects or shortcomings." The more I make an effort to be humble, the more I realize how it strengthens me and how it takes strength to be humble in the first place. Having been raised in a Christian home, I learned from an early age that humility is good and arrogance is bad. I find there is much strength in the ability to remain humble. It has a lot to do with me seeing the weakness in the opposite: arrogance. The arrogant will get an attitude, falsely believing that what they possess is strength. Oftentimes people have a skewed view of humility. They associate it with weakness, as if it's all about bowing down like a weakling in some self-degrading way before others; that's not what it's about.

Being humble is about recognizing that one is a sinner and, therefore, has shortcomings. It's about not being judgmental about past mistakes, but being rather matter-of-fact instead. There is a lot of strength in humility because it actually takes quite a bit of self-control to be humble, to resist the temptation to show off one's supposed superiority. I remember always being put off by the arrogant when I was growing up. God allowed me to experience being around them to show me how not to be, how ugly arrogance is.

Meek can be defined as "patient and mild" or as a synonym of humble. Either way, there is no weakness in meekness. On the contrary, there is only strength in meekness and humility. It is too easy to succumb to the flesh and man's ego by being arrogant when tempted by one's fellow man. I used to think like the world and get a somewhat arrogant attitude when I was attacked by a hurt person. I learned to be matter-of-fact about things. I came to realize that peoples' verbal assaults on me were due to some hurt in their past, not because of something I had done to them in the previous five minutes. God taught me that those people were hurting, not walking in the joy of the Lord, not praying for wisdom, and didn't know about Christian strength. As the world sees the meek and humble as weaklings, they seek not their company.

I make an effort to seek out their company. I know that the meek and humble tend to be more real. They are often not putting on some show of feigned strength. I am more likely to get the truth out of them when I converse with them. The arrogant, with their typical attitude of entitlement, will tend to seek out the "finer things" in life. They tend to be honing their skills at living the superficial lifestyle to a T. They often go about misled, thinking they are living as strong individuals, but actually need to have that arrogance broken off of them. Usually, but not always, the meek and humble have already experienced some cathartic moment which prompted them to seek a meek and humble existence. They might have been arrogant people at one time who just got tired of trying so hard to be "strong." Oftentimes, especially in the U.S., people just need to get out of the rat race and live humbly. For me, personally, I found out years ago after purchasing my first home that my financial situation was much better as a result of seeking a meek and humble lifestyle. Surely I was working hard to make money, but I wasn't getting overstressed because of some societal pressure to keep up with the neighbors. Remember, it is often your neighbor who prompts you to do what you do. Are you coveting what he/she has? You just may find that hanging with the meek and humble will bring a peace that can be had only by those who choose not to acquire the traits and things that go along with the arrogant lifestyle. Remember, the more you see the strength in humility and meekness, the more you will want them. The more you get them and avoid arrogance through self-control, the stronger you will become.

Psalm 25:9 says," The meek will he guide in judgment: and the meek will he teach his way."

Chapter 15

A strong Christian keeps sexual purity until marriage

Flee fornication. Every sin that a man doeth is without the body; but he that commiteth fornication sinneth against his own body. - I Corinthians 6:18

Admittedly this may be one of the hardest things for a Christian to do, but it can be done. I remember from an early age being taught that our bodies were holy temples which were not to be defiled by pre-marital sex. There would be a certain uncleanness about fornication that I did not want to experience. There is a certain purity that the virgin possesses that sets him/her apart from those who have fornicated. Clearly the disease risk factor should be one huge deterrent to fornication. One also should be aware that he/she is dishonoring God as well as desecrating his/her temple. Sometimes people don't care about honoring God. Sometimes people are mad at God and want to take it out on him by fornicating.

Recently at work, I was conversing with a man who nonchalantly told me, "But, Tim, everybody is fornicating nowadays." He was telling me about a strip club in the area that I did not know about, trying to entice me to go. He said that they don't have bright lights and it's hard to tell it's a strip club from the road. Those to me were big red flags. Any Christian place does not feel the need to keep a low-key, clandestine-type appearance. Christian places are not typically dimly lit and don't entice one to succumb to fleshly sexual desires without regard to one's marital status. One has to wonder if the people working inside the strip club are seeking to honor God with their temples. Probably not.

I recently was talking with a friend in her car about a gym where she used to work. She had told me that the gym owner, a married man, was having an affair with one of the fitness instructors there. Ultimately, the man lost his marriage, his gym, and his family fell apart. Oftentimes people seek that instant gratification that can come with sin, but they are too foolish to foresee the far-reaching consequences and ripple effects that their fornication will have. Families get torn apart, jobs are lost, wallets are emptied, souls are lost, sinners will grieve and so on.

It is often too easy in our society to procure pre-marital sex. And we must remember that the sin is not cohabitation; the sin is fornication. All too often I will see people ignorantly assuming that just because people are living together, they must be having sex. That isn't necessarily the case. I personally have lived with two of my girlfriends in my lifetime but did not have sex with either of them. I told them from the get-go that I wanted to wait until marriage to have sex. They reluctantly agreed to live with me anyway, in spite of my commitment to God to take care of my temple. Did this cause conflict? Sure it did. But if your significant other can't respect your commitment to God to take care of your temple by not defiling it with fornication, then maybe you should seek someone who does respect your belief.

Remember, the weak will succumb to the flesh, for they do not have the strength that it takes to withstand the pressure to fornicate. There is no power in having as much pre-marital sex as possible. There is a lot of weakness in it, though. The strong will remain pure until marriage, deciding to honor God with his/her temple, and God will reward him/her for his/her obedience. And, if you have fornicated, and you truly repent and seek God to cleanse you anew, He will do it. God seeks a truly repentant heart in this area. He is gracious and willing to forgive and wants to show you how good He is. If you do decide to remain pure until marriage along with your boyfriend/girlfriend, that person will be your king or queen, for God honors those who honor Him.

I Corinthians 7:2 says, "Nevertheless, to avoid fornication, let every man have his own wife, and let every woman have her own husband."

Chapter 16

A strong Christian prays to God even when
things are going well

Pray without ceasing. - I Thessalonians 5:17

I remember one night several years ago I had
gone into a baseball card and toy store. I traded
some old baseball cards of mine for a figurine of
Jesus Christ. He was dressed in a white robe
with a blue sash. It was my version of a Jesus
painting that many Christian families have in
their home. I put my figurine on a shelf in my
house as a reminder that He is always there for
me. This seemed fine and dandy, but the
problem, oftentimes is that we have a tendency
to pull Jesus down off the shelf only when we
need him to get us through some current
predicament or problem.

We need to pray to God daily, not just when
things are going awry. Maybe you don't have
something to ask for. Maybe you should just
converse with Him and tell Him what's on your
heart. When you try to have a heart-to-heart
conversation with God, He will gladly reveal
how He feels about what you are saying to Him.
He wants you to know His heart. You could tell
Him of all that you are thankful for. You could
tell Him how you want to grow in your daily
walk with Him. In fact, tell Him you don't want
to just walk with Him, but that you want to be
running partners! Since my favorite book in the
Bible is Proverbs, I enjoy reading it and ask God

regularly to impart more and more wisdom to me.

It has been said that prayer is one of the most powerful weapons we have. Satan, as he always does, has twisted the concept of prayer so that people will feel discouraged about doing it. Oftentimes he will have us thinking that if we don't get what we prayed for, then prayer must not work or that God is holding a bitter grudge against us. God answers all prayers according to His plan. Imagine how chaotic things would get if everybody got what they prayed for! All the lottery winners we'd have. All the "marriages made in heaven" we'd have. All the healthy people running around. It seems great to the untrained eye, but oftentimes God keeps us from the desires of our heart in order to protect us because we are often too nearsighted or blind to see how those things could harm us.

The weak tend to pray to God only in times of need. But the fact is we need God all the time. When a crisis hits is when most people bring Jesus down off the shelf to pray to Him. Using Jesus only when the manure hits the fan is not a real relationship. Did you ever have that one person in your life that called you up only when they needed something? Is that someone you enjoy having a "relationship" with? Is that a real friend? The strong realize that healthy relationships work 50/50. If you want to understand God, you need to pray to Him and spend time with Him regularly. If you look at people who don't pray regularly, more likely than not they apply a mediocre commitment to most, if not all, relationships in their lives. Strong Christians tend to be the loyal ones you can count on to pray for you or with you when you need it. They tend to understand wholehearted commitments. They tend to talk with God regularly, when things are going well. They know that if they talk with God when things are going well, it won't seem unnatural to talk with Him when things are not going well. You can be that strong Christian who prays daily to God, the one Being who will always be there for you. There's joy in such a relationship!

Chapter 17

A strong Christian uses spiritual weaponry to fight spiritual battles

Wherefore take unto you the whole armor of God, that ye may be able to withstand in the evil day, and having done all, to stand. - Ephesians 6:13

Did you ever find yourself wanting to knock out an annoying person? Probably so. We all have been there. Really what we are up against is an evil spirit which resides in the other person. Their spirit is conflicting with our spirit, whatever they may be. We want to squish that spirit inside of them, and we want to strangle the physical person to do so. Sometimes words simply don't work. Jesus's words were proof enough that speaking good words to people sometimes just doesn't do the job. They crucified Him anyway. The problem is that beating all the annoying people isn't going to get rid of the evil spirits inside of them. Therefore, we must use the spiritual weapons at our disposal.

I remember when I was threatened by the manager at the supermarket where I worked in 2012. I told him that I would use the weapons of love, prayer, and forgiveness to battle this problem. Naturally with him being a non-believer, he went to Human Resources to report my "threat" since I had mentioned weapons. The flesh inside of me wanted to strangle all the idiots who saw my comments as threats. Instead of strangling them, I prayed about the issue and for God to open the eyes of the blind. After I was fired from that job, I ended up getting a job in a natural food warehouse lifting heavy boxes all day -- something I love doing! I got paid more at the new job, too. Had I punched the manager's lights out, the end result would have been different, as you can probably imagine. How would it look if I, as a representative of the Kingdom, went around bashing people's skulls in just because they were annoying? Surely, I could spend all day doing it, but is that being kind to my fellow man?

The weak think their battles are against the flesh, but they aren't. The flesh operates based on spiritual leading. Therefore, it only makes sense to address the spirit when the flesh goes haywire. I recall as a child I would try to attack the flesh of every annoying person I felt led to attack. I hadn't grown in strength yet. The weak will succumb to the temptation of attacking the flesh, when, indeed, they need to be on their knees in prayer for the people that do them wrong. If you go around looking for physical confrontations with all those that wrong you, you will soon grow tired. You will probably end up in jail, too.

It may be difficult to see love, prayer, and forgiveness as weapons, but they can be used as such when you are in a spiritual battle. When we are attacked spiritually, we need first to discern this (that this is indeed an attack). Then we need to forgive the wrongdoer. What makes it easy to forgive is knowing that the wrongdoer was not operating in strength or superior wisdom when they wronged us. Knowing that we have control over our emotions at this point is our strength, and there is a joyous feeling accompanying this knowing. With a loving heart we are then to pray for the person who clearly was operating in a weak mindset. Let us pray for the person to get right with God and wise up.

Ephesians talks about putting on the WHOLE armor of God so that we can stand against the wiles of the devil (6:11). Each piece of armor on a physical warrior is equated to in a spiritual sense in this chapter, and we are to apply to our lives what it says therein. A girter of truth, a breastplate of righteousness, feet shod with the preparation of the gospel of peace, the shield of faith, the helmet of salvation, and the sword of the Spirit (word of God). A strong Christian walks with this armor on to do battle in this world. The chapter goes on to say that we ought to pray always with all prayer and supplication in the Spirit. Prayer must always go along with our fight. If we think we will win the thing with just our physical presence, we will come up short on the day of battle.

Ephesians 6:12 says, "For we wrestle not against flesh and blood, but against principalities, against powers, against the rulers of the darkness of this world, against spiritual wickedness in high places."

Chapter 18

A strong Christian realizes that he/she will
always be victorious with God as his/her partner

*But thanks be to God, which giveth us the
victory through our Lord Jesus Christ. - I
Corinthians 15:57*

There is not a person in this world who does
not go through some sort of struggle. We all
have our spiritual struggles, no matter how well
off one may seem in this world. Some struggles
are big; some are small. Either way, if we walk
in righteousness, with God as our partner, we
can be assured that we will come out victorious
after all is said and done.

I remember in May of 2008, as my 3-year
probationary period was drawing to an end, I
had chosen to run in my first marathon. Why did
I choose to run 26.2 miles? Because I was
determined to let the enemy know that he was
not going to get the victory over me. I was not
going to go down defeated. He was not going to
get the best of me. I was knocked down for a
while, but I refused to stay down. Even though I
was going through depression and was still
somewhat mad at God, there was a part of me
that was determined to get back up, dust myself
off, and do what was necessary to build myself
up, stronger than ever before.

Defeat takes place in the mind. It's when you
decide that you are defeated and that the other

guy (your opponent) has won. You feel hopeless. One way to avoid defeat is not to compete in the first place. However, sometimes we are in spiritual battles we have no choice to fight in. We can get spiritually defeated if we are not properly prepared for battle. The devil will come at you with all sorts of tricks to trip you up, to get you to do anything that is displeasing, dishonorable, or against God.

As I was running my marathon, Satan tried unsuccessfully to get me to give up. He tried in vain to get me to focus on how much my body hurt and that I was too weak for the event. I knew I had not trained that much physically for the marathon, but I was mentally determined to finish the race. It wasn't about coming in first. It was about not giving up; it was about finishing. When you give up, you don't win. When you don't try you are guaranteed failure. As long as you are trying, you are achieving some degree of success. God doesn't do anything halfway. He doesn't try to do anything; He either does or does not. If you choose to have Him with you during your trial, you will come out victoriously. This doesn't necessarily mean that the jury or judge will rule in your favor. I was convicted of an assault I didn't even commit. The victory came later when God got the glory through my testimony. The victory was displayed by my going on to live more successfully and stronger than before. The victory will often manifest in us showing through our living that we have defeated that which tried to knock us down for the count.

The weak will go around moping, claiming defeat. It's easier for them to blame their defeat on God than to man up and partner with God to get what God wants for them to begin with. The strong choose to partner with God, for they know that He will not let them be defeated. He will always provide an opportunity for victory on the battlefield. The strong choose to live righteously, knowing that they will ultimately be victorious for having done well in their partner God's eyes.

Chapter 19

A strong Christian recognizes that God's good and that only good proceeds from Him

Teach me to do thy will; for thou art my God: thy spirit is good; lead me into the land of uprightness. - Psalm 143:10

I recall as a child being mistreated on many an occasion. I didn't like the way I felt as a result of others' mistreatment, and I just accepted their mistreatment as normal. I was too young or, perhaps, too uneducated to understand that the way they treated me was not prompted by God. When I was a kid, I remember two facts about my being mistreated: 1) People saying "When you act like an adult, you will be treated like one."; 2) Me saying, "I get treated like a child because I look like one."

It is important for us to realize that any mistreatment we might be subjected to is not prompted by God, no matter how authoritative, educated, tough, burly, or serious our adversary might seem to be. As children we are taught to trust in adults and to see them as authority figures who know what they are talking about. God is one of those authority figures we see as our heavenly Father. Man tends to lean on his own understanding, thinking he has it all figured out regarding a matter. Then he typically goes around acting as if he has nothing left to learn in life, telling people what he knows as if it came from God's own mouth. Many times we do say what God has said, but often times we are simply being headstrong and are too quick to want to know a matter before we speak about it. So, we end up speaking what we feel heated about in the moment of heat instead of responding like Jesus would respond.

We need to realize that nothing bad, in word or deed, ever comes from God. "Bad" things that happen to you are never what God intended. I remember rebelling against God for not getting me out of the legal mess I was in in 2004. The fact was that God was still good and that He allowed me to go through the mess so I would be strengthened because He has great plans for me. My perception of the mess was that it was bad. That's what I was calling it. And it was, indeed, a bad experience. But, good did come from it. I am much stronger now than I was eleven years ago. It wasn't part of God's plan for me to not use wisdom to avoid getting into the mess to begin with. That was my mistake, not God's. I used discernment to see that evil lay ahead for me, but I failed to use wisdom to walk away from it.

Any time we are mistreated we must admit that the mistreatment did not originate with God. For example, if someone is scolding us, the person's intentions might be good, but if he/she is not acting good, we must look to God to inquire as to what is good regarding the matter. A strong Christian sees that no evil or mistreatment proceeds from God. Evil proceeds only from man and Satan. Good can proceed from man but so can evil. That's why we must use discernment, which we will talk about next.

Jeremiah 29:11 says, "For I know the thoughts that I think toward you, saith the LORD, thoughts of peace, and not of evil, to give you an expected end."

Chapter 20

A strong Christian uses righteous judgment to discern good from evil

Ye shall do no unrighteousness in judgment: thou shalt not respect the person of the poor, nor honor the person of the mighty: but in righteousness shalt thou judge thy neighbor. - Leviticus 19:15

To use righteous judgment, one must first understand what it is. It is using biblical standards to decide if something is good or evil, versus worldly judgment, which is using one's own standards to decide what is good or bad. Usually people are referring to worldly judgment when they talk about judging others. For example, if I say that little Tommy is stupid for wearing red shorts instead of blue shorts (because I love blue and hate red) then I'm using worldly judgment on him. There is no biblical standard having to do with the color of one's shorts. The fact that I hold Tommy's behavior (wearing red shorts) against him indicates that I am using worldly judgment on him. This type of judgment is most notably marked by a grudge of some sort. It's when we hold a perceived offense against someone that we know we are judging him/her. Remember it like this: grudge = judge; it rhymes.

Now, if I simply make an observation -- Tommy is wearing red shorts -- then I am just making an aphorism. I'm simply observing a truth. I'm not necessarily judging him, in the worldly sense. People tend to think we are judging others by our tone of voice when we make such statements. People seem to speak begrudgingly when they are using worldly judgment on others. However, we need to be careful not to assume that someone is making a worldly judgment just because they state something that is true, especially in writing, since then you can't hear the writer's tone. Oftentimes I have written things and people have assumed that I was judging, but they couldn't hear my tone of voice when I was saying the things because those things were in writing, not spoken aloud. Usually people's guilty conscience is what prompts them to act defensively and accuse another of passing judgment. Simply making an observation, or noticing something, is not the same thing as judgment. They are two different acts.

Worldly judgment is what we as strong Christians want to stay away from. Many have foolishly chosen to believe that they were called by God to go around using worldly judgment on others. We all, I believe, have done it at some point. Man oftentimes likes to believe he has been equipped with "the superior human mindset" or "superior judgment." He hasn't. The road of worldly judgment often leads one to justify the following: gossip, being a busybody, unforgiveness, condemnation, persecution, arrogance etc. As stated previously in chapter 8, a strong Christian realizes his/her time is too precious to waste on worldly judgment. Then what do we do with our time? We use it on righteous judgment.

A strong Christian chooses to follow the road of discernment which often leads to the following: avoiding foolishness, counseling others, correction, exhorting others, avoiding trouble, forgiveness, compassion, encouragement etc. Notice how the road of worldly judgment is all about bringing people down, including oneself, oftentimes, whereas the road of discernment is about wisdom and building people up. The whole purpose in using righteous judgment is not about holding an offense against anyone; it's about discerning good from evil so we can make wise choices in our lives and in the lives of others. You are using righteous judgment when you discern foolishness in the life of your neighbor and choose to avoid it. You can even choose to approach your neighbor and encourage him/her to cease from his/her foolishness so he/she can rise up in strength by not succumbing to temptations. For example, I have a neighbor who gets drunk often and smokes tobacco daily. The Bible is the standard against which such behavior is measured. It says that such things are foolishness. I could stand around all day condemning him for being a substance abuser, or I could counsel him on how avoiding such things would make him wiser and stronger. Knowing this particular neighbor the way I do, I feel that I'd be more successful by being an example of someone who is not a substance abuser and how I am stronger for it. And that's

OK. Sometimes people aren't receptive to your words. Sometimes your actions will speak louder to them. We should pray for the weak-willed, as well. Pray that they will find the will to overcome foolishness and to walk in strength.

This righteous judgment stuff is designed to protect us from evil. Don't be afraid to call things what they are because of probable repercussions from those who think you are judging. One of Satan's greatest tricks is to convince man to tell you you should feel guilty for calling evil what it is. Evil is allowed to continue more so because of man's unwillingness to call it out and to address it. As a strong Christian you are called to utilize God-given discernment to weed out the evil from the good. The weak are too afraid to do this, for they fear being labeled as judgmental. You, as a strong Christian, are not to walk in fear of potential labels that could be placed upon you by people who were never called by God to begin with to label you in a negative way. The more you choose to use righteous judgment to discern good from evil, the stronger you are, for you are called to be a mighty Christian warrior who quashes evil.

Hebrews 5:14 says, "But strong meat belongeth to them that are of full age, even those who by reason of use have their senses exercised to discern both good and evil."

Chapter 21

A strong Christian remains faithful to God when it seems the deck is stacked against him/her

Be strong and of a good courage, fear not, nor be afraid of them: for the LORD thy God, he it is that doth go with thee; he will not fail thee, nor forsake thee. - Deuteronomy 31:6

Oftentimes those of small strength will turn their back on God and walk away from Him when things seem not to be working in their favor. As I've mentioned before, God allows adversity in our lives so that we can be strengthened. It is rather childish, but many adults daily turn from God when adverse circumstances arise; I've done it myself. Once you are mature and have clarity, you can look back at some of your so-called adverse conditions and realize that your own stupid mistakes led you to your predicament. God wants you to see what happens when you walk away from Him so that you won't want to do it again.

I can remember hundreds, if not thousands, of times that I ended up in a mess because I failed to use good judgment. I used discernment to distinguish good from evil, but I failed to avoid the evil, foolishly thinking that I'd make out alright because I could rely on my own understanding to get me through something. That was my ego at work. Isn't that how we tend to be? I foresaw evil spirits in the children on the church bus prior to my legal crisis. But I thought I'd be alright even though the Holy Spirit was warning me not to ride the bus home that fateful Sunday afternoon. My strength was small at that time in my life. I quickly rebelled against God and blatantly sinned, yelling at God, "When you make things good for me and remove all these difficult people from my life, then everything will be just fine!" I didn't have the foresight at the time to see that God was allowing me to experience that crisis to build me up and that my great ministry would come from my darkest hour. At that time, I had a grudge against God and chose to be unfaithful to Him, which did me no good.

In the Bible, Job was not a Christian, for Christ was not yet on the Earth, but he would have been a very strong Christian. If you read the book of Job, you'll see that the deck was seemingly stacked against him, but he remained faithful to God, didn't rebel against Him, and Job made out better than before. Not long after my legal crisis began in 2004 did I begin to see that God remains faithful to us no matter what. No matter how rebellious we may get against Him, He doesn't hold childish grudges. No matter how much we misbehave, He still provides opportunities for us to come to Him and to see the light. That's what strength is about -- not acting weakly when faced with adversity. Even in the early rebellious days of my legal crisis, I could see God working on my behalf by guiding me to certain individuals who would take me under their wing to build me up.

Once I realized that God is not against me ever, then I quickly reasoned that I should never be against Him either, for it would not do me any good.

Remember, the weak will walk away from God begrudgingly when adversity hits, as if God allowed it so they would have a bad time. The strong realize that God allows adversity for our benefit, so we'd be strengthened, more disciplined, knowing how to respond when evil comes our way. The strong are the ones who don't let their faith waver, for they realize their faith can grow once they use their strength to overcome the adversity.

I Peter 3:15 says, "But sanctify the Lord God in your hearts: and be ready always to give an answer to every man that asketh you a reason of the hope that is in you with meekness and fear:"

Chapter 22

A strong Christian seeks comfort in the
Scriptures and in godly counsel

*A wise man will hear, and will increase
learning; and a man of understanding shall
attain unto wise counsels: - Proverbs 1:5*

I recall as a youngster I did not have a
personal mentor in my life, so I sought one.
That's what one typically does when one does
not have a mentor. In our youthful innocence,
we seek someone or, sometimes, some group
that seemingly has "the answers." We look for
answers about life. Those who don't have a
close personal relationship with God, tend to
look for answers from people who are living in
the world and for the world. We ought not be
looking for answers from anyone outside of
God.

I remember in 2008 when I was living in
Costa Rica, I learned about "stray puppy
syndrome." Every morning, as I was working at
a job site building a house, around the same
time the same stray puppy from the
neighborhood would show up where other
volunteers and I were working to "ask for" food.
It was about lunch time and he would wait
patiently until one of us fed him. He wasn't
concerned about the character of the people
feeding him, he just wanted to be fed. Weak
humans tend to do the same thing by seeking
comfort in ungodly people who don't follow, or

even know, the Scriptures. This is dangerous living. That's why it is of utmost importance to seek our comfort in the Scriptures and in godly counsel: because they won't lead us astray.

A strong Christian does not seek comfort in health-disturbing vices such as smoking, the drinking of alcohol, and other foolish things that would please the flesh of some. The weak will succumb to these things. I have done it myself. I used to seek comfort in chocolate pudding. I would devour a 22-ounce tub of it day after day in about 20 minutes. Had I sought comfort in the Scriptures during that time, I would not have acquired an eventual allergic reaction to sodium the way I did. People want to feel good, and they tend to follow those who seemingly can make them feel good. If we are ignorant and look to the ungodly for answers, we can easily be led into danger. We are blinded by our fleshly desire for instant comfort. We tend not to see the destruction at the end of the road we are being led down. As the smoker ends with lung cancer and the drinker with liver disease, so too will the blind perish for lack of vision. Vision is seeing what's ahead of you. Upon reading the Scriptures, you might not know what lies ahead, but you can be rest assured it's for your good if you do what the Bible says to do. This is the comfort that a strong Christian seeks.

A strong Christian knows the Scriptures, and godly counselors will lead them to good things. This is what sets the weak apart from the strong.

You too can be a strong Christian who seeks comfort in these things, not in the things of this world and the people who don't really have "the answers." So, now the question is: will you choose strength and go to those who are godly for your comfort, or will you be a stray puppy, disregarding the character of those who seemingly can feed you?

Chapter 23

A strong Christian utilizes proverbial wisdom in daily decision-making

Say unto wisdom, Thou art my sister; and call understanding thy kinswoman: - Proverbs 7:4

Once we get into the Scriptures to find comfort, we should study the book of Proverbs for how to live on a daily basis. Proverbs is my most favorite book in all of the Bible, probably because it has so much good advice in one place. I read a lot of the verses in Proverbs and think how I could have avoided a lot of calamities if I had utilized proverbial wisdom in many of the decisions I had made in my life. I thought about studying human psychology at one point, but then God told me that all the psychology I need to know can be found in the Scriptures.

On the street people tend to learn street smarts, thus they know about the street mentality. But in Proverbs wisdom is taught. By looking at the proverbs in this book, one can see the psychology of street smarts and apply it to real life. Proverbial wisdom isn't antiquated at all; it is applicable nowadays. I utilize it daily when discretion is needed. I deal with difficult, ungodly people on a daily basis at my warehouse job, so proverbial wisdom comes in handy when deciding what to do or what not to do when I'm with them. Certain people ask for a knuckle sandwich on a regular basis. I have to choose whether or not to feed them that sandwich. On the one hand, I can satisfy the flesh by feeding them (and probably end up in jail), or, on the other hand, I can keep quiet for it does no good to argue with a fool (Proverbs 23:9). I may be right if I present a valid argument containing proverbial wisdom, but certain people choose to be unreceptive to it. That's why sometimes words do no good. Sometimes it's just best to keep quiet and let the fool do his thing, so as not to provoke him to further foolishness.

We wake up every day with choices to make. We can choose to utilize either wisdom or foolishness. The weak tend to rise up and choose foolishness over wisdom. They either consciously or unconsciously choose to do the foolish thing with regularity. Usually the foolish person does not realize that he/she is being foolish. Usually, if he/she is wise, he/she will look back on his/her foolishness and see that it was just that. Oftentimes, though, this doesn't happen. The fool typically commits foolish acts repeatedly, thinking he/she will somehow get a good result if he/she simply persists. I see this at work all the time. One individual who has been at my work for five years continues to exhibit the same behavior day in and day out, foolishly expecting things to improve. The person regularly complains, insults people, and criticizes others yet provides no solutions to any perceived problems. A lot of his and company time is wasted on tearing down others. That time could be spent wisely by looking for different ways to do things, by looking for solutions that bring positive change. Instead, the fool returns to his folly and those who have to watch the fool feel sorrowful, for the blind fool walks in ignorance.

The strong choose wisdom on a daily basis. The strong know that wisdom will lead to longer days and greater health. Utilizing wisdom will help to keep one out of trouble and help those who are already in it. The strong know that Jesus utilized wisdom while here on Earth. It may not keep you trouble free, but often it will. It can lead you as to what to say or what not to say. It can lead you to whom you should associate with and who to stay away from. Recently I have thought about how utilizing proverbial wisdom has helped me through some difficult situations and I just say to God," Thank you, Lord!" You too can rejoice in the victory that can be had when one utilizes wisdom on a regular basis. It will have to be your decision, though. What will you choose in your daily decision-making: wisdom or foolishness? Remember, man's ego is what drives him towards foolishness. The Holy Spirit is what prompts us to utilize wisdom.

Proverbs 8:11 says, "For wisdom is better than rubies; and all the things that may be desired are not to be compared to it."

Chapter 24

A strong Christian allows the Holy Spirit to guide his/her daily walk

For the LORD shall be thy confidence, and shall keep thy foot from being taken. - Proverbs 3:26

What or who guides you daily? I remember back in about 2007 I was walking around a paved walkway at a nearby park. I walked on this walkway with regularity and began to see something symbolic as the Lord spoke to me: the circular walkway represented the circle of life. I noticed that when I stayed on the pavement only, I was safe. It's like God was saying to me that if I stayed on the narrow path I'd be safe. We tend to be safe when we allow the Holy Spirit to guide our daily walk. I had a vision that Jesus was walking beside me on the pathway. He was keeping me safe because I was close to Him. The Holy Spirit was guiding me along the path even when it started to get dark. I noticed that when I strayed from the path I ran into thorn bushes. These represented the trouble I can get into when I decide to deviate from the Holy Spirit's leading. As I collided with the thorns, I felt pain and regret.

Oftentimes we like to be led by our ego. This is what the weak do. If we are ego-driven, we tend to go it alone, so to speak. We go through life trying to manhandle the various obstacles that stand in our way. We often get led by our senses and seek the things that will bring pleasure to the flesh. Sin, they say, feels good for a season. This is considered true by those who seek to please the flesh. How many times have we gone through life saying to God, "I'm OK, God, I got this. I don't really need you now, but thanks for offering to help!" This sort of mentality ultimately leads only to trouble.

I recall in 2000 I was having conflict with a live-in girlfriend. As young couples do, we saw things differently. I thought I could fix the relationship on my own, by using my own smarts; I couldn't. We ultimately broke up on bad terms. Neither one of us was trying to let the Holy Spirit guide us. We each had our own idea of how things should be in the relationship. It wasn't something that could rely on man's brain alone. The Holy Spirit would have had to come in and led us to a harmonious accord. The spirits that were in me were in conflict with the spirits in her. When two people are in a relationship and both are being led by the Holy Spirit, there is harmony. This is what we want: harmony. But, we think we can create it without the Spirit's help; we can't. If left to our own devices, we will run into a dead end. The weak don't realize this. They stubbornly refuse to let the Holy Spirit guide them and they continue in their folly.

The strong Christian realizes he is deficient in spirit and needs the Holy Spirit to guide him/her if he/she is to achieve goodness. If you want to be that strong Christian, pray to God and ask Him to send the Holy Spirit to lead you.

This is what He desires more than anything besides accepting His Son as Savior. What is the point in being a "Christian" if you are not going to follow Christ's ways and be led by the Spirit? The Spirit will not do you wrong. You may be uncomfortable with some areas He is leading you to or through, but rest assured it's all for your good. The Holy Spirit will not lead you into any temptation or any sort of sinful activity. In fact, He leads you away from it. Oftentimes we end up in a mess because we don't let the Holy Spirit lead. We want to lead and then call on the Spirit when we are in trouble. That's not how it is supposed to work. We are supposed to let the Spirit go first and then follow. If you are on a wilderness expedition in unfamiliar territory, would you try to lead the pack? Of course not. You'd let the guide go first, because he knows the way. You trust in him to lead you. It works the same way with the leading of the Holy Spirit.

Christian strength in this area is about letting go of one's ego and saying, "Holy Spirit, you know what you are doing. If I try to lead in this thing, I will surely mess it up." It comes down to a daily decision of who you want to lead you through your day: your defective ego or the righteous Holy Spirit.

Chapter 25

A strong Christian seeks to keep his/her eyes focused on the Lord

The fool hath said in his heart, There is no God. They are corrupt, they have done abominable works, there is none that doeth good. - Psalm 14:1

Satan knows the potential good that man can accomplish when he keeps his eyes focused on the Lord. That's why he tries to distract us with as many things as possible so that we will avert our gaze from the Lord. Satan knows that one of our sins can be to idolize other people, so he'll lure us into looking at people who seemingly have it made, so that we take our eyes off the Lord. We can get so caught up with television, electronic devices, magazines, toys, hobbies, and countless other things that bring no fruit. I've been there myself many times.

I could give many examples, but I'll stick with one in particular here. One of my favorite shows in the 1980's was Knight Rider. I fantasized about having a Trans-Am like the one used on the show, and souping it up so that I'd have a super car. In early 1996 I was able to buy a Trans-Am from a friend's uncle for about $1,300. My dad said he'd paint it for me, provided I buy the equipment to paint it. I bought the equipment and, shortly thereafter, modified the front end so that a red scanner that I had bought, like the one on the show, could fit in and be seen. My dad painted the car for me and installed the red scanner. I was well on my way to having my very own Knight Rider replica. Shortly after the car was painted, I lost interest in pursuing the conversion project because I was saving money to buy my first house.

Years later, in 2011, I traveled to Las Vegas from Maryland for a Knight Rider convention. There I saw and took pictures of Knight Rider replicas that other fans of the show had made, met actresses from the show, and got their autographs. In retrospect, I had wasted a lot of time, effort, and money idolizing that show. I still think it's a great show, but I don't waste my time anymore watching it with frequency. After I returned from Las Vegas, God instructed me to give away my Knight Rider DVD's as well as a Knight Rider book that I had bought. The fact is the celebrity actresses that I had met and whose autographs I had gotten don't give two hoots about me. How could they make time for one fan out of thousands that they don't really know? The whole time I was mesmerized by the show and the people on it, I had been keeping my eyes on a distraction, something that kept me from doing the Lord's work. It was a valuable learning experience; one of many.

My experience with Knight Rider is a bit like the stray puppy syndrome I mentioned in chapter 22. People not really grounded in biblical principles can easily be led astray to follow distractions that will keep them from godly things. Satan knows people very well and thus how to entice them to follow ungodly things. Satan likes to imitate God. While God wants to lead us to the things of His kingdom, Satan wants to lead us to things that are perceivably good, but really aren't. Anything that Satan can or does lead you to leads to a dead end. The things of God lead not to an end but rather only to good. You can see that my idolatry with Knight Rider led to a dead end. I didn't produce any fruit for the kingdom because of it. The weak will follow distractions and be lead to dead ends. Satan knows the fruitlessness of you walking around with your eyes off of God. Satan's whole agenda is about getting people as distracted as possible, so as to keep them from doing God's work. Satan holds a grudge against God, and he's all about getting God's children to be disobedient to God.

The strong Christian recognizes that Satan will try to get man's heart set on the temporal things of this world, since man tends to pursue the things in his heart. Knowing this, the strong Christian sets out to keep his/her eyes focused on the Lord because he/she knows that doing this will help him/her to avoid heartbreak later on. He/she also chooses to avoid wasting time on the fruitless pursuit of ungodly things, knowing that they lead only to dead ends. The strong Christian chooses to keep his/her eyes focused on the Lord because he/she wants to produce only good, God-honoring fruit. You too can be that strong Christian. Will you choose to be distracted by images or false gods that lead only to dead ends or will you choose to focus on the Lord, knowing that you need Him to lead you?

Chapter 26

A strong Christian recognizes that that which God provided at Creation is all he/she will ever really need

And out of the ground made the LORD God to grow every tree that is pleasant to the sight, and good for food; the tree of life also in the midst of the garden, and the tree of knowledge of good and evil. - Genesis 2:9

My Knight Rider materials were just a few of the many things that God told me to get rid of. In fact, He said this, "Tim, I want you to get rid of anything that does not contribute to the furtherance of my kingdom." I knew a few years back that I wanted to be a missionary. Slowly I began to wean myself off of the things of this world that I did not need. I did a lot of introspection, analyzing, contemplating, reasoning and so forth. It didn't happen overnight. It took years to justify what I did and did not need. I sold things and gave things away. I knew that as a missionary, I'd have to travel light. I had to re-examine my priorities and put them in proper order. Once I did this, my life became simpler and I found it easier to discard the superfluous from my life. If our priorities are out of whack, then how will we know what to get rid of? We won't. Instead, we spend lots of time debating. Sentimentalism is the biggest obstacle to people's getting rid of stuff. So, it's a heart issue. I have stated before that man tends to pursue the things in his heart.

There are a group of people in this world I call one-day people. These are the people whose favorite expression seems to be, "one day I will use it." Ten years later they still haven't used the thing they said they were going to use ten years earlier! When I ask them why they haven't used said thing yet, their reply is something like, "Oh, but, one day!" By not acquiring the fruitless things of this world that don't contribute to the furtherance of His kingdom, I have been able to save a lot of time, energy, and money. The weak are the ones who choose to pursue the fruitless things that they don't really need. Satan, in his subtlety, has convinced many a man to get and keep things he doesn't really need. He has sold man a lifestyle he doesn't need, nor is good for him. In the United States of America, many people are sold on the idea that they need luxury. People have been convinced that they need luxury this and luxury that and all sorts of superfluous, fruitless nonsense. People have forgotten how to get by on the basics.

I remember my first house I bought when I was 21. I wasn't in pursuit of luxury, I just wanted the basics: a roof over my head and peace in my household. I had to gut out almost the whole inside and redo it so that it would be livable. I bought just the basics as far as paint, carpet, and a countertop went. I didn't even buy kitchen cabinets. I used one big storage cabinet for my dishes and my tools. My living room "table" was actually an empty egg box. My "TV stand" was an egg box with a board on top which doubled as a shelf for my movies and VCR. I didn't have any wall decorations. I was completely content and comfortable, knowing I had my needs met. God saw my heart and that I wasn't in pursuit of fruitless things, that I was content with just the basics while paying only cash for the things I needed. He decided to bless me about 6 years after I bought the house: I sold it for over 3 times the price I paid for it!

The fact is we need very little in this lifetime. God revealed to me that what He created when He created the world is all we will ever really need. We have health. We have air. We have materials to make shelter and animals for clothing. We have natural materials to make transportation. We have the ground to make food. We have the rain to make our food grow. We have fire to keep warm in the winter. We have the sun to provide light and energy. We have the mountains for our cardiovascular exercise. The list goes on. It's when we decide to go outside of these things that we get into trouble. We can get into all sorts of debt and trouble with our fellow man over the superfluous things of this world, things that are man-made.

The strong Christian is able to suppress the desire to acquire the superfluous things of this world. Like stray puppies, many men will be lead by Satan to pursue things and a lifestyle they don't need. The strong Christian sees this trap and chooses to avoid it. Will you choose to live humbly and be content with God's creation and provision, or will you succumb to filling your life with things you were never called to have to begin with?

Chapter 27

A strong Christian refuses to prognosticate a person's future based solely on the person's past

Lie not one to another, seeing that ye have put off the old man with his deeds; - Colossians 3:9

A lot of people who aren't deeply grounded in Christian principles like to prognosticate or foretell others' futures by solely looking at the people's past. This is not a healthy practice. They tend to see limited potential in others. God has worked many a miracle through seemingly average or inferior people. If we can do all things through Christ, then our potential is virtually limitless.

I recall in elementary school I would be made fun of for slurring my words. I wasn't unintelligent; I was lazy. I had the most difficulty with Language Arts and English classes. The way those subjects were taught was not suitable for my learning style. Then one day in the fifth grade, I was in a spelling bee for fifth-graders. We had to repeat a word that was dictated to us, spell it aloud, and then repeat the word again. I made it to be one of two finalists. It was me against one of the gifted and talented kids who had made fun of me. The final word was "chair." I thought this would be easy for the other kid, since it was his turn. I stood right next to him as he repeated and pronounced the word. The teachers who were judging us had a look of doubt on their faces, so they asked him to do it again. Again he repeated and pronounced the word. I thought he did fine, but the teachers shook their heads and said that he was wrong. I was the only one left, so I repeated and pronounced the word well and ended up winning the spelling bee in front of all those who had made fun of me. I didn't realize it at the time, but God was with me at that moment. 15 years later, when I was in college, I ended up writing a book in Spanish having to do with English pronunciation.

Before I wrote that book, however, I had had my struggles with English classes in high school and in college. I was perusing the dictionary at home one day when it finally clicked. It took an English dictionary and a Spanish idioms book for me to realize how language works. I tend to learn most easily with structure. I pick up patterns easily and seem to have an uncanny ability to memorize lists and be able to categorize and organize information. Once I broke down language into sensible units that fit together like puzzle pieces in a big picture, things started making sense for me, linguistically speaking.

In the first grade I recall memorizing the names of all of the Presidents of the United States of America. It wasn't planned. I just opened an encyclopedia one day and did it. It took several days, but soon I was reciting all their names with regularity. Social Studies teachers in school would even get tickled pink by having me recite them before the class. I saw two other people in my life who recited the Presidents' names as well. Years later God revealed to me that He had me memorize those names so that I would have a reminder that I was smart, because He knew that a lot of people would try to make me feel dumb throughout the years.

The weak can be quick to write people off as has-beens or lost causes, having little foresight regarding their future. Oftentimes the people who do this have little success in their own lives. They don't typically have a clue when it comes to disassociating the perceived failures of the past from the potential future greatness of people. The strong Christian refuses to use someone's past to dictate his/her future. The strong Christian knows that a person's past does not have to dictate his/her future. In fact, it's those things of the past that deem us to be strong. To get strong you must come from weakness first. You must admit that you are more than you were before. If I had listened to the naysayers that said I had no ability for language mastery, I wouldn't be where I am today. You can be that strong Christian who refuses to prognosticate your own or someone else's future based solely on the past. Trust God and trust that He will make a way for you that is God-honoring.

Chapter 28

A strong Christian develops strategies based on God's leading and his/her talents

Now concerning spiritual gifts, brethren, I would not have you ignorant. - I Corinthians 12:1

As I mentioned in my Introduction, when I was living in Mexico in 2006, I taught a soul-winning course alongside the pastor of the church I attended. I had translated it from English to Spanish the previous year when I myself took the course in Maryland. I didn't have to translate it or teach it. I felt led by God to do so, even in my rebellion. I used my talent as a translator and developed a strategy in Mexico to teach the course in Spanish. It was a twelve-step program to show one how to lead others to Christ. I got about halfway through the course when it was time for me to leave the country, since my 3 months were up. The pastor continued my work after I left there.

All the time I see people who are talented in an area and using those talents to do God's work. When I was in Mexico, the former bodybuilder who ran the gym I frequented is an example. He was talented in exercise and fitness and had some godly knowledge, too. So, he opened a gym there and coached people on those things. He chatted with me quite a bit and gave me some good advice, which I needed at the time. I know another Christian friend who is talented in dealing with little kids and works as a pre-school teacher. She uses her talent with tact and diplomacy to instruct young minds and lead them towards the kingdom of God.

The focus here needs to be on strategy. Simply using your talents is one thing, but strategizing with them is another. Strategizing involves creating a workable plan with certain involved factors to bring about a harmonious outcome. At my one job, I see failure to strategize on a daily basis. As a result, chaos occurs. A lot of backtracking and double work has to be done. You've probably heard that failing to plan is planning to fail; it's true. A lot of time can be wasted by failing to plan. God doesn't want us to waste time. He wants us to be successful. We can be successful by developing a strategy by looking at the talents of the people involved to determine how those talents should be actuated. The creation of an intelligent plan should eliminate the possibility of wasting time, too.

When I wrote my English pronunciation book in 2003, I strategized: I wrote the book, self-published it, and then marketed it to about 5 different Latino stores who then sold it. I used my talent with the Spanish language, which I was mastering at the time, to write an academic-level book which could be used for top-notch information and instruction regarding English pronunciation for speakers of Spanish. By writing that book, I had proven that I had overcome a lot of self-doubt that I had struggled with throughout my formative years.

A strong Christian wonders how he/she can assist. He/she looks at a situation and thinks how he/she can use his/her talents to assist when assistance is needed. You ought not be simply gung-ho about it, though. One should develop a strategy. Doing so should reduce or eliminate potential damage, minimize (or in some cases maximize) energy expenditure, and bring about fruit. If your efforts are fruitless, then you are wasting your time. When God is leading you, rest assured the strategy is to be used for His purpose(s). The weak won't expend the energy to create a strategy. They will just go in acting macho about the situation, thinking they have everything all figured out; they don't. You should want to be the strong Christian that comes on the scene with an intelligent strategy that will bring about a harmonious fruitful outcome. Plan, put your ego aside, consider others as contributors, and think about the fruit. Your action should be God-glorifying and others should see this in you when you go into motion.

Chapter 29

A strong Christian leads by example, not by force

For I have given you an example, that ye should do as I have done to you. - John 13:15

Juan Gonzalez was the man's name. He was the goldsmith I met at the church I attended while living in Mexico. I visited his house several times. On one of the visits, he told me that his workers that he employed to make gold jewelry for him at first did not show up for work on time. They would always be there but late. Naturally he didn't like this, so he decided to set an example for them. He himself would show up at the time his workers were supposed to be there at work. Day after day he did this and slowly the workers got the message that they too should show up for work on time. They began showing up for work earlier and earlier until they began coming in every day at their scheduled time. Juan was a Christian man who did not force people into doing good; he set an example for them.

And so it is with strong Christians. Jesus did not force anybody to do anything. He went around living as a diligent admirable example of how people ought to live. The weak, even if well-intentioned, often have their priorities out of whack. They tend to place too much importance on the wrong things (or the right things, too). I remember in my early twenties I worked for McDonald's, the fast food restaurant. I remember working in the grill one day and feeling a sense of being in charge, even though I was not technically in charge. I told another worker to do a task. He refused to listen to me, so I tried to physically force him to do the task. It only created momentary animosity between us and a write-up for me. I had chosen not to speak to him gently. Had I asked him in the form of a question with gentleness, I might have gotten a pleasant and obedient response from him. Of all things to force someone to do, my "high" priority was that of making hamburgers!

Years later it would sink in that I should not be like a busybody – concerning my interest and emotions in the behavior of others. The only person I should try to control is myself. People don't like it when others try to control them. They intuit that mankind is not supposed to behave this way. I'm sure the Holy Spirit's convicting power has something to do with it also. There are exceptions when it comes to physically controlling others. When it comes to safety, sometimes physical control must be exerted. But normally, leading others with your own example is the way to go.

Recently I was listening to the radio and heard, "Values are not taught. They are caught." There is truth to this. What it means is that you can preach and teach values to people all you want, but people will "catch" your values by the ones they see you living out. We live in a monkey-see-monkey-do society. People tend to imitate the behavior they see. Deep down people want to feel in control of themselves. If you allow them to observe you and the values you live out, oftentimes they will *willingly* follow your example, like that of Juan Gonzalez. Jesus had 12 disciples. He didn't have to manhandle or coerce any of them into following him. They liked what and whom they saw and wanted some of that. Multitudes followed Jesus in His day. He was the gentlest of people. People followed Him because of the example He set for them, not because of a dictatorial command.

The more you feel the need to control others, the less control you actually have of yourself. If this is you, you have work to do. The strong Christian has great self-control and knows he/she is most responsible for his/her own behavior. The more you are willing to lead by example (controlling only yourself), the stronger you will be.

Chapter 30

A strong Christian can laugh at what the
naysayers say, realizing he/she serves the God
of the impossible, not the possible

But Jesus beheld them, and said unto them, With
men this is impossible, but with God all things
are possible. - Matthew 19:26

There was a time when I was somewhat
inclined to listen to what the naysayers had to
say; not anymore. The naysayers typically are
people of little or no faith. They don't
comprehend that God is almighty and
omnipotent and can therefore do all things. He
created the laws of physics and can override
them at will to accomplish His will. A miracle is
something that is accomplished when one of
these laws is either seemingly or actually
overridden. God still performs miracles today
for a number of reasons. Whatever the reasons
may be, the important thing is to have faith in
His ability to do the impossible.

Many times in my own life people said it
would have been impossible for me to do certain
things. One such example is when I bought my
first home. I was twenty-one years of age and
working 2 jobs, both of which paid less than
$7.00 per hour. I worked full-time at a grocery
store overnight and part-time at McDonald's, the
fast food restaurant. It didn't seem like I was a
likely candidate for a home purchase, but God
made a way because there was a lot He wanted

for me. I was in college at the time and God made a way for me to pay for my home and finish school during the six and a half years I owned that home. I sold it right after I turned 28 and thus was able to pay off my school loan and pay cash for my next three homes that I owned. This is just one example of what the God of the impossible can do. There are so many others in my life that I laugh now whenever I hear someone say that something is impossible. I will even quote what Jesus said in Matthew 19:26. People that don't know God's character will have their doubts. I don't laugh derisively at those people. Instead I laugh at what they say, knowing where they are coming from, for I too was in disbelief about God's abilities at one time.

"Ignore the naysayers" is one of the best pieces of advice I've ever received. Some of us have the mindset that when someone tells us that something can't be done, we set out to prove that it can be done. It's not so much about proving the naysayers wrong so they will feel bad as it is about building up their faith in God. It's not a competition about who's right and who's wrong. As strong Christians we should look to point out examples of the things God has done so they too are prompted to build up their faith.

Sometimes the naysayer is us. Satan wants us to be naysayers because he knows that God can do and does do the impossible to this day, and that we are likely to call on God to do such if we have such faith in Him. Let us not be weak naysayers who go around doubting God's ability. The naysayer sometimes will have such a faith that he/she believes God can do only the possible. The strong Christian, however, realizes that God can do that which seems *im*possible as well. God is limitless. The strong Christian realizes this and that is why he/she prays for God to do the impossible -- because he/she knows He can. Let us not keep our eyes focused on the things that limited man can do. Instead spend time with Him and watch Him do things through people and for people that only a God of the impossible can do.

Chapter 31

A strong Christian goes boldly where God sends him/her

Now therefore go, and I will be with thy mouth, and teach thee what thou shalt say. - Exodus 4:12

At eighteen I would have been terrified by the prospect of me traveling abroad by myself to a country where Spanish was spoken. It was at that age that I had just begun to study the language. I am now quite fluent in the language, but during my high school days I suffered from self-doubt, especially when it came to foreign languages. Not many people know this (now they will, though), but the only time I cheated on an exam in high school was in Spanish class. I was in the ninth grade and was taking a short exam on Spanish pronouns. I had studied for the test and had memorized pretty well the pronouns, but had so much self-doubt that I actually copied some answers from another student who was doing well. I didn't really need to copy, but I did it anyway.

The first time I traveled abroad was in 2002. I took a touristy vacation to Costa Rica and was already fairly fluent in the Spanish language, since I already had several years of its study under my belt. Of course it was my first time really being around native speakers of the language, since up til then I had only heard Spanish on cassettes. I got the opportunity to hear street Spanish for the first time. Boy, was it different. I caught on rather quickly, starting to understand television commercials after only 3 or 4 days there. Usually most people can hear a foreign language better than they can speak it. It was just the opposite for me. I always could speak it better than I could understand the spoken word. Now I'm so advanced in both skills that neither is a problem for me in most situations.

In 2012, ten years after my initial visit to Costa Rica, I ended up traveling to a few different churches in that country to give personal testimonies and speak briefly about my upcoming ministry there, all in Spanish. I was adamant about learning the missionary lifestyle and was excited about speaking in Spanish to the Costa Rican people about what God had done in my life. I wasn't as bold about the upcoming ministry part because it had been sprung on me at the last minute, plus the fact that God had revealed very little to me about the ministry up to that point. So, I didn't have much to talk about, and my talks were rather short! It's a different story now, though. Now I have a lot of information about the ministry, mainly lessons God has taught me along the way.

There is a degree of weakness when we doubt that God will be with us when He sends us somewhere. We want to try to avoid that weakness. That's why it is so important to learn God's character to know that He will accompany us wherever He sends us. The strong go boldly, knowing that the God of the impossible is with us and will accomplish His will through us wherever He sends us. If God sent me to Nicaragua, I'd go boldly, knowing that He will be with my mouth and will give me what to say. I might not know what all will go on down there, but the emphasis is on the "going boldly" part. If God doesn't send me to a place, then I'd have reason to be hesitant about going there. It's the boldness in going to the places that God sends us to that we should emphasize. He won't send you unaccompanied into a place. His Holy Spirit will be there to comfort you and will fill your mouth with the words that you need to survive.

It's like this: the more boldness you have about going to where He sends you, the stronger you are. The less boldness you have, the more you need to work on that thing. You can work on it by praying for Him to show you how to have the kind of faith you should have regarding this matter of going boldly. Either way, you can rest assured that He has your back wherever He sends you, regardless of how ill-equipped you may think you are. I may not speak quite like the natives of the places I'm going to, but my faith is in Him to fill my mouth with the words He wants me to speak. If He gives you the words, then He will give understanding to those who will hear them.

Chapter 32

A strong Christian worships, praises God, and
testifies of God's goodness publicly

*Whosoever therefore shall confess me before
men, him will I confess also before my Father
which is in heaven. - Matthew 10:32*

Your lifestyle, your prayers, your singing,
your exaltations of God, your preaching, your
testimonies that you give and anything else you
do to please, glorify, and honor God are all
pleasing to God. It's about your intentions. God
looks at the heart. Your motives. He's looking
for a servant's heart. Someone who wants to
serve Him because He is good and loves us.
Doing these things publicly will set you apart as
a strong Christian.

Doing these things in private is fine, but it is
an attestation of one's heart when one is bold
enough to go public with such things.
Oftentimes we are somewhat reticent to go
public with our praise and worship because we
are concerned with what other people might
think. If this is you, there is probably a degree of
fakery in your character. What I mean is that
you probably are a performer: you behave a
certain way to win the approval of spectators.
People that do this are typically still under the
belief that their fellow man has been put on
Earth to judge others. If anything, you should
feel sorry or empathic towards those who do
believe they were put here to judge or give

approval to their fellow man, for they are missing out on the joy that can be experienced by publicly praising and worshipping God.

I have a close friend who is a flagger. She is one who moves flags around freely as an act of worship. She does this privately and publicly. She didn't always have the boldness to do this. But over time she felt emboldened to do flagging publicly more and more. I myself have flagged a couple of times and want to do it some more when the opportunity arises. There is a certain freedom that one feels when he/she is convinced that he/she does not have to perform for others. We need to recognize that God is our audience and it is Him that we should try to please.

It can be a small thing such as a post on the Internet. When you testify, you want to make sure you word your statement(s) in such a way that the reader is prompted to believe that God is good and worthy of our praise. It's even better if you can word it so as to prompt the reader to want to worship God. People like to copy other people. Imagine what might happen if people saw you gleefully praising God and His goodness in public. They might want to join in and do the same. This stuff happens. If you are tired of how people are acting – complaining about their problems – then testify to them how God in His goodness has helped you in your life. People are hurting out there and longing for a strong Christian to come along with an encouraging testimony to help lift them up. You can be that strong Christian.

Remember this: the more you worship and praise and testify publicly, the stronger you are. It's often a matter of overcoming the weakness there is in trying to be a performer for those who were never called to judge or approve you in the first place.

Chapter 33

A strong Christian speaks unabashedly of the Kingdom of God to others

Go ye therefore, and teach all nations, baptizing them in the name of the Father, and of the Son, and of the Holy Ghost: - Matthew 28:19

I recall a pastor saying a few years ago that "there is no shame in the Kingdom." It is true. Anything you do as a Christian has no shame to it. Oftentimes, if we are weak, we aren't grounded deeply enough in our Christian beliefs to stand up for them. I once heard a man say that your actions will always follow your beliefs. This is true too. People act according to what they believe. Just as I mentioned in the previous chapter, many people have trouble speaking about the things of God due to what others might think. This is foolishness.

If what God thinks matters most, then that should supercede what man thinks. Man hasn't been put here to judge you. The world will try to convince you that you need to be a "performer," but that is not your calling. Your calling is to speak unabashedly of the Kingdom of God to others. Never should you be ashamed of the Man who died for you, nor for the One who sent that Man. I actually feel empowered when I speak of God's Kingdom to others. There is a joyousness in it. I know there is strength in doing this, for I have experienced the weakness in not doing this. That's what tickles me pink:

doing the opposite of the weak thing, knowing that I'm showing strength.

If you really believe in the Kingdom, you will speak of it. People speak everyday on all sorts of things they believe in: sports, politics, education, human rights etc. If we are here to build His Kingdom, then doesn't it make sense to speak of it to others? How else will they know what His Kingdom is like if we don't tell them about it? They might experience an epiphany out in the desert, but they might not, too. Satan wants you to feel bashful and/or ashamed about speaking about God's Kingdom to others. He wants you to think that it's all some mushy mumbo jumbo that you should associate with weakness. There is no weakness in speaking of God's Kingdom. There is only strength. How do we know this? We know this because Jesus spoke of the Kingdom and exhorts us to do the same, to be "fishers of men." Jesus never would ask us to do anything that required weakness. There is only strength in doing that which Jesus would do.

Remember this: the bolder you are about speaking of His Kingdom to others, the stronger and more Christ-like you are. Just keep in mind that God calls us to do only strength-enhancing duties, not things that will weaken you. Weakness is made so by disuse and neglect. The more you use your mouth to speak of His Kingdom, the more you are refusing weakness to increase in your life, and the more your Christlikeness will be made manifest.

Chapter 34

A strong Christian displays his/her true emotions

Without natural affection, trucebreakers, false accusers, incontinent, fierce, despisers of those that are good, - II Timothy 3:3

Nowadays we are yet subjected to another one of Satan's ploys to get us into fear mode: show true emotion, go to jail. This is what I was taught while living in Maryland. Society in the United States, with the way that it is set up, tends to dissuade people from displaying their true emotions. Satan knows that the truth is likely to come out of people when they show their true emotions. Therefore, he wants people to hide their emotions. So, he has promoted a culture that tends to punish or ridicule those who do show them.

This has been actually one of the hardest traits of a strong Christian for me to live out. In American culture, men are discouraged from being sentimental or crying. They are told to man up or to be macho, that only sissies cry. Jesus wept. He didn't weep because he was some weakling whose feelings were easily hurt. He wept mainly because God's children refused God's love, because they wanted to keep God at a distance. Jesus understood the sorrowful mindset of those who were not yet on board with the strong Christian mindset. And something similar happens today when we give into the defeatist mindset. We cry because those who are set against us are against love. Nothing can be more unhealthy to the soul than being against love.

When I was on trial, my lawyer advised me that if I went on the stand, that I could cry or show any other emotion than anger. He admonished me not to show anger on the stand. I retorted, "But I'm supposed to be angry. I am being accused of something I didn't do!" So, to me anger should have been natural, but to him and the judge, anger would have been seen as something that I had a "problem" with. After the trial was over, and I was in anger management class, I was told that I had an anger problem and that I shouldn't get angry at other people. At the psychologist's office I was told pretty much the same thing. Funny thing about that psychologist though. As I was driving to his office for our first session, the Holy Spirit spoke to me and told me word for word of a conversation that the psychologist and I would have that day. He said Dr. Raznick will ask you, "Tim, do you think you have a temper?" You are to reply, "Yes, I certainly do. Just like every other human on Earth, I do have a temper." The conversation, indeed, happened that way, word for word. Needless to say, the doc was not pleased with my response to his question. His idea was that I had an anger problem and that I needed to be fixed. The fact is I didn't have an anger problem. He refused to believe that I was innocent of the crime of which I had been accused.

The strong Christian, if angry, shouldn't be afraid to show his/her anger. Jesus himself got angry when he turned over the tables in a holy place of His Father. That is righteous anger, which is anger that is borne from some offense against godliness. Unrighteous anger is that which is borne from some offense against the unrighteous standards of men. The latter is sin. For example, if a father beats his child for drawing a pony with a marker on some bed sheets, that is unrighteous anger because it's not biblically approved. The anger is understandable; it's just not righteous, though. Nothing was desecrated or was sacrilegious about the child's drawing.

The fact is that there is weakness in being afraid to show one's true emotions. We fail to do so either because we are afraid of consequences or because we don't want to be seen as weak or vulnerable. It actually takes a great deal of strength to put yourself out there emotionally speaking. But, once again, there is something greater than how we are seen by others. Once again, their judgment is not what we are to fear. The weak will go around acquiescent, being afraid to show their true colors. The strong will show their true emotions, knowing that in doing so, they are expressing a degree of truth and strength as well. The more true emotion you are willing to display, the stronger you are. Just keep in mind that it's not others' job to judge you based on which emotions you display. Their job, whether they realize it or not, is to learn from the strength- and truth-expressing example that you set by showing your true emotions.

Ephesians 6:24 says, "Grace be with all them that love our Lord Jesus Christ in sincerity. Amen."

Chapter 35

A strong Christian encourages others

Wherefore comfort yourselves together, and edify one another, even as also ye do. - I Thessalonians 5:11

About a year ago I was at work working with an individual who was having a moment of self-doubt. We were talking about acquiring the physiques we had when we were in high school. We both lifted weights and played sports. He played soccer, and I played baseball. He was 34-years-old at the time and said longingly that he wished he could have back the body he had at 17. I quickly asked him, "Who told you you couldn't?" He quickly bowed his head and became silent, having no response for me. I began to tell him that I myself was 17, 20 years earlier and that I accomplished some weightlifting goals recently that beat my lifts of when I was 17. I had deadlifted, squatted, and bench pressed more weight now than I had 20 years earlier. In fact, I recently dieted and lost 50 pounds to get down to the weight that I was at when I was 17. Sometimes all it takes is words of encouragement from someone else who has succeeded in order to motivate us forward.

Why do we want to encourage others? Because God wants us to. Because it feels good knowing that we lifted another child of God up. Because we can quickly get distracted by the bombardment of worldliness around us and lose sight of the godly path that we could be on. It happens. We need daily reminders oftentimes because we are hit so hard with the world's propaganda that our eyes become set on it rather than on godly things.

What is the main cause for us not wanting to encourage others? It's actually that we are afraid to encourage others because we think they might get "ahead" of us. We are afraid that others might become more "successful" than us if they act on our encouragement. That sort of thinking is had by those who are still in that competitive mindset. Those people still feel the need to be number one, dominating their fellow man. Again, it's not a competition. We aren't called by the Almighty to compete with our fellow man. We are called to encourage one another. We all need encouragement. Nobody is so sanctimonious that he/she is above daily encouragement. We need it because our eyes and minds tend to run astray. It's the job of the encourager to try to get others back into a proper perspective, so they won't run astray and do Satan's work.

When we encourage others, the thing we want to make sure of is that our words are truth-filled. We don't want to just say nice things to people for the sake of saying them. Tell them the truth. Remind them of their potential. Remind them of the good that's in them. Oftentimes when we see that others see potential and the good that is actually in us, we feel inspired to live out our potential and our goodness. Sometimes we just need to bring it out of others. We aren't technically reaching in to bring it out, but we are prompting them to do it to themselves. We are prompting them to tap into something that is already in there and would be awesome if it were on display.

The people who shy away from encouraging others tend to be negative naysayers who aren't notably successful in life. They typically live in misery and themselves aren't surrounded by those who typically give positive reinforcement, words of encouragement, and constructive criticism. Their lives will typically reflect the absence of those things. The strong Christian, however, has no problem with the idea of encouraging others. He sees nothing wrong with his fellow man acting upon his encouragement to do well, for he knows it's not a competition. The more we eliminate competitiveness and focus on encouragement, the stronger we will become. You too can become that strong Christian that goes around encouraging others as we are exhorted to do. Examine your own heart. Are you stuck in competition mode or are you willing to encourage your fellow man so he can be successful too?

Chapter 36

A strong Christian corrects others when they speak the untruth

For whom the LORD loveth he correcteth; even as a father the son in whom he delighteth. - Proverbs 3:12

Oftentimes we hear others speak something that is untrue, and we want to correct them, but we are afraid to say anything. We needn't be afraid of what they might think of us. If you have a desire to correct someone, it's probably because you care for him/her. You just might love that person and want the best for him/her; that's good. If you walk away not caring, then that is not good.

It is important to correct others when they speak things that are not the truth. People tend to follow the things that they believe are true. If they have some misguided religious beliefs, that can lead to disastrous results or consequences for those affected by the behavior of the person with the misguided beliefs. Let's say that someone believes that if he commits suicide by bombing himself along with bystanders, he is pleasing God. The truth is that God isn't pleased by suicide. Suicide is a tragedy. A suicidal bombing often brings grief and suffering for those affected by it. The suicidal bomber was simply operating on his belief. He was never convinced that his belief was the untruth. He believed what he was doing was right in the eyes of God. It wasn't.

The example of the suicidal bomber is just one of many. The weak are often too afraid to speak up, fearing that they will offend the person who says something that is untrue. We must put that fear behind us. We must speak up. If that untruth is allowed to prosper, the person will continue going around astray and his/her beliefs could perpetually worsen, affecting himself/herself and others. How you say the truth may be more important than the truth you say. Usually we needn't be overbearing or pushy in correcting others unless there is imminent danger. Let's say someone wants to dive into a pool that is only three feet deep, but believes that it is nine feet deep. Then you can be pushy when correcting her about the thing she believes. We should normally try the gentle approach, with sincerity and expressing a desire to see better in the life of the person we are speaking to. The person's receptiveness often will depend on our approach to him/her.

The whole goal in correcting others is to lead them to the Truth. If they speak the untruth, it's because they were led by someone or something that was not of God. The strong Christian is not afraid of getting the truth out there. It's the love in the heart of the strong Christian that prompts him/her to speak against untruth. If we follow Jesus, we can rest assured that we will know the Truth. He will never tell us anything that is untrue. We should be spirit-led when correcting others. We don't want to correct others just for the sake of correcting them because of some ego issue of ours. We sometimes have to resist the sinful urge to feel superior to others by showing off our "superior" knowledge.

You can be the strong Christian that comes along to correct others lovingly. Your correction can be followed up with words of encouragement to let the person know you have his/her best interest at heart. When people believe you are for them, they often will be more receptive to your approach. Let them know that you are interested in their success. People are looking for answers, and those who are truth-ready will often receive your correction gladly.

II Timothy 3:16 says, "All scripture is given by inspiration of God, and is profitable for doctrine, for reproof, for correction, for instruction in righteousness:"

Chapter 37

A strong Christian is willing to forgive anyone

Then said Jesus, Father, forgive them; for they know not what they do. And they parted his raiment, and cast lots. - Luke 23:34

So, forgiveness seems to be one of the hardest things for people to do. It's people's ego that makes it seem difficult to do. It actually is easy once you understand the psychology of it. I understand all too well a heart of unforgiveness. I had a heart of unforgiveness for a long time, against many people. I allowed their misdeeds to dictate my emotional state. I saw forgiveness as the go-ahead for my offenders to screw me over again.

Unforgiveness is when we hold a grudge against someone for his/her offense against us. The unforgiveness agenda is rampant and is spread by Satan, oftentimes, through background checks. We often get lulled into a false sense of security when we do background checks on people. We foolishly believe that if we find that a person has a clean background, then we can rest assured of that person's future behavior. I am quick to remind people that all serial killers at one time had a clean background. The underlying idea of the background check is to hold a real or a perceived offense of someone's against him/her so that he/she can't get ahead. People think they shouldn't provide an opportunity to someone who has done wrong in the past. Well, if that's the mindset, then we are all guilty. That's why the Bible says that all have sinned and fallen short of the glory of God, and that the wages of sin is death. We all deserve to die for our sins, but God is merciful and has been gracious, and has thus provided Jesus as a way for us not to die spiritually, as the way for us to go to Heaven. And that's how we are to be towards one another: merciful and forgiving one another's faults, perceived or real.

Allowing another's behavior to control our feelings can be a dangerous mindset. We need to understand that people that need forgiveness don't have some sort of spiritual advantage over us. They are weak-minded sinners who are hurting and need to be shown the ways of the strong. Strong people don't go around committing offenses for which forgiveness will be merited later on. Forgiving someone isn't saying that the offense was OK. It's saying that you realize that the offender was in a weak mindset and didn't know better. People that know better, do better. Jesus knew that the people who were against Him didn't realize spiritually what they were doing. They saw with their physical eyes, but their spiritual eyes were blind. Today when people try to offend us, we need to realize they are spiritually blind. The key here is "try." It's not about your feeling offended; it's about their trying to offend you. If you feel offended, that's something you need to work on, and I will discuss it in a later chapter. For now, understand that the weak are those who give a sort of power to those who they haven't forgiven: the power to control their emotions.

I walked in that weakness for years. Having suffered abuse, derision, attacks, arrests, and innumerable other personal offenses, I refused to forgive people, thinking that forgiving them would be the same as agreeing with their offensive behavior. Unforgiveness has been compared to a sort of personal prison in which the unforgiving person suffers from a hardened heart, much the way the incarcerated suffer from not being able to live freely outside of a prison. It was about five years ago when I attended a workshop by actress Lindsay Wagner that I first started to be nudged towards forgiveness. I had adored her and her work on the Bionic Woman. I was not walking in forgiveness at the time, so normally I would have blown off her advice about it, but I looked up to her as a role model, so I was quite inclined to listen to her advice. A little while later, I began to explore the psychology of the whole forgiveness matter while alone with God, and God eventually led me to the point where I could justify forgiving people. That's it. It's the justification that people struggle with. Why? Because their egos get in the way. Because they don't understand the psychology of forgiveness and unforgiveness. Because they don't assign the proper definitions to these terms. Once you allow God to minister to you about this matter, the way I did, you can get to the point where forgiveness is no big deal. You'll see offenses as being committed by people who are spiritually blind and will be thankful that God has opened YOUR eyes to what actually goes on.

You can be that strong and mighty Christian that goes around, with gladness in your heart, forgiving people left and right for things. It can be kind of like the guy in the parade who passes out candy left and right to all the kiddies. Instead of candies, you could be handing out little business cards that read "You are hereby gladly forgiven. Only I control my emotions. As a strong follower of Christ, I forgive you too!" It feels good and empowering to do this. Try it. You'll be blessed. Your health will improve. It's rather incomparable the joy you can feel when you are in that mindset wherein you are willing to forgive anyone.

Proverbs 11:17 says," The merciful man doeth good to his own soul: but he that is cruel troubleth his own flesh."

Chapter 38

A strong Christian denounces and abstains from foolishness

The thought of foolishness is sin: and the scorner is an abomination to men. - Proverbs 24:9

As we have the choice each day to employ either wisdom or foolishness, the fool employs foolishness. Why? Because he believes his ego is smart enough to carry him through a situation; it's not. The wise choose wisdom, for they know that foolishness leads to a dead end, whereas wisdom leads to success. We mustn't be afraid to denounce foolishness and call it what it is when we notice it. I have yet to meet a person who ended up being successful because of employing foolishness. Surely foolish people can achieve the world's definition of success, but they don't achieve God's definition of it. Success in God's eyes is living for the Kingdom. The more you live for the Kingdom as a royal son or daughter of the Most High, the more successful you are. This is the success that matters.

Jesus pointed out examples of wisdom versus foolishness on a number of occasions. One such occasion is found in Matthew 24-27: "Therefore whosoever heareth these sayings of mine, and doeth them, I will liken him unto a wise man, which built his house upon a rock: And the rain descended, and the floods came, and the winds blew, and beat upon that house; and it fell not: for it was founded upon a rock. And everyone that heareth these sayings of mine, and doeth them not, shall be likened unto a foolish man, which built his house upon the sand: And the rain descended, and the floods came, and the winds blew, and beat upon that house; and it fell: and great was the fall of it." The point is that we need to denounce foolishness right from the get-go and choose to stay away from it. As I hinted at earlier, the two main reasons we choose foolishness is: 1) we are afraid of what others might say or do if we denounce it; 2) we think we will make out OK if we go by our ego, not believing that we would be dumb enough to do the foolish thing. The wise man foresaw potential for disaster if built his house on sand, knowing that it'd fall. The foolish man chose to avoid wisdom and trusted in his ego to carry him through. Satan wants you to trust in your ego, to think that you don't need godly wisdom. God knows that wisdom is for your good and wants greatly that you have it.

We need to pray for wisdom and discernment. Discernment is when we differentiate wisdom from foolishness. We are wise if we listen to our discerning voice that the Holy Spirit equips us with and act accordingly. We can have discernment but still not *use* it. Having it isn't enough. We must use it and then act on it. I foresaw and discerned many foolish things and still went ahead and did the foolish thing. Why? Because I let my ego lead me, foolishly thinking I'd make out alright. I never did make out alright when I acted foolishly. You'd be better off having imperfect people upset with you for your decision to abstain from foolishness than you'd be if you pleased them by dishonoring God with foolish behavior.

It's time for us to step up and boldly denounce and abstain from foolishness. The fool doesn't count on God's leading to get him/her through a situation. The fool counts on his/her ego. This is weakness. We aren't called to participate in weak activities. We are called to employ strength. We employ strength by doing what the weak are not willing to do. The weak aren't willing to denounce and abstain from foolishness. "As a dog returneth to his vomit, so a fool returneth to his folly" (Proverbs 26:11). The weak and foolish return to foolish things, foolishly thinking that if they try foolishness again, success will be had; it won't. The strong realize this and thus make an effort to stay away from foolish things. How strong are you? Will you speak up and call out foolishness? Will you make an effort to abstain from it, knowing the end thereof?

Remember that in Proverbs it says that the thought of foolishness is sin. This doesn't mean if the word foolishness or a foolish thought pops into your head you've sinned. It means that if you spend time thinking about foolishness, contemplating doing it, you've sinned. You shouldn't even entertain the notion of contemplating foolishness. As soon as you notice something foolish, you should zap it down. Call it out. Choose immediately to abstain from it. It's foolish to even contemplate doing foolishness. The fact that you'd even ponder doing something foolish indicates you have doubt about the validity of God's word. You should never doubt God's word, even when you don't understand it. Just trust that He knows what He's talking about. Trust and obey. That's all you need to do.

II Timothy 2:23 says, "But foolish and unlearned questions avoid, knowing that they do gender strifes."

Chapter 39

A strong Christian assuages others' hostility with truth-filled words of kindness

A scorner loveth not one that reproveth him: neither will he go unto the wise. - Proverbs 15:12

I'd agree if you told me this is one of the hardest traits to master. Sometimes our temper can be one of the hardest things to tame. It's often because of our ego. A lot of times when we are in hostile situations, we feel the need to "outanger" the other person. We think that if we demonstrate that our emotions are stronger and that we aren't willing to back down, then the other person, or our "opponent," will give in or give up. I've seen this scenario played out hundreds, if not thousands, of times. I've seen it with couples fighting, friends fighting, hostage situations and so on.

The carnal thing to want to do is prove to the other person that he/she is wrong and/or defeated and that we will be the victor and/or are right. How about if we first chose to understand the other person's emotions and what led to his/her hostility. This is called empathy. Jesus made an effort to understand people's situations and their temperaments. In Mark 14 Jesus assuaged the anger of those who noticed the woman who broke an alabaster box of ointment to anoint Him. He simply said, "Let her alone; why trouble ye her? she hath wrought a good work on me. For ye have the poor with you always, and whensoever ye will ye may do them good: but me ye have not always. She hath done what she could: she is come aforehand to anoint my body to the burying. Verily I say unto you, Wheresoever this gospel shall be preached throughout the whole world, this also that she hath done shall be spoken of for a memorial of her."

This is what we are to do: speak truth-filled words of kindness to people. However, we need to be aware that people won't always reciprocate kindly. Right after Jesus spoke these words, Judas Iscariot went unto the chief priests to betray Jesus. Evil doesn't like it when good is spread. Evil seeks to quieten good. There was evil in the heart of Judas. People will come against us no matter how kind we may be to them. We aren't to fight evil with evil. Good is what quashes evil. We ought to pray for the weak-minded who devise evil against us.

The weak feel the need to outanger their hostile opponent whereas the strong control their temper and empathize, realizing that the hostile person feels under attack and that he/she feels that he/she is losing control of a situation. A hostile person isn't always hostile. He/she uses hostility as a defense mechanism. We need to understand this in order to minister to them. We need to address the hurt. As strong Christians we should be glad that we have been chosen by God to undertake the task of addressing the hurting person. Most likely the hurting person has had hurtful words slung at him/her. Let's be strong and approach the hostile hurting person with kindness and words of truth and empathy to lead him/her to a place of peace in the Lord.

Remember that the more you can control your emotions and your tongue when dealing with hostility, the stronger you will be.

Proverbs 26:5 says, "Answer a fool according to his folly, lest he be wise in his own conceit."

Chapter 40

A strong Christian shares with others the Good News which includes letting them know they are sons and daughters of God meant to rise up and become mighty Christian warriors

The Spirit of the Lord is upon me, because he hath anointed me to preach the gospel to the poor; he hath sent me to heal the brokenhearted, to preach deliverance to the captives, and recovering of sight to the blind, to set at liberty them that are bruised, - Luke 4:18

Oftentimes man is ashamed to share with others the Good News about Jesus, mainly because he is more concerned with what his fellow man might think. This is part of that mindset that others have been equipped with superior judgment. If others have been equipped with superior judgment, then what sense does it make to evangelize or minister to them? More often than not, your fellow man isn't well-informed when it comes to his role in the Kingdom.

People have a tendency to live out the roles that they think they are most meant to play in this world. Mothers act like mothers. Fathers act like fathers. Firemen act like firemen. Accountants act like accountants. Thieves act like thieves. Prostitutes act like prostitutes. It's all about what role people think they are meant for, what life has led them to believe. When people aren't led to believe they are sons and daughters of God meant to rise up and become mighty Christian warriors, then they typically don't play the role. I've been there myself. I recall wandering aimlessly through life with a desire to play the one role that was meant for me. Now I'm playing it because God led me through the circumstances he wanted to lead me through to get me to where I am.

I see myself as a bilingual operative going on missions in God's army to strengthen others so they might follow my lead and become more Christ-like. Before assuming this role, I played a number of dead-end roles, like most people do. We do have certain secondary roles in this lifetime: our jobs at work, our jobs at home, little league coach etc. But our main role is the one we are to play all the time. That is the one of mighty Christian warrior. This is a role we must play and get better at til our dying day. Jesus said for us to carry our cross daily, not just from time to time. We are to grow in strength and use that strength to fight evil on a daily basis. A warrior fights. This fight will include a multitude of tasks such as prayer, ministering to hurting people, healing the sick, raising the dead, and preaching the gospel.

We are to have intimate relation with Jesus and ask him to empower us to heal the sick and raise the dead, just like He did with His disciples. Let us not be afraid to minister to the sick. When we minister to them, we have an open door to present the Good News. Jesus did not come for the healthy. He came for the sick, the hurting. One is made strong by coming out of weakness, out of sickness. We can be the strong Christians that come along to help strengthen the sick and the hurting. But, first we must let them know they are meant to play the role of strong and mighty Christian warrior. If they aren't convinced they are meant to play this role, they will seek out another role. The weak will let them go whereas the strong will pursue adamantly the lost sheep, for they know they are called to do so, that that is part of their role.

Remember that the more you share the Good News with people, the stronger you are, for you are not overtaken by the spirit of timidity.

Matthew 4:23 says, "And Jesus went all about Galilee, teaching in their synagogues, and preaching the gospel of the kingdom, and healing all manner of sickness and all manner of disease among the people."

Chapter 41

A strong Christian seeks to capitalize on the unification of God's resources for the betterment of mankind

And Noah did according unto all that the LORD commanded him. - Genesis 7:5

God has placed His people where He wants them to be to fulfill His purposes. He placed the waters where they are. He placed the mountains where they are. He placed the trees where they are. He placed the Sun, the Moon, and the stars where they are. He placed man and animals in their corresponding biomes, all according to His divine plans. The strong Christian realizes this and seeks to capitalize on these placements of resources in order to help out mankind.

When Noah was building the ark, God gave him all the resources he needed to build it: the building materials, the energy, the daylight, the space, the tools etc. God sent both man and animal to Noah so he could put them into the ark so that life could continue after the flood. We are to use what God has given us to help out mankind as well. Instead of this, man, in his greed, will often try to exploit God's resources. He will seek to maximize his profit margin so he makes out financially instead of using God's resources for the betterment of all. This is why we all too often see bosses of organizations making tons of money while the "little" people do most of the labor for little pay. God does not want us to be selfish like this. The sociopathic person who does this knows what it's like to be without money, so he fights to keep a system going in which the money and power flow to him and the workers remain virtually helpless. This is why unions are formed: so that everybody gets a fair share of the pie.

That combining form *uni-*, in union and in unification, indicates *one*, as in one body coming together for a cause. Jesus called specific resources together to be His disciples. He called Judas Iscariot, knowing that he'd be the one who'd betray Him. This was in accordance with the Father's plan. The disciples served not only as those who'd do His work, but also as bodyguards, in a way. Jesus would have been in much more danger had He not had twelve men accompanying Him during His ministry. God sent those twelve resources to accompany Jesus until it was time for Him to go to the cross. Jesus went to the cross for the betterment of mankind. Now, man can call Heaven his eternal home if he gets saved. This wasn't so before Jesus came to Earth.

The strong Christian finds out the purposes of the resources God put in his life, and thinks of how he can capitalize on the unification of those resources for the betterment of mankind. The emphasis should be on the betterment of mankind, not on the betterment of one's bank account because of greed. It's alright to increase our bank account so long as we don't have to put our fellow man down a notch to do so. The strong Christian isn't looking to outdo his fellow man. He/she knows that we aren't called to compete, that is, to put others beneath us. Capitalizing on God's resources should be done so that God gets the glory for our action(s) and so that man is better off. After all, God's resources are here for our benefit. They are here so that we use them in such a way that God will get the honor and the glory that He deserves as a result of our using them. We are called to be Christian MacGyvers (like from the TV show) using our resources to save the day in a God-glorifying way.

Remember, the weak seek to gratify themselves and to inflate their bank accounts through the exploitation and misuse of God's resources whereas the strong Christian seeks to glorify God and to better mankind through the proper unification of those resources. Will you choose to ignore the purposes of God's resources to satisfy your selfish motives and ambitions? Or, will you look out for your fellow man and other God-supplied resources to enrich the lives of others? The more you seek to honor God and utilize His resources according to His will, the stronger you will be.

Chapter 42

A strong Christian seeks friendship even with the impoverished

The righteous considereth the cause of the poor: but the wicked regardeth not to know it. - Proverbs 29:7

I recall in 2007 I was living in the Dominican Republic doing a 12-week volunteer project, coaching kids in baseball. I had spent eleven weeks there when I decided I was not going to leave the country without doing something to really help God's people. I set out to feed the homeless during my last week there. One morning I left my apartment in Santo Domingo, the capital city, to buy food for the homeless people living on the streets. I only had about $1.35 on me, so I was only able to buy a bunch of bananas from the one street vendor who was open at that time. It was 5:30 a.m. and still dark. The first person I came across was a twenty-seven-year-old woman whose family didn't want her. She was unkempt, missing teeth, and living on the streets. I cheerfully gave her a banana and we chatted for a few minutes. She wanted to touch my hair, and I let her. She appreciated the food, but I think she appreciated my gesture of friendship even more. My genuine interest in talking to her and treating her like a worthy human being might have made her day, for man's greatest longing is to have another love him and to show that he is loveable.

I made my round giving out one banana to each person I saw sleeping in the open air. I felt good, as though I had done service to God's people. I wanted to feel that way again, so I headed out the next day to give again. Only this time it was in the afternoon and unplanned. I was walking through the Colonial Zone when a homeless American man approached me for help. He told me his story of how he ended up living on the streets there, and I decided to feed him. I walked with him into the local Kentucky Fried Chicken restaurant and approached the counter. I thought "what can I order for him that won't be too expensive?" I suggested that he get the number one combo. He ordered the number one, but I found out when the cashier told me the total that he had ordered the number one in the family size, which was clearly more expensive than the number one individual meal. The man looked down, his countenance replete with utmost humility, hoping that I'd buy him the bigger meal. I felt compassion and agreed to buy him the meal, which was more than he had eaten all week, along with a meal for myself. He thanked me for the food and went on his way. I sat down to eat and got about halfway through my own meal. I remembered that I had dinner waiting for me back at the apartment, so I thought about whom I could give my remaining chicken to. There was a lady who lived at the end of the street in a cardboard box. I left the restaurant and walked along the busy street towards her. As I approached her home, she reached out her hand, seemingly anticipating that I'd come along with a bag of food for her. I handed her the bag of food as she smiled at me with white teeth that were brighter than mine. I almost asked her who her dentist was! I returned to the apartment and ended up conversing with a roommate who knew of my food giving that week. He said that I'd have good karma, that good things would happen to me because of all the good I had done that week. In my rebellious mindset still, I retorted back sharply, "I don't believe in that! Most likely I will get stabbed in the back!

A few days later I returned home to the United States and began to open all of the mail that had accumulated during my 12-week stay in the Dominican. One of the first things I opened was a letter from a mortgage company. I recognized the name of the company but thought that it was strange for them to send me something, considering that I had paid off my loan with them a couple of years earlier. The letter started something like this:

Dear Mr. Hicks,

As you know, you had a loan with us a few years ago, and it was paid in full. However, we recently were going through some old paperwork and found that even though you paid us the money you owed us, it turns out you paid us too much. So, if you will kindly fill out the enclosed papers and return them to us, we will send you a check for $1,345.00.

That was approximately 100 times the

amount I had spent on the man's fried chicken meal and 1,000 times the amount I had spent on the bananas. God taught me a very important lesson with that: You take care of my people, and I will take care of you. God always reimburses us when we give cheerfully to the impoverished. I not only gave my money but also my friendship. Jesus never discriminated. Man looks on the outside and categorizes others based on their perceived economic class. God looks on the heart and doesn't categorize man based on his bank statement. Jesus sees people as sheep. He came to save the lost, so it only makes sense for Him to seek friendship with the impoverished. He wants to enrich peoples' lives spiritually. As Jesus befriended the poor, so should we. The weak go around with a separatist mentality, classifying and categorizing people according to finances. We, as strong Christians, are to seek out the treasure that's inside of people. When the poor find out that we have a genuine interest in friendship, we end up enriching our own lives with their friendship. Let people know that you love them. This is what people are really longing for. The strong Christian will authentically have a heart-to-heart conversation with the impoverished. God will see your heart in this and reward you accordingly.

Proverbs 28:27 says, "He that giveth to the poor shall not lack: but he that hideth his eyes shall have many a curse."

Chapter 43

A strong Christian remains unperturbed in the face of those who fail to appreciate his/her contribution

And ye shall be betrayed both by parents, and brethren, and kinsfolks, and friends; and some of you shall they cause to be put to death. - Luke 21:16

Loyalty is a funny thing. It often seems to be had by those who don't deeply investigate the character of the people they are loyal to. Oftentimes people are loyal to those who would sell them out in a heartbeat. As strong Christians, we aren't to let others lack of contribution dictate our contribution or control our emotions.

At work, I've seen a certain scenario a thousand times. A person on one shift will leave a mess instead of cleaning it up to help out the next shift. The next shift will come in, see the mess, and won't clean it up. They will often leave the mess and/or create an even bigger mess for the first shift, thereby acting perturbed by the behavior of those on the first shift. This mentality focuses on man seeing the behavior and being the rewarder of the behavior. It's God's eyes who are on everything we do. God is the one who sees our hearts when we do any behavior. Even if man doesn't reward us for our good behavior, God will in His own unique way. God wants us to be diligent and not change our behavior to be like those who aren't diligent. We, as strong Christians, are to be exemplary in conduct. The weak are those who haven't been convinced that diligence is good for them. Be humbly diligent in their face anyway.

Jesus was betrayed by Judas. He still died for Judas and people like him. He didn't grow bitter because Judas failed to appreciate what Jesus was going to do for the world and for him. In like manner, people today are like they were back then in biblical times. They will fail to see the strength in our actions. They will think there is something wrong with us if we act diligently and care about doing things well. They will fail to appreciate our contributions in this world. Press on anyway! The weak will give up, thinking their contribution won't matter. But, maybe someone will notice your efforts. You may be inspiring someone unknowingly. There are many men who have inspired me. I saw their contribution and wanted to follow in their footsteps. It's alright to follow good behavior, so long as it is Jesus-like. We want to be careful not to fall into idolatry, which makes man like a god to us.

By remaining unperturbed in the face of those who fail to appreciate our contribution, we are not letting others control our emotions. We are still in control of them. If we harbor negative emotions towards them, we give them control of our emotions as well as fail to remember that they aren't strong like us yet. The strong Christian keeps in mind that the weak don't know any better, that the weak don't understand Christian strength. We are to press on regardless of others' lack of appreciation.

Watch your loyalty. People's loyalty tends to wane or to grow based on their feelings towards others. If you let others know of your intention to remove your loyalty from them, mention that you noticed a heart issue with them. This should cause them to introspect. The weak will grow more withdrawn and resentful towards you whereas the strong will examine their heart and the reasons why they failed to appreciate your contribution in some area in the first place. Be that strong Christian who appreciates others' contribution. Be the strong one who sallies forth unperturbed, not allowing others to dictate or to determine your emotions and your future contributions.

Chapter 44

A strong Christian refuses to compromise
his/her Christian principles

*As ye have therefore received Christ Jesus the
Lord, so walk ye in him: Rooted and built up in
him, and stablished in the faith, as ye have been
taught, abounding therein with thanksgiving. -
Colossians 2:6,7*

It seems to be becoming increasingly
difficult to stand up for one's Christian
principles nowadays with all of the persecution
that's going on. People are being sent to jail,
being beheaded, being fired, being beat up,
being harassed, being attacked in many ways.
Our forefathers probably couldn't have foreseen
how religious freedom would be used against us
in this era. I was wondering recently where one
draws the line.

I asked God and He told me that even though
we may be contributing to sin, we are not to
enjoy it, as we continue in it, and we are to seek
a way out of it. For example, the bartender who
converts to Christianity who wants to stop
serving alcohol to people, because he doesn't
want to contribute to others' sin, is to keep doing
his best Christian duty as a bartender until he
finds a better, God-honoring line of work.
Another example is with my part-time job. I
merchandise pizzas and ice cream. I believe
God got me this job to bless me and to teach me
things. However, I can't help but think that the

products I am shelving are contributing to someone else's sin, mainly their gluttony (probably). We even have one pizza called Diablo, which means "Devil" in Spanish. I know that greater employment awaits me down the road, but I am to remain in this position until God has called me to the greater position. Does it mean that I set out to sin just because my job contributes to another's sin? No. It simply means that I do my best not to enjoy my contribution to their sin while I'm doing my job. I still smile and work cheerfully, but I don't boast or praise my contribution to others' sin.

As I stated in the Introduction, I got fired for refusing to compromise my Christian principles. I said I would use the weapons of love, prayer, and forgiveness in this spiritual battle, for I knew I was up against spirits, not flesh and blood. I was purportedly seen as a threat due to my mention of weapons. I was subsequently fired. You ask if I'd do it again. You bet I would. We need to remember that God won't leave us hanging if we take a stand for Him. He's not going to say, "I appreciate what you did, but you're on your own now, kiddo!" No! God will take us to a better place. God got me a better job that was closer to home after I got fired from that supermarket job. He will do the same for you.

There is nothing that tickles Satan pink more than when a Christian publicly dishonors God. Conversely, nothing pleases God more than when one of His children stands up for Him publicly. When a Christian refuses to compromise his/her Christian principles in public, God is thrilled. We aren't called to timidity, to walk in fear. We are to walk boldly, not backing down when threatened concerning our Christian principles. Satan will try to play on human fears to get people to back down. This is where Christian strength comes in. The weak will back down fearing consequences or what people might think. The strong will refuse to compromise, knowing that God is omnipotent and will have their back. We aren't to be more concerned with what the ill-advised and the uneducated might think. Naturally evil doesn't want you to stand up for Christ because it knows that it will be exposed. Evil doesn't like to be exposed. Christ doesn't need or want to hide. However, we must act wisely when defending our principles. We don't want to back down, but we don't want to try to increase our propensity for danger, either. The strong Christian will use wisdom to defend his/her Christian principles in a God-honoring way. You can be that type of strong Christian. The question is: what spirit will you follow, the spirit of boldness or the spirit of fear?

Chapter 45

A strong Christian refuses to play the role of weak and quiet victim

Watch ye, stand fast in the faith, quit you like men, be strong. - I Corinthians 16:13

Evil has an agenda, and it doesn't like to be uncovered. As it is now, that's how it was thousands of years ago when Jesus was sentenced to death. He was seen as a threat. He was a threat ... to evil. He remained quiet when asked certain questions that He could have answered to defend Himself and His life, possibly. He wasn't playing the role of weak and quiet victim. He was going along with the script that His Father had written. We can follow the example of Jesus today if we want.

I asked God a few years ago to clarify the whole bullying thing for me. He said bullying boils down to one thing: man has a sinful desire to feel superior to his fellow man. Man is led to believe, not by God, that if he puts his fellow man down, he himself will feel better, superior. If he pushes around, coerces, is condescending towards, or threatens his fellow man, the latter will feel inferior and the former, superior. If he can get his fellow man to feel defeated, then he is assured victory. The bully wants his fellow man to play the role of weak and quiet victim. He wants him to shut up and to accept defeat like a weakling. Nothing will kill the spreading of the Gospel more than the Christian's willingness to obey evil's command for him/her to play the role of weak and quiet victim.

To be strong Christians, we need not give in to the bully's tactics. We need to be outspoken and to stand up for the truth and righteousness. The weak and quiet victim is the one who gives in to fear and doesn't speak up. Jesus focused on the heart and people's motives. If you are being bullied, you need to focus on the bullies' motives. Ask them questions that point to the motives in their heart. We know there is a heart sickness and that the bully probably feels insecure about himself/herself. Maybe he/she is being threatened by a bully who is higher up and is passing on the threat to you. Get at the root of that thing. Getting to the root of the matter, i.e., the heart, you should arrive at the truth. Once you know the truth, healing can begin. But, evil must be cut off first. It's like when you have a disease. The sick part must be removed first, then health can be recovered.

When I was fired from my frozen lead position at the supermarket in 2012, I was bullied by a manager on the phone. He was fed some false information about me and was passing on a threat from higher up. He was feeling bullied, but, in order not to have to be the final one bullied, he passed on the threat to me. I stood up for myself and my Christian beliefs, refusing to play the role of weak and quiet victim. As per our phone call, he wanted me to play the role of weak and quiet victim. I would not. I told him I would use the weapons of prayer, love, and forgiveness in this battle against evil. I was immediately seen as a threat because of my mention of weapons. The fact is I was a threat ... to evil. Only evil will feel threatened by love, prayer, and forgiveness. I could have chosen to keep my mouth shut and thereby keep my job. We are not to keep our mouths shut when it comes to bullying. We are not called to keep quiet when it comes to evil and bullying. We are to call those things out when we notice them and to address them. We are to ask questions, like Jesus did, that lead to the motives in the hearts of those involved.

Remember, evil wants you to keep quiet. Evil wants you to bow down to it. Evil wants you to be a defenseless victim. By using the whole armor of God, we can fight evil and come out the victors, not the victims. That's what a strong Christian does. You can be that strong Christian. It's your choice.

Chapter 46

A strong Christian refuses to bow down to satanic authority

Submit yourselves therefore to God. Resist the devil, and he will flee from you. - James 4:7

"Bow, sucka!" I remember repeatedly hearing that line in a movie years ago. A bully martial artist was attempting to get another martial artist, who was humble, to bow down and kiss his shoes as a way of admitting that the bully was the superior one at martial arts. That line comes to mind any time I see an instance of satanic authority trying to have its way with people. In a way it's both easier and harder to stand up for Christianity nowadays. With all the persecution of Christians that's going on in these last days, the Christian is really being put to the test.

Jesus said that he who loses his life for His sake shall find it. We tend to get caught up with so many things of this world as we are bombarded with worldliness on a daily basis. Abandoning the worldly things and living for Christ's sake is what He was talking about when He mentioned finding his life. The more we get attached to the things of this world, the more leverage Satan has to influence us. Satan can see the attachment we have to the things of this world, so he threatens us. He basically says that if you follow Jesus, you will lose the things of this world that you hold to be precious. So, it shouldn't be surprising that in the Unites States, as materialistic as it is, people find it harder to follow Christ, because they have that internal debate about giving up a lifestyle Satan sold them some time ago. That's why in other countries where people have few material things, they find it easier to follow Christ, because they have less to give up. People tend to be so set on clinging to the little that they have that they actually turn down Jesus to maintain that which they can see with their physical eyes.

As strong Christians, we can actually have life more abundantly if we follow Jesus. If you'll notice, a lot of the things we do on a daily basis have to do with keeping up a certain ongoing lifestyle. I pay auto insurance, drive to and for work, buy gas, get repairs, and do other things just because I have chosen a certain lifestyle that requires that I do those things. Oftentimes there is a direct correlation between the lifestyle we choose and the amount of surrender we offer to the Christian lifestyle. It follows that the more we choose a non-Christian lifestyle, the more likely we will bow down to satanic authority. What exactly is bowing down to satanic authority then? It's admitting that Satan is ruler over your life to a degree. What makes it hard not to bow down to his authority is our unwillingness to follow Jesus. Our desire to follow the things of this world and store up treasures for this life is what keeps us from that abundant life we could have if we followed Jesus. Abundant life is walking with the joy of the Lord in your heart and being grateful for the blessings He has bestowed upon us. It's about experiencing a Jesus walk as we deal with the things and the people of this world while we are here. It's not always going to be pleasant. Things in Jesus' life were not always pleasant, but He lived abundantly because he embraced the lifestyle the Father wanted for Him while on Earth.

Not surprisingly, the weak are the ones who choose to bow down to satanic authority, whether they realize it or not, so they can pursue that elusive trouble-free life, filled with the things of this world. The strong know they will have trouble. They will get fired, get written up, get their tires slashed, get their mailboxes crushed, get beat up etc. We are to press on anyway and tell the truth. The captives are set free by agreeing with the truth. Once you know the truth and how it is healthy for you, you will feel inclined to fight lying, satanic authority. Authority is valid only if people agree and submit to it. If nobody agrees to submit to it, then the authority has no power over people. This is where Christian strength comes in. Christians need to unite and refuse to bow down to satanic authority. Rest assured God will have your back if you do so. It may get ugly for a bit, but that's how it is on this planet ruled by Satan. Refuse anyway, like Jesus did.

Chapter 47

A strong Christian is undeterred in calling out a wolf in sheep's clothing

He that deviseth to do evil shall be called a mischievous person. - Proverbs 24:8

There is, perhaps, no greater threat to good than the individual who chooses not to call out a wolf in sheep's clothing. Jesus said He'd be sending out His disciples among false prophets who inwardly would be ravening wolves (Matthew 7:15). He said that they'd be known by their fruits. Good men bring forth good fruit; evil men bring forth evil fruit. We are to call out those who devise to do evil. Jesus knew that those against Him would be like hungry wolves attacking meek sheep (His disciples). That's why He told them to use their discernment among the wolves (for their protection).

Probably more often than not, people are afraid to call evil what it is and evil people what they are. Those who are afraid are members of what I call "the do-nothing management team." It's because usually those in authority positions are the ones who fail to call out evil. As individuals we are to call it out, too, but it's worse when someone in charge turns a blind eye to evil. There is an extremely dangerous mentality that such people tend to have: a little evil isn't so bad. I see this mentality in place all the time. People let so many seemingly harmless things slide, thinking that "a little evil never hurt anybody." Satan wants you to think like that. But, it's the snowball effect that he employs to dupe people. Why? Because people tend to notice contrast, not the subtle changes that come along. Just fifty years ago, a lot of the things that are on TV nowadays would not have been permitted on TV. Women's navels and certain cuss words were not permitted then, but now they are. Standards have changed little by little. If standards change drastically overnight, people are all up in arms about it, but, people tend to react with less resistance when standards change slowly.

I can recall many times when people failed to call out sheep in wolves clothing. I myself was guilty of it. If we go along with evil, it's usually because we agree with it. For years smoking indoors was permitted and many people did nothing about it. Little by little changes came about and places began to ban indoor smoking. The question is, why did it take years and years for that to happen? It's because nobody took it seriously enough to do something about it right from the beginning. People had to labor intensely to convince those in charge to do something about the evil behavior because those in charge were thinking "a little evil isn't so bad." This is a dangerous mentality because of the snowball effect which allows evil to perpetually worsen and not show people the contrast between presence and absence. It's dangerous because even a little evil can and does destroy people. Nobody was an alcoholic with just one drink. They became alcoholics because a little evil was allowed to perpetually worsen and was probably not called out (although it might have been).

If people devise to do evil, call them out on it. Years ago I was traveling with a Costa Rican pastor from church to church in Costa Rica while learning a little about missionary work. We had to cross some water on a ferry. The pastor told me he'd pay for our ferry trip on the way back as long as I paid for it the first time. I agreed and took him at his word. A few days later when we were about to embark for our return trip on the ferry, he changed his mind and said I'd have to pay for the return trip because he'd paid money, behind my back, to another pastor with whom we stayed for a few days. I never had been told of any such agreement. I only knew of him telling me he'd pay for our return trip on the ferry. He was going back on his word. I told him directly that he was going back on his word and he got upset and spoke very little to me all the way back to my hotel room where he dropped me off. Four years later and he hasn't spoken to me since. I don't hold grudges, nor do I regret calling him out on his evil motive. I had learned through a friend of his that members of his church had called him out vociferously when they learned of his plot to acquire church land for his own personal gain. That pastor lost a lot of his congregation over that. This is one of the biggest things we can do to overcome evil: call it out!

As strong Christians, we are not to walk in

fear of potential repercussions over calling out evil and wolves in sheep's clothing. Knowing the snowball effect should prompt us even more to call those things out. Did you ever suffer because of the actions of an evil person? Of course you did. We all have. We suffer because that evil was never addressed from the get-go. It was allowed to perpetually worsen. Someone who could have done something about it just let it slide. If people are speaking lies, call them out on it. Whatever evil you discern, call out the doer, the deviser. If you are attacked because of calling them out, that's your confirmation that you were doing the right thing. You will be disliked or even hated by those whom you call out. But, remember, your motive in calling them out is to put a stop to evil and to prompt the deviser of evil to become a doer of good; it's never to destroy people. You're calling them out because you care, and you care because you have love. Jesus wasn't afraid to say to his disciples that one of them would betray him. One of them was a wolf in sheep's clothing (dressed as a disciple). He was betrayed anyway. Be the strong Christian by calling out evil when you discern it.

II Thessalonians 2:3 says," Let no man deceive you by any means: for that day shall not come, except there come a falling away first, and that man of sin be revealed, the son of perdition;"

Chapter 48

A strong Christian boldly takes a stand for God when others are not

Suffer me a little, and I will show thee that I have yet to speak on God's behalf. - Job 36:2

Jesus said that the laborers would be few. When it comes to taking a bold stand in the name of God, few will labor in this area. Many will be afraid of getting stoned, ridiculed, or attacked in some way. They believe more in being afraid of man than they do in God being in control. With all the affliction that came upon Job in the Bible, he had more "reason" than other people to distrust God. He stayed faithful to God, and God blessed him abundantly for it. As other people turned from God when things didn't go their way, Job remained steadfast in his loyalty to God. He knew that God wasn't against him. Admittedly, this is, perhaps, one of the hardest strong Christian traits to live out.

I remember one evening a few years back, I was in church for a special class that the head pastor was teaching. At one point during the class, he asked, "Who here would like to pray for the sick?" I almost raised my hand but, instead, I looked around for someone else to raise his/her hand. I remember thinking, "Raise your hand, somebody!" I wanted to pray for the sick, but I grew up always expecting someone else stronger than me to step up to the plate, so I chickened out. Nobody raised a hand. After that

I did some introspection, and God spoke to me, as well. He encouraged me to be the strong Christian in that kind of a situation by insisting to pray for the sick. I said to myself, "From here on out, if ever again I am asked to pray for the sick, I will stand up boldly and say that I will be the strong and mighty Christian warrior who will pray for the sick!

The Bible tells us that many will be persecuted for Jesus' name. People will be persecuted, martyred, tortured, beaten, whipped, ridiculed, ostracized, and isolated for taking a bold stand for God. This is happening now more than ever in this world. Pastors are being jailed for preaching the Word, Christian groups hold services in hideouts, and believers are being beheaded. Those who want to remain safe either say nothing or bow down and pledge allegiance publicly to the enemy. Those who speak out will face opposition to some degree. The majority don't want to take a bold stand because of the consequences. They are letting fear win. They are actually still living a lie, the lie that denying God and/or Jesus is the way to go; it's not. While we are to use discernment and wisdom when choosing our words, we aren't to deny our God before men.

Jesus said in Luke 12:8,9, "Also I say unto you, Whosoever shall confess me before men, him shall the Son of man also confess before the angels of God: But he that denieth me before men shall be denied before the angels of God." The decision is yours. Will you decide to take a bold stand before men for God's sake, or will you succumb to the fear of those who would oppose you (who really oppose God)? The more you take that bold stand, the stronger you are. Remember, it's God who is the rewarder of good and evil deeds. You will receive your reward in due time for taking a bold stand in His name.

Chapter 49

A strong Christian spots weakness in others and sets out to strengthen them

Even so ye, forasmuch as ye are zealous of spiritual gifts, seek that ye may excel to the edifying of the church. - I Corinthians 14:12

God spoke to me a couple of years ago and said, "The main reason people don't want to strengthen others is that they are afraid that others will become stronger than they are." Man's fear of feeling inferior to his fellow man is the biggest thing that holds him back from setting out to strengthen others. I remind you that we aren't called to feel superior to our fellow man. Our emotional status should not depend on our perceived level in comparison to our fellow man. We aren't called to look at ourselves as being above or below others. Once you remove that comparison mindset, you can clearly focus on spotting weakness in others and strengthening them.

It has been said that some school teachers feel insecure towards certain students who show promise of excelling to a level of expertise potentially beyond that of the teacher. If we are teaching others, we needn't be concerned with others excelling beyond us. Being absent of the comparison mindset, we can focus on the joy of strengthening others. There is indeed joy to be experienced upon watching another person overcome weakness. We should be glad that another is overcoming weakness and entering into strength. They are essentially coming out of a lie that kept them in some bondage. Remember, there is no weakness in strength. There are varying degrees of strength, but weakness cannot be present when strength is present. It's just like how darkness cannot be present when light is present, and vice versa. They can coexist but not in each other. In other words, they can't overlap. One is one, and the other is the other. As long as you are making an effort to be strong, you are showing some degree of strength. Refusal to apply any degree of effort entails weakness.

Jesus said in Luke 22:32, "But I have prayed for thee, that thy faith fail not: and when thou art converted, strengthen thy brethren." Jesus said this to Simon, but it applies to us as well, for what He wanted for Simon, he wants for us all today. Noticing weakness in others is not judging them. We are called to observe both weakness and strength in others and the good and the bad in them. Spotting weakness for the sake of wanting to strengthen them shows your own strength. It shows you are not in that comparison mindset. Strengthening others involves doing what you know how to do to convince them that doing the "Jesus thing" is what real strength is all about. In other words, doing what Jesus would do is where real strength lies. It's about looking at things from a Jesus perspective and handling life's situations and obstacles the way Jesus would.

You may have noticed that some traits in this book seem harder to live out than others. The fact that you are doing this should tell you that you have a heart issue. We all have this issue of the heart. We all have the flesh pulling at us on a daily basis. It comes down to daily decisions: to do the Jesus thing or not to do it. And, if we do the Jesus thing, to what degree? Your degree of strength will be in direct proportion to your willingness to carry your daily cross. Some days you might be in one of those moods where you get discouraged and forgetful about your identity in Him and that you are supposed to do the Jesus thing. It happens. That's why we need to be diligent in our daily efforts to strengthen one another, the same way Satan attacks us daily to get our eyes off of Jesus. Satan attacks daily because he knows how quick we can be to forget the things of Jesus if he bombards us with lustful images of worldliness. Satan doesn't take a day off and neither should we. It's up to us to spot the absence of strength in others and to encourage them to go after real strength, which is doing the Jesus thing. Satan is doing his utmost to distort people's view of strength. He will have people comparing themselves to one another and having them think that if they dominate their fellow man, then they are strong. The fact is real strength involves strengthening others which is what Jesus has called us to do. How far will you choose to go in this area of strengthening others. The more you set out to strengthen others, the more your own strength will increase.

Proverbs 3:27 says, "Withhold not good from them to whom it is due, when it is in the power of thine hand to do it."

Chapter 50

A strong Christian realizes that offenders were acting only in ignorance

So foolish was I, and ignorant: I was as a beast before thee. - Psalm 73:22

A strong Christian does not get offended, for he/she realizes that the offender was acting only in ignorance. The offender is spiritually blind, unaware of the spiritual ramifications surrounding the offense. As a strong Christian, in order for me to get offended, I have to value what the offender says above what God says; that won't happen. Some things will be said with the mouth, others, with actions. Either way, the offender foolishly thinks that he/she will be one-upping me (somehow) by offending me. Usually the offender's intention is to get me to feel either defeated or inferior (or both). Offenders walk in ignorance because they are still not convinced -- maybe because they are unaware of the truth -- that truth-handling is the best way to go.

I understand the mentality of those who still go around claiming that offenders "know better" as if we've all been equipped with some higher reserve of thinking called "knowing better" that we are to call upon when making decisions. "Knowing better" is actually a misnomer. Usually when people say that someone knows better, really what they mean is that someone "believes better" or "believes the way I believe." We see others and assume they have the same knowledge, education, ethics, beliefs, and morals that we do. The fact is no two people have the exact same upbringing and knowledge, education etc. However, there is, indeed, such a thing as knowing better: When people know better, they do better. If they do worse, it's because they don't know better. In other words, they don't believe that what YOU consider to be better behavior is better behavior for them. Those who do better, know the truth and apply it because they see and believe it's good for them to do so. Those who do better don't look at it as knowing better; they just do what they know to do. All the time I see and hear judgmental people complaining of an offender who supposedly knew better. The fact is they don't know better. That's why Jesus said, "Father, forgive them, for they know not what they do." The people coming against Jesus were blind to the spiritual ramifications of what they were doing. Once Jesus died, God opened their eyes and people repented because then they knew what they had done. They saw with their spiritual eyes at that point.

Jesus knew that people who didn't accept Him would be blind to the Truth. He had compassion on them, for He knew they were ignorant. He knew they would accept His ways if only they had their eyes opened. That's why God allowed man to receive eternal life while he was still alive, and to receive eternal damnation if not. Knowing that offenders walk in blindness should prompt us to have compassion on our fellow man. As strong Christians we needn't walk around presuming that all others know and believe the way we believe. They might not have arrived at our level of Christian maturity. When Jesus counseled people, He focused on their doubts. Their doubts came from their lack of knowledge about the Truth. People then were uneducated and ignorant regarding the truth, so they went around being victims of their own ignorance and eventually perished. Some did get saved.

Today we see examples of people all around us who walk in spiritual blindness and end up suffering needlessly because of it. As a strong compassionate Christian, you can be the one who guides others to the Light, and the Truth, and the Way. We see how those who don't walk on a lit path fall by the wayside and into destruction. I've seen it countless times. It's very disheartening, but people do have their free will, and it's therefore a matter of choice. Help them to choose wisely. Use personal examples and testimonies of how you once walked in darkness and ignorance but now walk in the Light and want the best for them. Remember, he who claims that an offender knew better is typically given to unforgiveness, and unforgiveness justifies persecution and judgment, and we are called to stay away from saying that the ignorant knew better. We are to walk in compassion, realizing that offenders are blind to potential forthcoming destruction as a result of their offense or sin. Be the strong Christian who shows others how Jesus would not try to offend others in a situation.

I Timothy 1:13 says, "Who was before a blasphemer, and a persecutor, and injurious: but I obtained mercy, because I did it ignorantly in unbelief."

Chapter 51

A strong Christian refrains from holding people's past against them to hinder their future

An ungodly man diggeth up evil: and in his lips there is as a burning fire. - Proverbs 16:27

Just as God works through people, Satan does too. The latter will have those not under godly influence focus on others' past in an effort to hinder their future. The whole idea is that Satan wants us to believe that the mistakes of our past define our identities; they don't. If that were the case, then that same philosophy could just as well be turned against those trying to use it in the first place on others, and they wouldn't like that, now would they? The biggest tool Satan has people using is the background check. The ungodly will dig up whatever dirt they can find on those who seem to show promise in an effort to hinder their future. Satan has people do this because he doesn't want us to live as successful, God-serving Christians. He wants to do his utmost to ensure our efforts to serve God be hindered. Those doing background checks on others typically have an unforgiving heart. They think they can assure the safety of people by finding a squeaky clean background on the person being checked. Really what they end up having is a false sense of security, for nobody can assure safety merely by doing a background check on others. I am quick to remind people that every criminal in history, at one point, had a clean background.

Jesus was well aware that all sinned and that the wages of sin is death. But, the problem is that we try to convict people while withholding any sort of compassion, empathy, or forgiveness. People do deserve to die for their sins, but Jesus came along and was merciful. He saw that people didn't know better. He saw the intentions in people's hearts. He said in Luke 7:47, "Her sins, which are many, are forgiven; for she loved much: but to whom little is forgiven, the same loveth little." People today are quick to judge, for judgment gives them a feeling of power, and people like power. In an effort to keep power away from those who show potential, people typically jump on a judgment bandwagon and focus lots of energy on the condemnation of others for their purported sins.

I find it ironic how people, even Christians, have a tendency to jump on the bandwagon of the sin that they feel they are least likely to commit. Moms, fathers, and other pro-life advocates a while back were quick to jump on the anti-abortion bandwagon. Then, a while later, heterosexual marriage advocates were quick to jump on the godly marriage bandwagon. But then I noticed how when the gluttony bandwagon pulled into town, in front of people's homes, Christians were looking the other way, turning a blind eye, pretending not to notice it. Those that jump on the bandwagon are hypocrites. Jesus said so Himself in Luke 6:41, 42: "And why beholdest thou the mote that is in thy brother's eye, but perceivest not the beam that is in thine own eye? Either how canst thou say to thy brother, eye, when thou thyself beholdest not the beam that is in thine own eye? Thou hypocrite, cast out first the beam out of thine own eye, and then shalt thou see clearly to pull out the mote that is in thy brother's eye."

The weak follow Satan's command to try to hinder others' future. They are quick to judge and slow to forgive. The strong believe in giving people another chance, are quick to forgive, are compassionate and empathic. To keep it real, the strong Christian will introspect and thus realize that he/she has messed up in the past too. This introspection should lead toward empathy towards one's fellow man and a desire to see him succeed, not to hinder his future. Where is your heart regarding this matter? Are you being a busybody and spending precious time focusing on others' pasts or are you walking strongly by refraining from such foolishness?

Jesus said in John 8:7, "He that is without sin among you, let him first cast a stone at her."

Chapter 52

A strong Christian stands firm in spite of cultural difference

And be not conformed to this world: but be ye transformed by the renewing of your mind, that ye may prove what is that good, and acceptable, and perfect, will of God. - Romans 12:2

I remember from my school days that those who tried to fit in to be a part of the culture were called posers. I certainly didn't want to be known as a poser, so I made an effort early on not to be like one and not to be like the trendsetters. I like to do things my own way and think outside the box. I notice even today that when I go to certain areas, the people who are from those areas talk like they are from there. I am not talking about the obvious regional accent. I am talking about the kinds of vocabulary that people use. People in the ghetto tend to talk like the other people in the ghetto. People in the aristocracy tend to talk like other aristocrats and so on. I decided long ago to create my own idiolect, for I did not wish to sound like other people.

Jesus had his idiolect as well. That's why people used to say that they never heard anyone speak like Him before. Even though I grew up speaking standard American English in Maryland, I have acquired other accents and verbal peculiarities that manifest when I speak. Some words will come out sounding like they are spoken by a typical New Yorker. Other words will come out sounding like they are spoken by someone in West Virginia and so forth. Even though people, for the most part, understand me, sometimes people will ask me where I am from because of how I speak. Oftentimes when I speak Spanish, which is my second language, people will ask me where I learned it. This is because I speak it fluently, but I don't sound like another speaker they've heard before. When we speak, people should say, "He/She sounds like a Christian." The strong Christian will make a fervent effort at sounding like Christ when He spoke. Christ didn't try to speak or act in a certain way to try to fit in in a culture. He spoke the way the Father wanted Him to speak. As a strong Christian, your actions should speak for you as well. It won't just be your mouth that does the talking. The way you conduct yourself and deal with the world should indicate your adherence to a Christ-like lifestyle. We aren't called to conform to a man-made culture.

When I was traveling in 2012 with the Costa Rican pastor, he urged me to conform to the Costa Rican culture since I was living among Costa Rican people. I politely refused to do so. I knew that I wasn't supposed to conform and saw how people were being destroyed by following the culture like robots. Sometimes a culture can have positive things in it, but we aren't to pledge allegiance to any culture other than the Jesus culture, for there is only good in the latter. Costa Ricans, for example, drink coffee. It's what most of them do. It's considered a Costa Rican custom. I can go along with this, for I see the health benefits of drinking coffee in moderation. However, it's also a part of their culture to eat pork products. This is unhealthy. When I was there, the Costa Rican people tried to get me to eat pork. I would not do it. I care about my temple too much to be eating meats that contribute to unhealth. I was standing firm in spite of cultural difference.

The weak will succumb to peer pressure and try to fit in, going along with the crowd, going with the flow, performing ungodly tasks like some pre-programmed robot, incapable of thinking for itself. The weak typically suffer from stray puppy syndrome, not assessing their situations and the character of those involved to make a wise decision. The strong, however, choose to avoid foolish culturisms, even if it means being shunned by the majority. This is what a follower of Christ does. The majority will simply follow the crowd and choose to partake in the culture, for this requires no strength. If people are to say about us that we seem like strong Christians, then we must stand up and prove it. We do this by not conforming to this world, to cultures. We the strong shall choose to follow only the Jesus culture. Are you in or are you out?

Ephesians 4:23 says, "And be renewed in the spirit of your mind;"

Chapter 53

A strong Christian credits his/her attackers for prompting him/her to become strong

The discretion of a man deferreth his anger; and it is his glory to pass over a transgression. - Proverbs 19:11

I remember one time a lady said, "Nothing bothers your enemies more than when you forgive them!" I thought about that awhile and realized that attacks from enemies are usually psychological ones. The enemy tries to get into your head and make you feel defeated with his/her attack. But, the enemy himself/herself will feel unsuccessful when you show him/her that you refuse to accept/feel defeat. When you forgive your enemy and credit him/her for prompting you to become strong(er), your enemy feels like a failure because he/she then realizes he/she wasn't able to make you feel defeated.

One of the dangerous mindsets people get themselves into is this: I choose to let others have control of my emotions. Oftentimes this can be a hard one to overcome, but, with time and practice it can be done. You might have said, "That person is really pushing my buttons!" In another words, that person knows how to control you. Imagine a keyboard-type device in front of your enemy equipped with lots of buttons. Each button is labeled with one of your emotions. There is one for anger, one for joy, one for sadness, one for heartache etc. If you give control of those buttons to others, then they will soon discover that they can control you through your emotions. Certain sadistic individuals will take advantage of this and have you doing all sorts of foolish things, mainly act out on your anger. You may end up in jail as a result of this. I've seen it happen a thousand times. Understand that you actually have control of your emotions and you choose how to respond to life's situations. The more you let others dictate your emotional response to things, the more control you are giving them over your life. Jesus responded wisely to all situations He encountered. Sometimes he said nothing, for He knew it would do no good to argue with a fool (Proverbs 23:9).

The strong Christian has overcome grudge holding. He/she tells his/her attackers that it was they who prompted him/her to become strong. The weakling will hold a grudge against an attacker whereas a strong Christian has compassion, for he/she realizes that the attacker was acting in ignorance. The strong Christian lets his/her attacker know that it was because of prompting him/her through an attack that he/she decided to become strong (or stronger) and not hold the attack against him/her. By crediting your attacker, you are showing that you are strong enough not to hold a grudge. Hopefully your attacker will pick up on this and pay forth this attitude instead of trying to attack someone else. You aren't rubbing anything in your attacker's nose by forgiving him/her. You are showing him/her how Jesus would respond and that he/she was wrong in attacking you to begin with.

The weak will try to fight fire with fire and one-up their attackers with similar tactics. They are proving with their response that they aren't ready to forgive, that the enemy still has control of their emotions. The strong may ask compassionately, "What have they done to you?" People that are hurt hurt people. I've heard this saying. It is oftentimes true. People often want to go around hurting others because they themselves have been hurt. Since God seemingly won't take immediate justice on the attacker, the offended party goes and hurts someone else, oftentimes as a way of getting back at God. To get back at God, the hurt person takes it out on one of God's children. This is often why seemingly innocent people are attacked in society. Hurt people aren't responding in a strong Christ-like way, so they do what they know to do: hurt innocent people to get back at God since they can't get back at their original attacker. How will you respond to your attackers? Will you go on hurting others, or will you forgive them and credit them for prompting you to become strong and not act the way they are acting?

Chapter 54

A strong Christian realizes true freedom is caring about only what God thinks of him/her

And ye shall know the truth, and the truth shall make you free. - John 8:32

In the New Testament Paul writes a lot from a jail cell. He wasn't free in the physical sense, but spiritually he was. The freedom Jesus was talking about in John 8:32 was the spiritual kind. People live as slaves to sin as long as they choose to believe and follow the lie that sin is good for you. Jesus wants to set us free from that lie. We can be set free if we choose to follow Him and His ways. The problem man has is justifying Jesus' ways. Why? Because they go against the fleshly ways of this world. Man tends to lean towards the fleshly ways of this world because it feels comfortable to succumb to the flesh while we are in these bodies. While we are in these bodies there will always be a struggle between the flesh and the Spirit. By following the Spirit, we can experience freedom from the lies that the flesh brings.

It has been said that the only people who have a problem with you telling the truth are those who are living a lie. Many people go around living the lie that it's ultimately important what others think of us. There are a few instances when what others think of us matters: usually it's when we are on trial for something, and they need to know the truth about us so we can be freed. Out in the world, I see people all the time being led by the flesh because they are still deluded in thinking that the flesh knows best. They say they feel free because they can do what they want. They, in actuality, are unwittingly walking as slaves to sin. They haven't been shown how the truths that Jesus presents will set them free.

People in addictions are enslaved to their addictions. People say they are in control and that they can quit at any time. I say if it is good for you, then why quit at all? The fact is that addiction is controlling them. People want to feel in control of things, so Satan has created harmful, seemingly affordable addictions for people. For many people these addictions feel good to the flesh. People think that if they can afford them, then they are in control. If you have to go back to it, then it controls you. I used to be addicted to lasagna. I would go back to it night after night. I didn't feel complete without it. A dish of food was controlling me. I was drawn to it and seemingly couldn't say no to it. I no longer feel the need to eat lasagna. I feel good when I do eat it, but it doesn't pull at me like it did before. I am OK with saying no to it now. Now I say I am addicted to Jesus. I feel addicted to Jesus because I want to keep going back to Him. I keep feeling drawn to Him. This is a good addiction to have.

Oftentimes we live as slaves to the thoughts of others. The world has taught us to be more concerned about what others think of us than what God thinks of us. This is foolishness, for we spend so much time living as performers, trying to win the approval of an audience that was never meant to judge us in the first place. The world is an audience that has no say in our eternal destination, so why do we spend so much time, energy, and money to win their approval? Because the world has taught us to do so, to please those who seemingly have something to offer us so that we can remain in pursuit of some elusive dream we've been sold on. Once you let go of being a slave to the world, then, and only then, will you experience true freedom. I actually admire those whom I see in a church service worship freely with song and dance. I can tell they are only interested in one audience: God. Oftentimes people like this live freely, as opposed to those of us who live in constant waiting of judgment from some audience. I admire those who live not caring about what others might think of them.

Jesus wasn't a performer. He did perform miracles, but it wasn't to seek His own glory. He wasn't trying to please those seemingly equipped with the superior human mindset. He was simply doing His thing, being the embodiment of a strong Christian who practiced the I-got-you-covered attitude, which I will discuss later. He knew from the get-go that He'd be judged by man one day and unjustly crucified. He knew better than to seek man's judgment early on because He knew that man was not equipped with superior judgment. He exemplified freely how a Christian should live.

He focused on matters of the heart. Lots of His questions focused on what was in people's hearts, for He knew that by getting to the heart of a matter, the truth could be uncovered. And, once the truth was uncovered, people could be set free from lies that they might have been believing. Which are you more concerned about, what God thinks of you or what man thinks of you? The more you are concerned with what God thinks of you, the freer and stronger you will be.

Chapter 55

A strong Christian speaks from the heart

Keep thy heart with all diligence; for out of it are the issues of life. - Proverbs 4:23

I recently counseled a co-worker on an issue of workplace behavior. I noticed he was playing the busybody and was concerned with the perceived misdeeds of another co-worker. I told him I myself was going to mind my own business, for I was responsible for my behavior only, not that of another co-worker. He said that was a good idea and he followed suit. He told me how he was going to follow the book from now on, albeit begrudgingly, since our leader was not following the book and was being hard-nosed towards us. I told him that was a good idea (to follow the book). I've seen examples many times over the years of people not following the book and then complaining about corruption among the bosses. The bosses then point out the example(s) of the employee not following the book and use that against him/her. Then the employee shuts up and drops the issue. As strong Christians we should follow the Book from as early on as possible, not deviating from it, so that we are irreproachable down the road.

Jesus called out hypocrites in the Bible. People would have a right to call us out as hypocrites if we were to deviate from Christian living. That's why it's important to speak sincerely, from the heart, all the time. We can spend so much time trying to concoct a sugar-coated speech to protect the feelings of those who can't handle the truth. We aren't called to protect the feelings of those who can't handle the truth. We are called to speak from the heart, whether our listener can handle it or not. I have a hard time trying to imagine Jesus burning the midnight oil, trying to draft out a sermon for the following day, painstakingly coming up with sugar-coated wording that won't offend a single person in the congregation. Jesus didn't go around walking on eggshells trying to protect people's feelings. He simply told the truth. He spoke sincerely. He didn't try to offend anyone with His words. He knew He'd be rejected by some no matter what. We aren't to live in fear of those who might not be able to handle the truth that we should speak. However, we want to word things wisely so as not to seem like we are trying to be offensive.

There was one example in Matthew 17:27 where Jesus instructed Peter to cast a hook into the first fish that came up to get money to give to those in Capernaum so that they wouldn't be offended. Jesus did this to prevent a misunderstanding. People oftentimes get offended because of misunderstandings. I noticed this phenomenon as a small child. People would often get the wrong idea because not enough of the right kind of information was conveyed. I see this happen all the time nowadays: people are getting offended left and right because others aren't speaking enough truth from the heart. We can prevent this by speaking from the heart. But first, we need to make sure we have the truth in our hearts. Once we have the truth in our hearts, we can then speak it to others that they may know it.

The weak have been taught to hide the truth. Sometimes they get apathetic about speaking lots of truth to people because they see that others don't act upon it. I say speak it anyway. A strong Christian will speak truth from the heart and not try to misguide people with lies. As long as you do this, people can't condemn your speech. They who are weak, not being able to handle your sound truthful speech, have themselves something to work on: they need to learn to speak from the heart. You can be the strong Christian that comes along and encourages them to speak from the heart. Remember, it's not on you if others reject this idea of speaking from their heart. Their failure to do so will bring its own consequences to them.

Titus 2:7,8 say, " In all things showing thyself a pattern of good works: in doctrine showing uncorruptness, gravity, sincerity, Sound speech, that cannot be condemned; that he that is of the contrary part may be ashamed, having no evil thing to say of you."

Chapter 56

A strong Christian influences and persuades others with gentleness

Thou hast also given me the shield of thy salvation: and thy right hand hath held me up, and thy gentleness hath made me great. - Psalm 18:35

As I've stated before, I am responsible for only my behavior. I am not responsible for others' behavior. It's not my job to control others. Sometimes disciplinary measures must be implemented when there is stubborn resistance, but have you tried the gentle approach? As a young person, I followed Satan's commands to try to control the behavior of others, for I was convinced that things had to be a certain way. I was not convinced that God was in control. I felt like I needed to control certain people who were resisting order in order to achieve a certain outcome. Those people did not respond kindly to my control tactics. Jesus didn't try to manhandle anyone.

There were times when Jesus raised His voice, but He never tried to coerce or force anyone to do anything. Even though He might have come off as weak in the eyes of the world, He was anything but weak. Meekness and gentleness do not equate with weakness. Jesus got 12 men to follow Him as disciples. All of them He persuaded through gentleness. Jesus taught multitudes and influenced them to be His followers ... all through gentleness. People don't like to follow childish despots unless they themselves have evil in their hearts. When a leader is kind and gentle, the multitudes will want to follow him/her. People are influenced and persuaded when they believe they see the good in the heart of the person leading. People could see the good in Jesus and were therefore influenced and persuaded.

The controlling person is afraid of losing control. He/she feels that if he/she doesn't manhandle things or people, then control is not his/hers. We aren't called to control others. We only are responsible for controlling ourselves. We are to influence and to persuade others with gentleness the way Jesus did. If the stubborn refuse to follow, then that's on them. There are a few instances when the stubborn must be put under control: when people's safety is at risk. That doesn't mean that they have to be beaten. It means they must be prevented from getting out of control so that other people won't get hurt unjustly. The stubborn have demons that need to be dealt with. We should pray for those people and command the spirit of stubbornness to come out of them. Jesus was against stubbornness. It's the spirit of stubbornness that influences a person to reject Jesus, the Holy Spirit, and the Father. The stubborn person refuses to let go of his/her ego. He/she is running on ego, not on the Holy Spirit.

We can be the strong Christians that come along to gently influence and persuade those who aren't yet on board with Jesus culture. Remember, it is the weak who feel the need to manhandle their fellow man to get them to follow them. The strong do not feel that need and choose to have great self-control, influencing and persuading others with gentleness. If people reject your approach, they are ultimately rejecting Jesus, and there will be consequences for that decision, consequences for which you the strong Christian will not be responsible.

II Corinthians 10:1 says, "Now I Paul myself beseech you by the meekness and gentleness of Christ, who in presence am base among you, but being absent am bold toward you:"

Chapter 57

A strong Christian utilizes integrity exemplification as his/her motive, not monetary gain

The integrity of the upright shall guide them: but the perverseness of transgressors shall destroy them. - Proverbs 11:3

It's because of the pure, sickening evil in the heart of the child who threatened to sue me for "everything I got" that I decided that if I ever went into ministry, that I'd not do it for the love of money. All the time I see preachers and pastors who are into the ministry for the money. I can tell by how people live their lives if they are all about the money. If you are a pastor or a preacher and earn hundreds of thousands of dollars or even millions of dollars annually, do you live like it? Do your material possessions indicate your unwillingness to live humbly? If so, then you have a heart issue. I've seen firsthand the evil thereof and want no part of it. God doesn't give free passes on sin. He doesn't let any sins slide. The amount of suffering you incur for your sins will be in direct proportion to the amount of sin you commit. I see it all the time. People that live in gluttony and overeat, end up with bodily diseases. Those that live for pleasure, end up in poverty and so on.

I am not financially rich, but I do know how to get there. I need at least one of two traits (but having both helps). First, I need to be willing to take a lot of crap from my fellow man. I need to be his doormat. I've noticed a lot of people end up in high-earning, high-stress positions in life because they were willing to take a lot of crap from their fellow man. Lawyers, politicians, managers etc. Second, I need to be willing to manipulate my fellow man, to take advantage of him to squeeze all the productivity out of him that I can or to convince him that he should pay me as much as possible. I've seen this occur many times. In the warehouse where I work, the guy at the very top does the least amount of work while the people earning the least do the most amount of work, thereby making the guy at the top more money. The guy at the top doesn't even break a sweat because he's letting someone else do the work for him. Those that master the art of manipulating people and taking crap from them will go far in the financial world, I've seen. I have a friend from high school who barely graduated and now owns a construction company that earns in excess of a million dollars a year. In the 26 years that I've known him personally, my friend, who doesn't have a college degree, has masterminded his way to the top of his field through employing the two traits I mentioned previously. He's willing to take a lot of crap from people, and he's willing to manipulate just about anybody to get what he wants. As a result, he lives in an expensive home, drives nice vehicles, has expensive toys, and is also an atheist. Wait, did I say he doesn't believe in God? Yes, I did. He's not concerned in the least about serving God or walking in integrity. He's totally concerned about pleasing the flesh and getting as far ahead financially as he can. He even told me once, "Money is the root of all happiness."

I want nothing to do with the evil that is involved when monetary gain is the motive. I've seen it, I've been a victim of it, and I've seen it destroy people. Those who walk with monetary gain as their motive as they push aside integrity are like thieves. The thief says, "God will not provide, therefore, I will steal." The fact is God will provide in due time to those who believe in Him and are saved. Once we trust that God will provide, we need not walk in fear that He won't provide. I've seen this fear manifest many times. At the warehouse where I work, people aren't cared about; money is cared about. That's why the guys at the top push the workers to be as obedient and productive as possible. As a result, the workers tend to fear losing their jobs and all their behaviors become money-related. Once this happens. All the evil motives in people start to manifest. Co-workers begin to treat each other nastily so they can "make rate." All sorts of anger come out of people and are directed towards others who seemingly might lessen the pay of the angry person. Jesus could have been the wealthiest man on the planet with His ability to just touch people and heal them instantly of whatever infirmity they had. He could have opened a physician's office and had a line from here to Singapore filled with people waiting to get healed. He could have charged exorbitant fees for His guaranteed healing services. He charged nothing while He was here on Earth.

That's how we know He walked in true integrity, in true love. He didn't have ulterior motives. He loved people and this love can come out of us more easily when we decide not to see money as our motive.

Have you ever noticed at volunteer events how the volunteers tend to be happy and smiling? That's because things tend to be free there and they aren't out to get your money. They give cheerfully. They have a different motive. When we remove monetary gain as a motive and insert integrity we can be cheerful as well. I've done this before. It feels so good to serve others when I know that monetary gain is not my motive. It feels really great to walk in integrity in a situation, knowing that I am not lowering myself to an attitude of weakness. The weak will not trust in God for their provision. They will try to harm their fellow man in some way to get something from him. The strong, however, trust in God for their provision and value their integrity more than they do financial gain. You can be that strong Christian who trusts in God and walks in righteous integrity, refusing to take advantage of your fellow man. Remember, you are here to help build him up, not to take from him that which God has promised to provide you anyway.

I Timothy 6:10 says, "For the love of money is the root of all evil: which while some coveted after, they have erred from the faith, and pierced themselves through with many sorrows."

Chapter 58

A strong Christian expresses sincere gratitude

In everything give thanks: for this is the will of God in Christ Jesus concerning you. - I Thessalonians 5:18

How many times have you cursed God for the trials in your life? I used to do it plenty. I can recall yelling at God, "As soon as you stop putting stupid people in my life, everything will be just fine!" Like a lot of people, I grew up being self-centered. I was very judgmental and highly ungrateful for the blessings in my life. It was years later when certain blessings were taken away, and when I saw other people without my blessings, that I began to have an attitude of gratitude towards God.

To this day I am not happy when difficult people are around, however, I am thankful that God is with me when I have to deal with them. God has graciously given me lots of wisdom and strength to deal with the seemingly difficult circumstances, people, and problems that arise nowadays. Things that would have crushed me years ago I now laugh at because, comparatively speaking, I have overcome much greater difficulties. So, those things that seem difficult to some now, I can look at and say that I now have the strength to deal with and conquer. I see how others haven't achieved my degree of strength. I see the struggles others face and the defeatist attitude they have when difficulty arises. I empathize because I was once there too. Now I can take my experience and show others how to overcome obstacles. A lot of it has to do with self-confidence and the belief that God will enable you to handle anything He allows in your life.

When people are ungrateful, they usually aren't aware of how blessed they actually are. They're usually not aware that God has already made provision for them to be successful. Being successful in God's eyes has to do with one's obedience when it comes to following a Christ-like lifestyle. What the world deems to be success varies greatly from how God sees success. All the things that money can buy don't amount to a hill of beans in the Kingdom. How you act as a Christian is what matters to God. That's why it's easier for a camel to fit through the eye of a needle than it is for a rich man to enter into the Kingdom. The rich man tends to focus on what his money can do for him. The strong Christian tends to focus on the things he can do without money.

God would rather you go out and see what you can do without money, so you can trust in His provision. In Matthew chapter 10 Jesus sent forth His 12 disciples and commanded them to preach, to heal the sick, to cleanse the lepers, to raise the dead, to cast out devils, and to freely give. He told them not to take money along with them. The things that He asked them to do don't require money. He wanted them to be grateful for God's forthcoming provision. I remember when I was in Costa Rica in 2015 going to prayer meetings on a regular basis. But, before I arrived in the country, I had a vision that God would feed me wherever I went in the country. I found that was true. Once I was there, every time I went to a prayer meeting, I was fed afterwards. When I ministered to people there in that country, I was fed food. When I traveled one day to the countryside to scout possible locations for my ministry headquarters, I came upon free food and ate it.

Let us be strong Christians and thank God in every situation He has entrusted us to handle. Let us be grateful for our blessings. If another one of God's children blesses you, thank him/her for it. Let us not be resentful as if God were punishing us. A lot of times we end up in messes because we failed (not God) to use wisdom in the first place. God gave us the Earth and all of its elements for us to use for His honor and glory. Let's be grateful that He is our great provider.

Chapter 59

A strong Christian praises others for their good deeds

Let another man praise thee, and not thine own mouth; a stranger, and not thine own lips. - Proverbs 27:2

Once I developed an attitude of gratitude and set my ego to the side, I found it acceptable for me to praise others for their good deeds. However, this was many years in the making. I noticed as a child how it was good to praise others, but not to praise oneself. I would get compliments on my good deeds, my achievements, and my accomplishments. In a way this was good because I was being encouraged to keep up the good work. On the other hand, I felt pressured into doing more good when I sometimes didn't feel up to it. That was the flesh pulling at me to do bad. We should learn to recognize the voice of the flesh, so we can start to hush it up. If we are doing good, then we should feel encouraged to keep on doing good.

Having attended public school, I learned to be a performer, that is to say, someone who did good when I had to for a certain audience. The world had taught me to seek the praise of man. I had been taught that my fellow man was my highest judge of character, so I learned how to win the approval of him. I had a problem with taking compliments: I wasn't sure how to do it respectfully, for I didn't have true gratitude yet. I still felt that the world owed me something; it didn't. I had to learn how others viewed me and why they praised me to begin with in order to respond well to their praise. Once I learned this, I began to praise others following the same model. Once I got out of ego mode, I saw that it wasn't about competition and was OK with building others up through praise.

Oftentimes the weak will seek the praise of men instead of God's praise. They aren't living to please God. When you live for man's praise, you seek that kind of praise so that your ego will be puffed up. Even today I see men seeking the praise of other men. At strongman competitions I've attended, the participants will raise up both arms while facing the crowd to get people riled up so that the current competitor will lift more weight in an effort to ultimately please the crowd. We live in a society afflicted by approval addiction. We have been taught to be performers to seek the approval or the praise of others as if theirs mattered more than God's.

Getting praise for our good deeds from others is fine. The problem is when we go out and seek it just to have it. We shouldn't initiate any praise that comes from others. Let them initiate it. We aren't called to be performers for them. Do good because God wants you to, not because man might reward you somehow. Give credit where it's due. The weak withhold praise for the same reason they don't set out to strengthen others: they don't want others to gain an advantage. They don't want their fellow man to be someone that they end up envying. Praising others shouldn't be about glorifying the doers for some enviable deed that they did. It's about letting them know that you recognized their accomplishment so they don't feel it was in vain and so they can feel encouraged about continuing to do good. You can follow up your praise by saying, "Glory to God." Oftentimes we need others to praise us as a way of reminding us that we are to do good deeds. You can be the strong Christian that comes along and gives another the praise that he/she might need one day to remind him/her that a child of God is watching and recognizes the good he/she has done.

John 12:43 says, "For they loved the praise of men more than the praise of God."

Chapter 60

A strong Christian utilizes his/her ability to recognize the Jesus in all of God's children

Speak not evil one of another, brethren. He that speaketh evil of his brother, and judgeth his brother, speaketh evil of the law, and judgeth the law: but if thou judge the law, thou art not a doer of the law, but a judge. - James 4:11

As strong Christians we are to learn about the life of Jesus, His traits, and to recognize those traits when we see them in others. When we see non-Jesus traits in people, we aren't judging people. We are simply observing or noticing the lack of Jesus in them. Just as we are to notice the good in people, we are to notice the bad as well. It's for our good. It's to preserve us. It's about discernment. Using that discernment will help to keep us from people who might be likely to do us harm.

Sometimes people will tell you not to judge others. Be careful with these people. There is a good chance they don't understand judgment as I have explained it in this book. There's a good chance they are referring to worldly judgment, as opposed to righteous judgment. Jesus said in John 7:24, "Judge not according to the appearance, but judge righteous judgment." When I speak of recognizing the Jesus in all of God's children, I am referring to His traits and the way He handled things. Do the people you observe respond the way Jesus would?

Whenever I am in a new situation and am unsure of how to respond, I ask what would Jesus do? To know this, we need to read about His life in the New Testament and study His character. Once we know His traits, we can respond to a situation the way He would.

A lot of times man wants to look only at the outside. Other times he doesn't want to believe that bad people can have good traits. This latter one is the one you most want to overcome. Sometimes we look at people begrudgingly and say, "Well, that guy surely couldn't have any of Jesus' traits. He's a horrible person." Then one day you discover he's a loving father at home, caring for his children the way Jesus would. If we are looking at people begrudgingly, then we are still in that comparison-judgment mindset. We are still holding a grudge, and that grudge is blocking our acceptance about the truth regarding that person. The strong Christian does not hold grudges. He/she sees us all as sheep of the Shepherd with varying degrees of goodness.

You can be the strong Christian who uses righteous judgment to recognize the Jesus in all of God's children, even your worst enemies. Once you get over using worldly judgment on people, you should use your Christian strength to recognize Jesus' traits in others. Once you recognize these traits, you soon will be informing them of those traits.

Chapter 61

A strong Christian lets people know of the Jesus traits that he/she sees in them

Her children arise up, and call her blessed; her husband also, and he praiseth her. - Proverbs 31:28

Seeing the traits of Jesus in people is one thing; letting them know you see them is another. Why would we want to tell people of the Jesus traits we see in them? For one we want to build them up. Secondly, we need to remind people because people can forget quickly that they possess Jesus traits. When people tell me that they see Jesus traits in me, it's like they are confirming something I am probably already suspecting myself. Letting people know of the Jesus traits we see in them also serves as a subversive way of saying that we also notice the traits in them that are not Jesus-like.

In John 13:11 it says, "For he knew who should betray him; therefore, said he, Ye are not all clean." Jesus said this latter part about not being clean. He knew Judas' heart. Just as Jesus saw His traits in His disciples, He saw also the traits and hearts that were not like His. He knew that Judas had a dirty heart. I say because of this betrayal that those who love money enter into a very dangerous mindset. If Judas betrayed Jesus, of all people, for money, just imagine what most people would do to us sinners nowadays; they would sell us out in a heartbeat. We foolishly go around trying to impress people who were never meant to judge us to begin with, trying to show our loyalty, when those same people would have little or no loyalty to us. We need to stop trying to win the approval of man. Man cares very little about you, especially in these last days, for the Bible proclaims that in the last days men will be lovers of self. Very seldom do I see people in society make an earnest effort at caring sincerely for their fellow man. Usually when it is done, it's because they are being paid to do so.

Let's stop kidding ourselves and start telling people of the Jesus traits we see in them. When we do this, they should see that we are followers of Jesus and want what we have. People are tired of being bombarded with the news that they are worthless. God revealed to me a while back that many people today have very low self-esteem, which is why they carry themselves in such a crestfallen way with their heads down a lot of the time. People aren't normally approached by strong Christians who tell them that they have good in them and that it shows. Instead, people are approached by other people who are down and out and have nothing but negative news for them about how horrible their world is. So, it's no wonder people aren't thriving as strong Christians today; they don't know what strong Christians look like! Since strong Christians aren't the norm, when they are seen by the untrained eye, they are seen as anomalies or eccentric zealots who are strange. This is understandable. You could be the strong

Christian who comes along and influences that person to change his/her perspective about strong Christians. People who don't understand are the ones who are not yet educated in a subject matter. It sounds obvious, but sometimes people who aren't strong Christians are quick to forget that they shouldn't judge what they don't understand. You can be the strong Christian who sets them right.

Remember, the weak refrain from telling people of the Jesus traits they see in people because they are more concerned about potential judgment from people who might laugh and/or misinterpret what they say. The strong do not fear misinterpretation. They are constantly on the lookout for ways to build people up. One of the best ways you can build people up is to boost their self-confidence by letting them know you see the good in them, the Jesus traits. Oftentimes when people see that others see potential in them, they start to think that maybe they can take that good and run with it right down the road of self-improvement.

Chapter 62

A strong Christian focuses on human potential as a basis for rebuilding

I know both how to be abased, and I know how to abound: everywhere and in all things I am instructed both to be full and to be hungry, both to abound and to suffer need. - Philippians 4:12

As Jesus is the vine, and we are the branches, we need Him to do His work. The world will try to lead us astray, to get us to believe we don't need Him to get His work done. But, John 15:4,5 say, "Abide in me, and I in you. As the branch cannot bear fruit of itself, except it abide in the vine; no more can ye, except ye abide in me. I am the vine, ye are the branches: He that abideth in me, and I in him, the same bringeth forth much fruit: for without me ye can do nothing." Jesus is the one who gives us our potential. As strong Christians, we are to focus on that potential when looking to rebuild people.

To bear Jesus fruit, we need to follow Jesus traits. To bear worldly fruit, one needs only to follow the world. To achieve success in the Kingdom, we need to treat people the way Jesus would. The way Jesus would do things typically goes against the flesh. To those who aren't in the know, it doesn't feel good to do the Jesus thing in most situations. I can recall as a child feeling uncomfortable about helping those who were less fortunate than me. I was not yet taught that there is strength in helping those who need a helping hand. Years later I realized there is strength in helping those not as strong as me, and it feels good to do so. One can experience this joy when doing the Jesus thing. The joy happens, at least for me, when I realize I'm exhibiting strength. Doing the Jesus thing requires strength, for most people want to do the opposite (the easy thing), which is to bow out and choose not to participate. We should be the strong Christians that see ourselves symbolically as branches connected to Jesus the vine.

Branches get their nutrients and strength from a vine. If the vine dies, so do the branches. When the vine is watered and grows, the branches grow too. Branches also bear fruit. We are to bear Jesus fruit. If we bear His fruit, people should look at us and say, "I want to have some of that." Our potential as humans is only as strong as our connection to the vine. I have a mulberry tree in my yard. Several months ago I trimmed off some of the branches so they would not get in my way as I was cutting the grass around the tree. Only afterwards did I realize the tree would bear less fruit now. Thus it is in the Kingdom. As branches are cut off and die, so does the fruit of Christianity when people stop doing the Jesus thing. People tend to cut off or snub Christians because they are an inconvenience to those seeking a worldly lifestyle. If we leave well enough alone and let fruit multiply, no one will go hungry. If we cut down a tree that produces bad fruit, it will die. That's how it can be in the world. To get rid of evil, it must be cut off at the root so it dies. In your yard, when you plant lots of good grass next to weeds, the weeds die. Evil cannot thrive when it's outnumbered by good. We are to be the good that outnumbers evil. If we multiply our good fruit, good will be the victor.

To rebuild our fellow man, we need to focus on fruit production. Plant good seeds in others. Seeds come from fruit already in existence. If you have good fruit in you, take some of its seeds and plant them in people. Build them up by watering them with positive reinforcement and constructive criticism. Inspire them with testimonies that tell of people who realized their potential. People tend to become like those who water them. Water them with pure water. When focusing on yourself, plan to expound on your good fruit. Ask Jesus what more you can do to bear more fruit and to plant more seeds. He will open doors for you in this area, for He loves to see His fruit abound.

Chapter 63

A strong Christian recognizes that God does not create trash

And God saw everything that he had made, and, behold, it was very good... - Genesis 1:31

A while back God revealed to me that a lot of people go through life believing they are human garbage. Satan, in one way or another, has convinced many people that they are trash, and they go through life trying to live out that role. Sadly, many people come to accept this way of life as fact. I see evidence of it all the time. At my part-time job I am around a lot of customers in grocery stores. Many of them walk around with this look that says, "I am so done with life." Many have little to no self-esteem, for they don't know their true identities in the Kingdom. Instead, they walk around assuming a different identity (human garbage), one they were never meant to have.

Then God pointed me to Genesis chapter 1. At the end it says how God looked at everything that He had made and saw that it was very good. God doesn't create trash. Even our end product, excrement, can be used as fertilizer so that the life cycle can continue. He created producers and consumers for Earth. Scavenger animals were put here to take care of the remains of the dead. Their body chemistry was designed so that they wouldn't get sick from eating rotting carcasses. Our bodies' chemistry was designed for consuming God-honoring, temple-fortifying nutrients so that we could carry out God's marching orders. We get sick when we deviate from God's design, both spiritually sick and physically sick. Satan knows that we tend to be flesh-led individuals, so he implements all sorts of strategies to try to convince us that feeding junk into our bodies, to please the flesh, is the way to go; it's not.

I find to be quite disheartening the observations that I make on a weekly basis when I encounter my fellow man who blatantly disregards his temple. We oftentimes are sold on the idea that we must conform to a certain kind of lifestyle to fit into a society. I see people dishonoring God by getting drunk, smoking tobacco products, eating junk, getting tattooed, getting piercings, getting branded, getting "enhancement" surgeries, committing other sins of the flesh, and doing many other temple-altering modifications to please other people who were never meant to give their approval or judgment in the first place. Our temple is holy and should be treated as such. Weakness in this area of temple management is evidenced by one's willingness to succumb to aforementioned behaviors. The strong will avoid such behaviors. The more you can avoid them and not regard your temple as trash, the stronger you will be.

I used to have an addiction to chocolate pudding, so much so that my sodium intake was so high that I developed hives. I had gotten little red or pink dots on my palms and eventually elsewhere. I developed an allergy to sodium but didn't know it. The pudding I ate was all-natural, but I was being gluttonous about the amount I ate. At one point my lower lip had swollen to about 3 times its normal size. It took some trial and error, but I eventually narrowed it down to my gluttonous intake of sodium. I hadn't eaten God's nutrients in moderation and, therefore, suffered. I had been living to please the flesh. When I greatly reduced my sodium intake, the hives went away. If nature creates a problem, it will also create a solution to the problem. Oftentimes, eliminating the sinful amount of edibles is the solution. Treating ourselves like holy temples and not like human garbage disposals is key to honoring God and inviting good health.

Remember, the weak will regard the body as trash whereas the strong will see it as a holy temple to be used for God-honoring activities. How will you choose to walk daily? Will you see yourself as trash or will you recognize that God does not create trash, so, therefore, we should not live like we think we are trash? The strong will choose the latter.

Chapter 64

A strong Christian seeks to know (not assume) people's motives, including his/her own

But Jesus did not commit himself unto them, because he knew all men, And needed not that any should testify of man: for he knew what was in man. - John 2:24,25

Oftentimes certain people like to assume that they know other people and all of their motives without even getting to know people. This is what the weak do. They are led by their own understanding, their own ego. Jesus didn't do this. He knew people's thoughts and their motives. Matthew 9:4 says, "And Jesus knowing their thoughts said, Wherefore think ye evil in your hearts?" God was in Jesus, so He could do this. If you read Jesus' words throughout the Scriptures, you should notice that His questions are designed to lead people to the truth and to the motives in people's hearts. He didn't beat around the bush. He got right to the point. He was all about speaking truth and getting at it when evil tried to cover truth up. He knew that the truth was good for people, and therefore sought to free the people by leading them to the truth. It has been said, in this world, that the only people who have a problem with you telling the truth are those who are living a lie; this is true.

We must use discernment and wisdom in this world. Simply by reading Proverbs you should get a good understanding of how these tools can be used to keep us from unnecessary trouble, how to solve many of life's problems, and how to help our fellow man. We even need to use these tools on ourselves. We need to introspect, that is to say, to do a reality check, on a regular basis. We don't want to get to the point where we feel so sanctimonious that we are beyond correction. Sometimes I think I have a certain spiritual lesson down pat, but then I find myself not even listening to my own good advice. So, that means there is still a heart issue with me. It means I'm still convincing myself to follow the flesh. I had a brief spiritual attack the other night at work. The spirit of revenge tried to get ahold of me. It tried to wrestle with me, but eventually after a few minutes I was able to shake it off and come to my senses. It's not that I wasn't a Christian during those few minutes of attack. It's that the spirit of revenge was trying to invade me because of some words I had spoken about an individual I encountered in that area where I was some time earlier. Satan hears your words and knows the corresponding spirits that typically go along with certain vocabulary. Then he attacks you by sending out to you the precise type of demonic spirit that's needed to cause your downfall, to get you away from doing Kingdom work. If I had given in to the spirit of revenge, I might not be here now to write these words. That's why it's supremely important to know people's motives, for you could save your own life by discerning the evil ones.

In Matthew 10:16 Jesus says to His disciples, "Behold, I send you forth as sheep in the midst of wolves: be ye therefore wise as serpents, and harmless as doves." He knew that most of the people they'd encounter would stare at them like savages hungry for a kill when they presented the Gospel to them. He wanted them to be wise and not gullible. He wanted them to use wisdom and discernment to see if they were in danger. He was basically saying that you shouldn't trust everyone. He knew that man had a sinful heart, full of evil. He knew they'd be persecuted. In Matthew 10:23 He says, "But when they persecute you in this city, flee ye into another: for verily I say unto you, Ye shall not have gone over the cities of Israel, till the Son of man be come." We need to walk and talk with this same attitude. I grew up in Westminster, Maryland, but I had gained so many enemies in that town throughout the years because of my walk and talk with Jesus, that it was time for me to move on to the next town in a different state; it happens. If they run you out of town, rest assured it's not because God or Jesus is telling them to. Those people have their own demons to deal with. Pray for them.

Remember to use that wisdom and discernment that God has equipped you with. It's for your protection. It's for your ministering. The weak won't use these tools. They will automatically assume that they know you just by one glance, for they look only at the outside. The strong, however, get to know people and compare the fruit of their life with that of Jesus' life. Remember, the more people look like Jesus in their walk and talk, the less you need to be concerned. This goes for you too.

Chapter 65

A strong Christian seeks to keep his/her word without being a people pleaser

To have respect of persons is not good: for for a piece of bread that man will transgress. - Proverbs 28:21

A strong Christian makes an earnest effort at trying to keep his/her word. Jesus walked with such authority that He was able to keep all of His promises. Whatever He said He was going to do, He did it. He didn't do it to be a people pleaser. He knew that one's walk should match one's talk. The problem in this world is that people tend to overcommit themselves in an effort to appear more holy or better than they actually are. They might start off with good intentions, but they usually end up facing an obstacle that keeps them from keeping their word. The thing to understand is that it happens. We won't always be able to carry out the things we say we are going to do. Realize this so you don't overburden yourself with worry and anxiety over what people might think.

It's important to develop understanding in this area. Once we understand, we can have compassion and not hold people to an unrealistic standard. People are human and will fail. Especially in America people tend to set the bar very high. I myself have tended to be very hard on myself. I have eased up some over the years, but I was raised as a perfectionist. I was always very meticulous and methodical about doing things. I would get very angry when others did not meet my expectations when it came to doing things perfectly. It's good to have high standards, but at the same time Jesus wants us to be understanding, for many will let us down if we hold everyone to our high standards all the time. Whenever I am or I see someone getting worked up in this area, I recall Romans 3:23 which says, "For all have sinned, and come short of the glory of God;" This verse reminds me that others are not equipped with superior judgment and have no right to sentence me to death for making an earnest effort at keeping my word.

The weak will speak idly, having no intention of keeping their word. I come across these people all the time. I basically say to them something to the effect of "put up or shut up" or "put your money where your mouth is." Discernment comes in handy big time in this area. Many can talk the talk, but do they walk the walk? When one keeps one's word, it's usually because one has a heart of honesty and truth-handling. Did you ever notice how habitual people can be when they don't keep their word? It tends to be a habit in certain people. Those who typically keep their word, want to show a heart that is sincere. Jesus was sincere when He said to the guy on the cross that he'd be with Him in Paradise that day. He healed everybody He said He would heal. He did everything He said He was going to do. We should walk with the same kind of heart, trying to show sincerity in our actions, but not fretting if we fall short. In this regard, let us treat others the same, keeping in mind they may fall short too.

Remember, the people pleaser tends to do things for appearances' sake and typically has a level of commitment that is so low, he/she will prevaricate at the first indication of his/her audience's displeasure. The strong Christian, however, will try to be Jesus-like by walking the walk after he/she has already talked the talk. Jesus followed through with everything He said He'd do. Now it's time for you to follow His example.

Chapter 66

A strong Christian is confident, not cocky

I am that bread of life. - John 6:48

Jesus spoke matter-of-factly and with confidence. He was never wishy-washy. He rested assuredly in everything He did and said. He grew and matured in knowledge and so should we. I used to have little self-confidence when it came to foreign languages. But, the more I studied and learned Spanish, the more confident I became in using it. Now I don't fear holding a conversation with a native speaker. I might not understand everything they say, but I am not afraid to ask them to repeat themselves in a clearer way.

Confidence involves trust in something or someone. Jesus trusted in the knowledge His Father gave Him. He walked it and talked it confidently. In Luke 19 and 20 He said, "Behold, I give unto you power to tread on serpents and scorpions, and over all the power of the enemy: and nothing shall by any means hurt you. Notwithstanding in this rejoice not, that the spirits are subject unto you; but rather rejoice, because your names are written in heaven." He didn't want people to be cocky about spirits being subject to them. He wanted them to rejoice over their connection to the Kingdom, for this is where real power is had. He also said (John 8:12), "I am the light of the world," (John 10:11) "I am the good shepherd,"

(John 10:7) "I am the door of the sheep," (John 11:25) "I am the resurrection and the life," (John 14:6) "I am the way, the truth, and the life," (John 15:1) "I am the true vine, and my Father is the husbandman." Was Jesus being arrogant? No, of course not. He was simply telling people His identity, who He was. People have a tendency to treat you according to how they see your identity. If people have it wrong (your identity), it's up to you to set them straight about it.

Several months back at the warehouse where I was working, a Spanish-speaking man habitually called me "vago," which basically means "lazybones" in English. We laughed about it jokingly the first ten times he called me that. The eleventh time it wasn't funny anymore. I decided that I needed to set him straight about my identity, since he apparently had it wrong. So, one day I came across him in an area of the warehouse, and he called me lazybones in Spanish once again. I rolled up next to him on the forklift I was driving and looked at him seriously. I said in a confident, matter-of-fact, non-threatening way in Spanish "You are in error, for you know not the Scriptures nor the power of God. I am a mighty son of God who does not succumb to the spirit of defeatism, nor do I suffer from self-doubt. I can do all things through Christ who strengthens me. That is how a strong Christian speaks. That is who I am. Now the question is who are you?" He apparently was so dumbfounded by what I said to him that all he could mutter was "nobody" in

Spanish. If you think you are a nobody, then most likely you will walk around acting like a nobody. If you see yourself as a worthy child in the Kingdom, then your walk and talk should reflect this belief.

Remember, when Jesus spoke the way He did, people used to say that no one spoke like Him. It's probably because no one else walked a Kingdom walk the way He did. Remember, people will treat you according to how they see your identity. If they see you as crap, then most likely they will treat you like crap. Young teenage boys trying to court a girl they like will treat her like a princess or a queen because that's how they see her. If people have your identity wrong, set them straight. First you have to get your identity in the Kingdom figured out if you haven't already. Then you can tell people your identity. After that you can tell other people their identity if they don't know it already. Simply telling people who you are isn't being cocky. You may be perceived as cocky if you follow up your name with traits that indicate your connection to the Kingdom. You may be perceived as a threat, and rightly so. You should be perceived as a threat...to evil. It's alright. It's how Jesus was perceived. Be the strong Christian that is clearly confident and identifiable as a mighty child of the Kingdom.

Chapter 67

A strong Christian rests assured that he/she is a mighty son/daughter of God empowered and equipped to handle all God allows

That the man of God may be perfect, thoroughly furnished unto all good works. - II Timothy 3:17

People walk around in this life hungry and thirsty. They seek to satisfy that hunger and that thirst through anything but Jesus because Jesus feels uncomfortable to the flesh. People will turn to pornography, drinking, smoking, so-called body art, and a multitude of other sinful vices to fill that God-sized hole in their lives. One must get tired of what fleshly living has to offer to come to Jesus. Sometimes people will get tired, but they aren't tired enough. They simply want a temporary bailout. I've seen it before. People will come crying to Jesus, seemingly sincere about repenting and turning from their wicked ways. They just want to be bailed out of their current predicament, having every intention of returning to the sin that got them there in the first place. Those people are still walking in spiritual blindness. They will still be hungry and thirsty afterwards if Jesus is a part of their lives.

I have a friend who graduated from New Life For Girls, a Christian program designed to help rehabilitate women with addictions. My friend had a serious drinking problem before she went into the program. She also had a high-paying job and all the things that typically go along with the high-earning lifestyle. She went into the program and seemingly did well and then graduated after several months. She remained with the program and worked as the manager for the New Life retail store for a while. A little while went by and she left New Life to work back in the world. Soon the demons of alcoholism overtook her and she fell right back into the same predicament she had been in before. It's been about five years now and she is worse off now than she was before, having failed at several rehab attempts throughout the years. There is still a God-sized hole in her life that only God can fill. Only Jesus can satisfy her hunger and thirst. That's why she is never satiated through the drinking of alcohol. No alcoholic is ever complete just by drinking alcohol. Physical thirst may be satisfied, but we're talking about spiritual thirst here.

John 6:35 says, "And Jesus said unto them, I am the bread of life: he that cometh to me shall never hunger; and he that believeth on me shall never thirst." The strong Christian rests assured that Jesus is all the food and drink that we need in this lifetime. His love, principles, commandments, and way of life are all we need to handle what God allows in this life. If you feel disempowered or unable, ask Jesus to empower you to go and to heal the sick. He gets glad at willing hearts who care about people. He will equip the called. He doesn't send the weak out. He sends the strong out. Wherever He sends you, rest assured He will provide your needs, whether it be financial, linguistic, social, or material. In every country I've been in outside the United States (4 to date) God has provided the people I needed to get me to where He wanted me to be. The right resources will come along at the right time. When I'm far from home, people will ask me if I worry about having need. I simply chuckle and say, "God will provide, and He has equipped me." I rest assured in my empowerment that comes from Jesus, for He is the one who sent me in the first place. The fact that I'm here now today is indicative of God's commitment to provide all my needs. Many of my wants have not been provided, but my needs always have been. Get alone with God and make an inventory of all that you really need in this lifetime. It's not as big a list as you might think it is. Be the strong Christian who is satisfied with Jesus being the bread and drink of your spiritual life. The world will always leave you thirsting and hungering for more; Jesus will not. He will provide you with all the power and equipment you will need to do His work.

Chapter 68

A strong Christian tells it like it is without threatening people

...It is written, My house shall be called the house of prayer; but ye have made it a den of thieves. - Matthew 21:13

Jesus did show strong emotion and spoke vociferously, but He never threatened anyone. He was seen as a threat by those with an evil agenda. As I've stated before, evil doesn't like to be discovered; it likes to go unnoticed. People with good intentions don't mind their light shining, but people with sin in mind prefer darkness, literally and figuratively. When Jesus said He was the light of this world, He essentially was showing Himself as the prime example for us to follow. Light exposes darkness. That's why when you act as Jesus did, your good deeds will expose the evil deeds of evil people. We are to walk as bright lights so that man may become aware of his sin, if he is in it to begin with.

Jesus spoke matter-of-factly. He just told it like it was. In Mark 14:62 He says, "I am: and ye shall see the Son of man sitting on the right hand of power, and coming in the clouds of heaven." Was He being arrogant? No, He was simply telling the high priest a fact. He wasn't threatening anyone. He was simply telling a truth related to the authority in Him. We, as believers, have the authority to do Christ-like things like heal the sick and cast out demons, but we oftentimes don't take advantage of it because either we don't know we have it or because we don't want to be perceived as silly by our fellow man for speaking in such a way. Again, this fear goes back to the dangerous mindset of believing that our fellow man possesses superior judgment. He does not and therefore cannot use on us what he does not have. We spend more time following man than we do following Jesus and what He said we could do.

In Luke 22:67 Jesus was asked if He was the Christ. He responds by saying, "If I tell you, ye will not believe: And if I also ask you, ye will not answer me, nor let me go." He knew that nothing He said would convince them and that they were trying to get Him to blaspheme. The same people concluded that He was claiming to be the Son of God. Even though He was, He never actually said He was. He simply said, "Ye say that I am." Jesus wasn't one to have the wool pulled over His eyes. He knew they were up to no good. He knew they would try to pervert the truth of what was said in order to find Him guilty. This same spirit of dishonesty is with us in the world today. We need to call it out when we notice it. We need to be aware that, as strong Christians, we will be going out as sheep among ravenous wolves. The enemy will stop at nothing to quieten God's children. I was the scapegoat several times throughout my school years, perhaps because of my unwillingness to react like a loudmouth to defend myself. As strong Christians we need to be vociferous about righteousness and evil. If you see evil going on, speak up. It has been said that he who remains quiet before an injustice, agrees with the injustice. There is some truth to this.

Be the strong Christian who brings light to a situation where there is darkness. It's OK to be the whistleblower when there is evil going on, and it's OK, even wise, to remain anonymous in certain situations. Don't forget to use wisdom. Oftentimes we can go overboard and end up threatening people because we are so enraged by an injustice. Speak as loud as you want to, but remember that God is ultimately in control. His eyes see the evil that is transpiring. Just do your part and stand up for justice. That's what we are to do in this sin-filled world. Remember, the weak are the ones who remain quiet and consent to injustice. The strong call it out and tell it like it is, thereby letting their light expose darkness.

Chapter 69

A strong Christian utilizes the I-got-you-covered attitude

For God sent not his Son into the world to condemn the world; but that the world through him might be saved. John 3:17

Jesus personified to the max the I-got-you-covered attitude. This attitude basically demonstrates caring for one's fellow man. Jesus dying on the cross was His best example of this attitude. We can demonstrate this attitude in many ways in life. We can hold the door for people. We can allow another motorist to enter our lane on the freeway. We can lift a weight off of someone who is stuck on the bench press. We can bail someone out of trouble or out of jail. We can give a ride to a friend in need. We can provide a bandage to someone with a cut. We can feed a hungry person. We can tell someone all about Jesus. We can volunteer our skills to the poor or to a friend. Any act or gesture that lets another person know that you have got him/her covered is what we are shooting for here.

Jesus never let anyone down. He always healed people when someone approached Him for healing. He did miracles to feed multitudes. He did everything in His power to make sure He had people covered. His blood covers all our sins when we accept Him as Savior. Unfortunately, Satan has convinced many to turn a blind eye to their fellow man. He has convinced them to utilize what I will politely call the forget-you attitude. People cut other drivers off in traffic. People smoke in the presence of others. People mistreat their fellow man in a multitude of ways. They have a non-caring, negligent attitude towards life and people. They willingly exclude others from group activities. They ignore the needs and the emergencies of others. People's hearts have grown cold in today's world. The thing is, Jesus frowns upon this negative attitude. Holocausts, genocides, poverty, starvation and many other problems all occur because those who can do something about it choose not to utilize the I-got-you-covered attitude. Our fellow man is ignored to the nth degree in today's world. The people who choose the forget-you attitude tend to be stuck in their own little worlds, focusing on their lives only.

It is not hard to see how people end up suffering because they are ignored. People are left to rot and perish in jail cells. The elderly die alone in their homes. I'm not saying it's all to blame on other people. Sometimes we suffer as a result of the way we treat ourselves and the way we choose to socialize. Jesus was all about taking care of people. He never deliberately ignored anyone. If we choose to spend time with Him, He will reciprocate. Jesus came here to save the world. We can't save it, but we can act as heroes for our fellow man by helping them out in times of need. Even when they have little need, we can be of help. This attitude of caring can and does rub off. I admire people with this attitude. My earthly father is one of the greatest examples of someone with this attitude of covering people, mainly the people he loves. He has almost always been there for me in times of need. He has literally saved me thousands of dollars over the years on auto repairs. He is a mechanic, so he does a lot of my auto repairs for me. He does all the electrical and plumbing jobs that I need done in my home. This has helped me out tremendously. This attitude of caring of his has helped to keep me afloat. I see through his efforts the kind of caring I should have for my family when I get married one day.

There isn't much that's more heartbreaking than someone who willfully and disdainfully ignores his/her fellow man in times of need. I see it all the time, though. It saddens me, and it saddens Jesus. I believe Jesus wept because people refused to show care and/or love towards their fellow man. He came here to be and to show us love, and we turn around and act as unloving as possible towards our neighbor. We spend a lot of time judging others instead of looking for ways to take care of them. We look to see how we can take advantage of them instead of looking for ways to share with them. I don't have much more gratitude than I do in the moments when I know someone is genuinely covering me, for I know all too well what it's like to be ignored by my peers; it's very disheartening. I choose to be the strong Christian that approaches my fellow man and says, "I got you covered!" You can do this too.

People will notice this and see the strength in you. Hopefully you can spread some good this way. The world needs it. Be the strong Christian who approaches someone with a need, be it prayer, food, clothing or the like, and say, "I got you covered, for I am a strong Christian sent here by God Almighty and this is what I do!"

Chapter 70

A strong Christian refuses to allow would-be thieves to pull a switcheroo, replacing joy with discontent

Whoso is partner with a thief hateth his own soul: he heareth cursing, and betrayeth it not. - Proverbs 29:24

In this world there will be jealous haters that will see what you have – joy –, and they will try to take it from you. They don't want you to be happy with what they don't have. They will try to determine what you're joyous about, and they will try to eliminate that thing from your life. It could be that you are joyous about something material. It could be a person or a privilege that you are joyous about. People tend to think that they can steal your joy by taking away things. The weak allow their joy to disappear and become discontent when their joy-bringing thing is taken from them. It's like when a favorite toy is taken away from a toddler. The strong Christian, however, associates his/her joy with his/her relationship with God.

Your relationship with God, the Holy Spirit, and Jesus is something that only you can lessen. Others can persuade you to walk away from God, but God will never try to end His relationship with you. Joy is about enjoying that relationship. It's about basking in the love that God has for you. It's about recalling the things that Jesus has done for you and the pleasure you get out of serving Him. It's about your gratitude for your salvation. It's about your worship and praise and loving others as a strong Christian. These are all intangible things that no thief can take from you.

Discontent is another way of saying unhappy. Unhappiness typically depends on what one has or doesn't have in one's life. Your salvation, if you have it, is guaranteed. You can't lose it, and it can't be taken from you. Serving God is something that will always be your choice. No one else can make you serve or not serve God. The things that Jesus has done for you, it could be healing, for example, no one can take from you. It is possible to get sick again. Usually when one relapses or gets sick again, it's because the sin that brought on the infirmity in the first place was never addressed. People have been healed by Jesus of a dreadful disease and then got the disease again later. As a dog returns to its vomit, so does a fool to his folly. I see this all the time. My mom had quit smoking once she had her quintuple bypass operation. She went smoke-free for about 3 years and then started back up again around Christmas time. 2 weeks later she was dead. Died in her sleep. Her health never really improved after her operation because she chose not to live in a healthy manner. Sources have told me she had a relationship with Christ after her operation, but I have to wonder about the amount of joy she experienced, considering the unhealthy lifestyle choices I saw her make in her last few years alive.

Regardless of your physical condition in this world, you can always do something for the Lord. I had a friend who lived her life in a wheelchair. She told me she felt useless. I told her one time that she could be a prayer warrior. No physical ability is needed for that. People have experienced great joy by going around being prayer warriors. Some people find great joy in knowing they had a part in bringing about an answered prayer in someone else's life. I personally get great joy from knowing that, as I realize Christian traits in my daily walk, I'm superceding weakness. It thrills my soul to know that I'm not doing the weak thing which is succumbing to the world's way of doing things. You can refuse to allow would-be thieves to pull a switcheroo by not attaching your joy to things that can be taken from you. That's a big part of why Jesus instructs us not to lay up treasures here on Earth where robbers can come in and steal. Be the strong Christian that attaches joy to your walk with God. The more you serve Him, the stronger you will become. The stronger you are, the more joy you will experience.

John 16:22 says, "And ye now therefore have sorrow: but I will see you again, and your heart shall rejoice, and your joy no man taketh from you."

Chapter 71

A strong Christian distances himself/herself
from the in-crowd

My son, if sinners entice thee, consent thou not.
-Proverbs 1:10

Who exactly is the in-crowd? Typically, the in-crowd consists of those who seek approval and popularity. It typically consists of those that walk around with the arrogant elitist attitude by doing only those things which are deemed to be "cool." It typically consists of those who live for appearances by trying to epitomize the superficial lifestyle to a T. It typically consists of those who believe they've been equipped with superior judgment. It typically consists of those who tend to exclude those who don't seem to subscribe to their beliefs. It typically consists of those who refuse to act humbly. Jesus would not be biased by hanging with the in-crowd and ignoring all others. In Matthew 5:47 He says, "And if ye salute your brethren only, what do ye more than others? do not even the publicans so?

If you are ignored or excluded by the in-crowd, chances are you've been doing something righteous. In Luke 6:22 Jesus says, "Blessed are ye, when men shall hate you, and when they shall separate you from their company, and shall reproach you, and cast out your name as evil, for the Son of man's sake." As the in-crowd seeks that which can satisfy the flesh and all outwardness, Jesus insists that we focus on meat that endures forever. In John 6:26, 27 He says, "Verily, verily, I say unto you, Ye seek me, not because ye saw the miracles, but because ye did eat of the loaves, and were filled. Labor not for the meat which perisheth, but for that meat which endureth unto everlasting life, which the Son of man shall give unto you: for him hath God the Father sealed."

I recall that up until the 5th grade, I had worn clothes that were not considered stylish. One day during that school year, I asked my mom to buy me some stylish clothes, just so I could prove to the kids in my class that I could too be stylish if I wanted to. She bought me the clothes and I wore them to school the next day. All the kids in the in-crowd came up to me in awe and started talking to me like I was one of them. It wasn't in me to talk and walk like one of them, for I knew only how to be myself. That confirmed that there was definitely an act being put on by them, and I could not keep up with it, nor did I want to, for I saw that doing so would lead only to a foolish end. In John 15:19-21 Jesus says, "If ye were of the world, the world would love his own: but because ye are not of the world, but I have chosen you out of the world, therefore the world hateth you. Remember the word that I said unto you, The servant is not greater than his lord. If they have persecuted me, they will also persecute you; if they have kept my saying, they will keep yours also. But all these things will they do unto you for my name's sake, because they know not him that sent me." Rest assured the world will turn on you if you are not a follower of it.

To the parents reading this, you might ask your child some of the following questions if he/she seems to be running with the in-crowd. I have chosen "Katie Miller" as the sample name for these questions. I don't know anybody with that name. It just came to me as a sample to use. Has Katie Miller been equipped with superior judgment? Has Katie Miller been made privy to some esoteric wisdom that somehow has eluded the rest of us? Do you or does anyone you know feel the need to bow at the altar of Katie Miller? Is Katie Miller known for her high standards of integrity and honesty? Does Katie Miller talk and walk the things of Jesus? Is Katie Miller there for you in times of need? Is it likely that Katie Miller is speaking positively of you when you are not around? Would Katie Miller be able to bail you out if you were to get into some serious trouble? In what ways is Katie Miller a positive influence in your life? These are just some of the questions you the parent can ask your child as a way of prepping them for using discernment, to protect him/her from evil, and to see how he/she is currently viewing his/her relationship with Katie Miller. Remember, it is easier to train them up when they are small than it is to fix a broken adult.

Be the strong Christian who chooses not to run with the in-crowd. It will take strength to do this for some, for they are given to peer pressure. Remember, the weak succumb to peer pressure whereas the strong do the Jesus thing.

Jesus would talk with anyone. He didn't discriminate. However, Jesus was not one to be buddy-buddy with the "cool" people of His day. He knew they were all about the superficial. Jesus was one who constantly focused on matters of the heart, even though He did heal people externally. Study the questions of Jesus. They always pointed to the truth or to what was in the heart of people. Use discernment and be the strong Christian who chooses not to follow those who follow the crowd. Following the crowd only reinforces the idea that what the leader of the crowd is doing is right. If your leader is not following Jesus, then you may have to go it alone. It's alright. You won't really be alone. Jesus will never forsake you.

I Timothy 5:22 says," Lay hands suddenly on no man, neither be partaker of other men's sins: keep thyself pure.

Chapter 72

A strong Christian questions, analyzes, and assesses that which others perceive as difficult

I will go in the strength of the Lord GOD: I will make mention of thy righteousness, even of thine only. - Psalm 71:16

I remember reading a while ago on the Internet that lumberjack was rated year after year as the worst occupation. I was puzzled. I began to question, to analyze, and to assess that claim. Why would people choose that occupation of all things as the worst one? Some of the reasons mentioned were: the sheer physicality of the work (climbing trees, using a chainsaw etc.), the weather conditions, the bugs, and the low pay. I can understand the worldly mentality that leads to the conclusion that lumberjack is the worst occupation. I don't agree with it, though. For me, it is one of the best, greatest, and most satisfying occupations. One can get into great shape because of the physical and cardiovascular demands of this type of work. One's physical and emotional strength can increase greatly. It could be that one, like myself, gets great joy from the work because one sees oneself living out a fantasy. As a younger man, I developed this fantasy in my mind about me being a lumberjack, for it was something fantastic that I had seen throughout my life but had never actually participated in. Once I got to do it (logging) for the first time, I was overjoyed. I started with an axe and eventually worked my way up to a gas-powered chainsaw. Soon I bought my own first chainsaw which was electric. My face shone gleefully like that of a child on Christmas morning opening a gift that was longed for for much time.

I began to use my new chainsaw with much fervor, cutting away at tree trunks on my property that I had slogged away with an axe on for what seemed like forever. For me I was living out a fantasy. There was joy in it also, for I knew that by doing what I was doing, I was doing what the weak were afraid of. The weak are typically afraid of doing the Jesus thing. They shy away from the sick. They don't want to forgive offenders. They don't want to bless their enemies. They don't want to serve their fellow man. Jesus tells us to do all these things. Jesus would never ask you to do anything that required weakness. Anything Jesus tells or asks you to do is going to require some degree of strength. Have you noticed how in 2016 most people don't like to lift heavy things? Satan throughout history has been convincing man that hard work is the enemy. Hard work isn't your enemy; laziness is. God convinced me years ago that hard work is actually beneficial to His children. When I talk of hard work, in this instance, I refer specifically to heavy lifting. I've spent the last 27 years in and out of various gyms doing a lot of heavy lifting. I've concluded that God was right all along. Heavy lifting, if done properly, is good for one's health. I get my kicks from logging and from lifting heavy things because I know they require strength; I know that I'm avoiding weakness by doing those things. The weak will shy away from that which is perceived as difficult. Understandably, people tend to seek comfort and ease, places where strength is not required. The problem is that those people typically are unprepared for battle when the going gets tough. They will typically react primitively instead of utilizing Holy Spirit-driven strength to handle life's difficulties. I've been there myself.

I used to be that person that would literally run and hide whenever trouble or difficulty was present. In middle school I began to pay off the biggest kid in our grade, in baseball cards or in cereal boxes, to protect me from bullies. It worked up until 10th grade. Then I was on my own. It took a while, but eventually I gained enough self-confidence to stand up for myself. Counting on school administration was simply a protocol. It's not a real solution in today's world, usually, because schools can't implement punishment for the offenders; it'd be illegal for them to do so. They don't have enough patience to implement corrective behavior training. So, things typically spiral out of control until somebody gets hurt or killed. Children today typically aren't raised by Holy Spirit-driven parents. They are typically taught the world's views -- the walk and talk of the world. So, it's not surprising that they get the world's results. If you want to be a successful soldier in today's world, you'll need the proper training and views.

I don't like confrontations with trouble

anymore than the next guy, but I feel highly prepared to deal with life's difficulties because of the One on whom I count. I see myself not only as an ambassador of Christ, but also as an operative doing mission work in God's army. A pastor asked me one time if I was tired because of all the traveling that I had done in Costa Rica to preach my message to different churches. I chuckled because I knew that I was living out my fantasy as an operative, doing mission work. The same mentality I had while doing logging, I applied to the Christian walk. The world saw what I was doing as difficult, but I was getting my jollies from it because I was doing things that required strength. So, you see, perspective is everything. What mainly matters in how you handle something is how you see it. As a child I was in awe of displays of strength. I wanted to live out a fantasy one day as one who went on missions saving the weak, the sick, the victims of disasters and brutality. Now I am doing that. As an adult I threw into the mix the avoiding weakness factor. Just knowing that I'm avoiding weakness by doing the Jesus thing tickles me pink. It was mainly the legal crisis that began for me in 2004 that prompted me to do whatever it took to avoid weakness. Sometimes that's what it takes. Maybe you can think back of some crisis in your life that can prompt you to follow Jesus and thereby display your strength for His glory.

Nowadays whenever someone proclaims that something is difficult, I have to wonder first of all if Jesus would look at it that way. Secondly, I have to wonder if that thing would be beneficial and or good for one's health. In today's world, most likely it is beneficial or good for one. Lumberjacks are typically healthier than their sedentary counterparts. Most likely Satan has convinced someone to say that something is difficult or hard. You can be the strong Christian who goes and does that which others perceive as difficult. Your joy can be had in knowing that only strength is required of you when doing the Jesus thing. To the world, the Jesus life is difficult. You will be persecuted. It won't be a rose garden, but you can choose strength. Simply tell others, "I choose strength." If you are challenged, say, "I choose love." Love doesn't like to compete, but when it does compete, it always wins. Be a strong Christian winner by showing strength and love in life's difficult moments.

Chapter 73

A strong Christian speaks and expresses all godly wisdom and truth with assertiveness and authority

Then answered Jesus and said unto them, Verily, verily, I say unto you, The Son can do nothing of himself, but what he seeth the Father do: for what things soever he doeth, these also doeth the Son likewise. - John 5:19

Jesus did not doubt himself. He was not a lollygagger. He didn't walk down the street saying to people demurely, "They say I'm the Alpha and the Omega, but...whatever!" In Matthew 7:28, 29 it says, "And it came to pass, when Jesus had ended these sayings, the people were astonished at his doctrine: For he taught them as one having authority, and not as the scribes." As ambassadors for the Kingdom, we are to walk and to talk like Him. If we seem unsure in our doctrine, people will doubt us and, therefore, Jesus too. Satan knows this and will try to get people to trip us up with questions we can't answer. Don't worry about these situations, if God hasn't revealed the truth regarding the question asked. They tried to trip up Jesus, too. Jesus knew all Scripture by heart; we don't. If you want to speak authoritatively, become an authority on a subject. Spend time with God by reading the Bible and ask Him to pour wisdom into you. He pours wisdom into me daily. When you learn His vocabulary, you will start using it yourself.

In Luke chapter 4, Jesus rebuked a spirit of an unclean devil that was in a man by saying, "Hold thy peace (shut up), and come out of him." Jesus gave the devil a command. He didn't beg him like someone who was afraid. He had the authority to cast out demons. If you want to use that same authority, tell Jesus and ask Him for it. He wants to set the captives free. He doesn't want God's children to be possessed by demonic spirits. He knew the devil had no business being in that man. Why do evil spirits want to inhabit our bodies? So they can control what we do, so we can do Satan's work. Rest assured, anything evil that people do is started in the spirit world. Everything we do is spirit-driven. A spirit of some sort speaks to us and we act upon it. Whether it be a spirit of love, a spirit of vengeance, a spirit of wrath, a spirit of joy, we act on the spirits we decide to listen to. When an unclean, demonic spirit speaks to you, and you don't know what else to say, just say, "Love will win, and Jesus is Lord." Repeat that phrase over and over with assertiveness and authority. That phrase has power and can defeat whatever demons may be inside of you. It may take some practice, but the more you believe in what you are saying, the more convincing you will sound when you say that phrase.

In Luke 9:56 Jesus says, "For the Son of man is not come to destroy men's lives, but to save them." He spoke these words with assertiveness and with authority, not in a threatening way. He spoke matter-of-factly, like His Father. He simply laid out the facts before people. He spoke like His Father because He spent time with Him daily. Did you ever ride into the ghetto and then get out of your car and speak with people? If so, you probably noticed that pretty much everybody there sounded like they were from there. They spoke with ghetto slang and a ghetto accent. Then you came in and spoke "Christianese." People started looking at you strangely and asked, "You ain't from here, is you?" If you aren't speaking like the crowd because you are not following the crowd, it's probably a good thing. If you speak with assertiveness and authority, you are probably one of the few laborers.

If you are a teenage girl reading this, it might help you to repeat the following in case some boy is urging you to have pre-marital sex with him: I am (insert your name), mighty daughter of God who desires to honor God by keeping my temple holy until marriage. Any man who honors me will also honor my beliefs regarding my God-given temple. I have decided to preserve the holiness of my God-given temple by not fornicating. I have agreed to that pact with God. Are you in agreement with that pact? This same sort of speech can be used for guys with girls as well. I used it on my very first girlfriend (because she wanted to fornicate), and she was not pleased. It's OK. The preservation of your temple is far more important than pleasing a fornicator.

Remember, the weak will follow the crowd

and will speak like the crowd. The strong will speak like Jesus spoke and will be set apart, perhaps both literally and figuratively. Be the strong Christian who expresses all godly wisdom and truth with assertiveness and authority. You may be seen as a threat by the spiritually blind. It's alright. Evil will indeed feel threatened whenever God's language is used. You are called to use that language and to use it well.

Chapter 74

A strong Christian speaks against succumbing to retirement

If thou faint in the day of adversity, thy strength is small. - Proverbs 24:10

If Jesus had not been killed, I'm confident He would have lived for many, many years. Nowadays people throw in the towel early, cutting themselves short at the halfway point, typically. Genesis 6:3 says, "And the LORD said, My spirit shall not always strive with man, for that he also is flesh: yet his days shall be an hundred and twenty years." If man has the potential to live to 120, then why does he typically cut himself short? Satanic influence has a lot to do with it. People today, for the most part, don't live very healthy lives. They are brought up believing they are required to get old early and that that's just how it is. They are brought up on all sorts of unhealthy habits and then consider them to be normal for their lifestyle. From an early age, man is told to live a kind of lifestyle that will invite an early retirement so he can proudly arrive at D-Day.

D-Day is known as Declaration Day. It's the day when man can declare his independence from God. It's when he can declare that he has or will have enough money that he'll be able to buy his way through the rest of his self-declared existence. He chooses an age at which he thinks he will die and an amount of money he thinks he will need to make it to that foretold age of death. He doesn't seek to look to God anymore for His provision for his life, for he has the "plan." The "plan" will entail trusting in one's own finances to scrape by until his perceived date of death. A scary thought, if you ask me. The average individual with retirement in mind typically has succumbed or is succumbing to a lifestyle of exponential decrepitude. In other words, their lifestyle revolves a lot around getting old quickly. They don't plan on sticking around for the long haul, for they believe life is too difficult. This is a weak mentality. The people who think like this typically try to spend their lives playing it safe as much as possible, avoiding trouble at all costs, never learning how to walk in true Christian strength. They will live out habits that dishonor God and spend most of their early years focusing and prepping for D-Day. Instead of trusting in God's provision, they choose a non-humble lifestyle which requires much bowing down to Satanic authority and living for the world. Oftentimes a sense of entitlement is had by those people, and God is not entrusted with blessing them financially.

I know people who for years have proclaimed, "When I win the lottery, my life will be great." Those people are in their 70's now and still work full-time jobs and live in misery. For years they have bought into a lifestyle they were never meant to have. They also have bought into the idea that things will be wonderful once they are retired. The fact is more people die from retirement than they do from working. Stress is what kills people, not working. A bad attitude kills people. People that keep on working and have a good attitude typically are healthier than those who seek to die as early as possible so they don't have to deal with life's difficulties anymore. Many people spend their days in fear, foreseeing things that most likely will never come to pass. They spend a lot of time plotting how they could buy their way out of trouble and how they could pay off so-and-so to get by. A lot of the worrisome lifestyle has to do with not trusting God. You don't have to live a lifestyle that seeks to procure an early death. God can extend your days.

I Kings 3:14 says, "And if thou wilt walk in my ways, to keep my statutes and my commandments, as thy father David did walk, then I will lengthen thy days." If God did it for biblical people, He can do it for you too. The date of your death is not set in stone by God, so you shouldn't try to make it set in stone either. If our limit is 120 years, then we should try to make that limited time as productive as possible, not try to end our productive days as early as possible. I've noticed the people who most seek to avoid trouble try to retire the earliest. They don't want to deal with their fellow man and his drama. I understand this, but, instead of praying for an easy life, how about if we pray for the strength to endure a hard one. People miss out on so much opportunity for ministry because they want to avoid other people. I totally understand this. The fact is we are called to minister to our fellow man. It will drain us oftentimes. It's not hard work that drains your energy; it's emotional upheaval. It's the drama that people want to dump on you. I personally don't have the desire or the plan to retire. I want to experience as much as I can while I'm here on Earth. I don't want to be consumed thinking about D-Day. While I have a functioning body, I want it to be active for the Lord. I enjoy seeing God provide for me in a myriad of ways. I can see His goodness even more that way. When people get so independently wealthy, they tend not to pray to God for their needs to be met. They tend not to see Him move in their lives. They tend to trust in their money (which God gave them) and fail to give God the credit for their blessings. I don't want to be so independent of God that I start trusting in the things of this world, many of which are impractical.

The weak will succumb to retirement, failing to live fully as a strong Christian, seeking to avoid trouble, trusting in their bank account. The strong trust that God will provide until their dying day. I once was curious and asked God, "How much money does one need in this lifetime?" He responded, "One only needs enough to make it to the end." I thought about it and said, "You're right, God!"

Psalm 71:9 says, "Cast me not off in the time of old age; forsake me not when my strength faileth."

Chapter 75

A strong Christian bounces back from depression

Envy thou not the oppressor, and choose none of his ways. - Proverbs 3:31

Oftentimes Satan will show us images of people who seemingly are able to escape the consequences of sinful living. He tries to get us to envy them. First we covet what our neighbor has and then we envy them, which entails us desiring to be like them. If we think we can't be like them, we get depressed. Right? A strong Christian can get depressed, too. However, a strong Christian bounces back from depression, realizing that depression is something that is self-imposed. What is depression, then?

Depression can be defined as follows: an attitude of willful stubbornness in which a child of God refuses, to a degree, to live out certain Christian traits when one is mad at God when God seemingly does not make things go one's way. Thus, our "depression" is something we choose to impose on ourselves. It's not something that just happens. In fact, all of our emotions reflect our beliefs about our relationship to God and our identity in the Kingdom. The more we distance ourselves from God, the more likely we are to become depressed. Jesus never got depressed. He was sad, but never depressed. He never held a grudge against His Father because things "didn't go His way." The more we think God is against us, the more likely we are to get depressed. God is not against you; He is against sinful living.

I became depressed after my trial in 2005. I was found guilty for something I didn't do. I was determined to be in rebellion against God until my probation ended in 2008. I decided I was going to be depressed until June of 2008. I would go to the pizza shop and indulge myself with greasy pizzas and sodas, then sit in the mall for extended periods of time eating chocolates, accomplishing nothing fruitful. I was decided that I was going to live the depressed lifestyle until God started making things go my way again. Little by little God started showing me that what I was doing was not what I was meant to do. I felt miserable in my body because of the crap I had been eating and in my soul I felt rebellious, yet sorry at the same time for dishonoring God in that way. My emotions were still a wreck, but I began to come out of the depression and entered a weight loss contest at my gym. I came in second, having lost 30 pounds in just under 3 months. I began to read stories about athletes and other overcomers who overcame adversity and went on to accomplish great things. I wanted to accomplish great things, but did not set myself up for envy by setting my sights on people's accomplishments. I began to set my eyes on things above.

Slowly but surely I began to realize that Christian strength has to do with doing what the world oftentimes considers to be weakness. I was determined not to be defeated. Defeat for me was going downwards in my standard of living. Victory meant going upwards in my standard of living. I was determined to go upwards. I reasoned that the only way to go upwards was not to give in to weakness, that is to say, not go along with the world's ways. Jesus soon showed me that His way was the way of strength, for nothing He does involves weakness.

The weak will stay depressed and essentially, are still mad at God. The strong, however, will soon snap out of it (if they are in it at all) and realize God is not against them. Just because things may not go your way doesn't mean that God is trying to punish you. God doesn't try to punish anyone. Oftentimes we punish ourselves for not listening to Him in the first place. Been there, done that. Be the strong Christian that focuses on God and His goodness, and not the weak person who chooses depression to justify being mad at God.

Chapter 76

A strong Christian does not change his/her feelings when others become distant

And he commanded the steward of his house, saying, Fill the men's sacks with food, as much as they can carry, and put every man's money in his sack's mouth. - Genesis 44:1

Technically Joseph in Genesis was not a Christian, for Christ had not yet come to the Earth, but he did display Christ-like strength when dealing with his brothers who betrayed him. Christ-like qualities were made manifest long before He came to Earth. Joseph did not grow bitter and hateful towards those who became distant. He still loved his brothers, and he wept when he finally was in a position of power to help them. He wept for the same reason Jesus would have — because he knew his brothers had rejected God's love up to that point.

As strong Christians, we need to understand that those that distance themselves from us do so because they can't handle the Christ-like behavior we project. It's happened to me many times. People came into my life but then soon vanished, when they could have stayed. Those that reject you are really rejecting Christ and that will be on them. Those people are hurting and aren't ready to let God fill the God-sized hole in their lives. If we change our feelings because of their refusal to stay near us, we are giving them control of our emotions. We are basically admitting that they are operating from some position of power and with a superior mindset. Rest assured, no one who leaves you because of the Christ in you is operating from any position of superior thought or power. Those people need to come to Christ to find rest and peace. Jesus is the Prince of Peace. As strong Christians, we should encourage those people to come to Christ to find solace. We aren't to rub Christianity in their face and say, "I told you so." Those people are hurting enough already. Focus on easing their hurt by inviting them to get to know Jesus personally.

Joseph blessed his brothers with food and money. They had left him for dead and he turned around and blessed them. Jesus wants us to do this. I have a Christian friend whose ex-husband tried to milk her for all he could. He stole things from her house and sold them for money for himself to use on drugs and prostitutes. She knew he was doing this and lots of other dirty things to dishonor God. He ended up doing a year in the local prison for a crime. When he got out, he was to be on his own. He was without a car, and money, and family. She decided to bless him by giving him her old vehicle and some gas money so he could go back to his original family out of state. At first I thought, "Why are you giving him money, especially after all that he stole from you?" Then I remembered that Christ told us to bless our enemies and those who persecute us. Giving those things was the way she knew how to bless him. Even though she was not pleased with his behavior, she didn't allow it to change her feelings for the worse. The weak grow bitter and hold grudges against those who distance themselves from them.

Be the strong Christian who looks at people who distance themselves from you as hurting children who need love. Remember what Jesus said in Luke 21:17: "And ye shall be hated of all men for my name's sake." A strong Christian overcomes and defeats hate with love. You can be that strong Christian. Just keep in mind that what those people need is love, not more hatred.

Genesis 45:5 says, "Now therefore be not grieved, nor angry with yourselves, that ye sold me hither: for God did send me before you to preserve life."

Chapter 77

A strong Christian takes responsibility for his/her actions, repents, and moves on

For we ourselves were also sometimes foolish, disobedient, deceived, serving divers lusts and pleasures, living in malice and envy, hateful, and hating one another. - Titus 3:3

It surely seems that nothing ticks off a human being more than an attitude of unrepentance in another person. When people deliberately commit an offense against another person and show no sign of remorse, it seems nothing is more heartbreaking, disheartening, and maddening. A lot of times what makes the heart glad is true repentance on the part of the offender. When people say, "I'm sorry," a lot of times that makes or keeps a relationship on good terms.

Jesus says in Matthew 5:25, "Agree with thine adversary quickly, whiles thou are in the way with him; lest at anytime the adversary deliver thee to the judge, and the judge deliver thee to the officer, and thou be cast into prison." Jesus said this as a warning because He knew how detrimental it could be for one not to reconcile with our adversaries. Jesus probably could have apologized for saying the things He did and possibly could have escaped execution, but He chose not to, for He did nothing wrong. The same thing happened to me when I went to trial in 2005. I did nothing wrong and was subsequently delivered to the judge by my adversary and then was wrongfully convicted. The people that are truly wronged by us are looking for an admission of guilt, an apology, and repentance. Some people that we have not wronged are simply out to get us into trouble. Sometimes all we can do is pray for those people. Remember, you will be persecuted for talking and walking Jesus in this world.

In Luke 15:7 Jesus says, "I say unto you, that likewise joy shall be in heaven over one sinner that repenteth, more than over ninety and nine just persons, which need no repentance." Jesus likes this matter of repentance. He came to save those who would repent of their sins and would accept Him as Savior, admitting that they need Him as their Savior. The strong Christian knows he/she is not perfect like Christ and chooses to set aside his/her ego. The ego is what keeps one from repenting. The ego typically says, "I have done no wrong." I used to live that way, failing to admit that I could be wrong. Once I found out about Christian strength, I realized it was alright to admit that I screwed up in the past. To deny it would be foolish, for we all have screwed up in this lifetime (Romans 3:23).

The strong Christian doesn't dwell on his/her mistakes. He/she quickly confesses, repents for them, and moves on, trying not to make the same mistakes or commit the same sins again. Lots of people go around continually feeling guilty for what they have done. If this is you, you should go to whomever you have wronged and get that thing off your chest. Be honest. Tell what you did and ask for forgiveness in a sincere way. Almost every time, when it's one individual dealing with another in the street, the offended party will be willing to forgive when they see true repentance coming from the offender. In a court of law, they typically aren't as forgiving. That's because most judges have ended up with a judgmental attitude (considering their job), and are more into condemnation than they are into forgiveness. I've seen people confess and apologize for crimes and still get thrown into jail. This is ungodliness in action. Jesus knew that some people could get like this. That's why He urged us to avoid ungodly, sinful behavior -- because He knew how bad things might turn out for us.

Be the strong Christian who is quick to confess your faults, mistakes, and sins. Christ is on board with this. The weak will go around acting as if they are holier than thou and pretend that they don't make mistakes or commit offenses, at least not against other people. Baloney! We all mess up from time to time; it happens. Be wary of those who claim they need never to repent. They may just be the first one in line to accuse you the moment you seemingly commit an offense.

James 5:16 says, "Confess your faults one to another, and pray one for another, that ye may be healed. The effectual fervent prayer of a righteous man availeth much."

Chapter 78

A strong Christian puts Satan in his place when attacked by him

And Jesus answered and said unto him, Get thee behind me, Satan: for it is written, Thou shalt worship the Lord thy God, and him only shalt thou serve. - Luke 4:8

Even though I've come a long way in my Christian strength, I am still susceptible to spiritual attacks. Satan has studied me for years and knows my former weaknesses. He still likes to prod and poke at me in those areas. He noticed dangerous attitudes and mindsets I seemed to carry and tries to entice me to this day. He tries to get my eyes focused on the world, how everyone else is living, so that I will find a justification and/or a rationalization for doing things I normally wouldn't do anymore. For example, I used to struggle with the one-more-time mentality. I used to go around thinking that if I committed a sin "just one more time" before turning over a new leaf, it'd be alright. I'd be convinced that if I did it just one more time, there'd be no harm, since I was about to embark on a lifetime of sinlessness in that area, or so I thought. The problem was that I was not nearly disciplined enough to live sinlessly in the area in which I was committing sin. Satan could see this in my behavior and would tempt me and have me rationalize it by repeating the phrase "just one more time." "Enjoy this thing just one more time, Tim." In my weakness I acquiesced and succumbed to sin that I knew was wrong and still managed to find that sin-filled justification for it. He would get me to remember times when God went seemingly against me and say, "You see, Tim, God went against you, so it'll be OK if you go against Him this time, just so you're even."

I was under spiritual attack and, early on, didn't even realize it. In the early part of my rebellion against God, which was right around the time of my trial, I willfully went against God. I was quick to go along with Satan's nudging, for I still had a grudge against God for letting me go through what I went through. Later on, when I gained Christian strength, I began to treat God reverentially. I began to see that God was not against me and began to believe that He allowed difficulty in my life for my growth, so I'd get stronger; it worked. Once I concluded that I had a degree of Christian strength and that God was not against me, I began saying no to Satan whenever he attacked me. I'd tell him to go straight back to Hell. I'd remind him of my identity as a strong child of God Almighty. I'd remind him that he had no power over me and that he could not convince me that serving him would be better than serving God Almighty.

You may be one of those people who have trouble saying no to people. If so, Satan will pick up on this and try to use it against you. If you have trouble saying no to people, he figures you will probably have trouble saying no to him, too. This is where speaking authoritatively and assertively comes in handy. Jesus put Satan in his place when attacked by him, for He knew Satan had no place telling Jesus what to do or tempting Him. He has no business tempting us or telling us what to do either. We need to realize this. If we are lulled into thinking "Well, that's just what Satan does; He's going to tempt me.," we essentially will fail to stand boldly against him on the day of attack. We need to realize these attacks will come, whether we are strong Christians or not. Satan has been studying your weaknesses since day one and has a way of tempting you in those areas. I see people all the time succumbing, as if by automation, in their areas of weakness, exhibiting little or no self-control. Understand that you can and should recognize these attacks when they happen. You need to be prepared for confrontation with a wily devil. You need to get talking like Jesus talked and put Satan in his place when attacked by him. Tell him the truth. Satan tried, without success, to tempt Jesus more than once. Every time Satan failed because Jesus told him the truth and where to go.

You can be the strong Christian who tells Satan the truth and where to go. I gave in to his temptations because I failed to choose strength, for I did not know strength. I knew my weaknesses all too well and was not yet secure in my position as a mighty child of God who was willing to walk strongly in resistance to Satan's wiles. I failed to tell Satan the truth because I did not know the truth and therefore could not tell him something I did not know. Know the truth and tell it to Satan. Once Satan sees you know it and are sticking to it steadfastly, he will flee from you, for he knows there is no way to overcome a child of God that is standing firmly in the truth.

Chapter 79

A strong Christian remembers the good that once was and pays it forward

Depart from evil, and do good; seek peace, and pursue it. - Psalm 34:14

Jesus did three years of ministry and was barely here thirty-three years on Earth. He urged His disciples to carry on His work. He came as an example of how we are to live. Every bit of the way He treated people screamed, "I got you covered!" He wants us to remember the good that existed previously and to pay it forward. We are to treat people in a loving way, as Jesus did. The reason we remember the good that once was is that it may not be present now. If we look around us nowadays, we aren't likely to see a lot of good; at least I don't see much.

One way I remember the good that once was is to experience retro things such as movies, TV shows, books, and songs. Those things tend to take me back to a place in time when life was simpler and education was more refined and greater. The vocabulary in books and TV shows from yesteryear was more erudite, and proper English was used more often the further back in time you go. It's a far cry from what's out there nowadays. The majority of young people nowadays are brought up on current shows and songs, so they don't know anything different. I like to show them how things used to be so they can get a proper perspective. Manners, ethics, and morals were taught and conveyed on a lot of TV shows back in the day; nowadays, not so much. Children were taught to write coherent sentences and paragraphs. Standards have slipped quite a bit since the era of technology took off with the proliferation of the Internet. The more technology does the thinking or doing for people, the lazier people tend to become. Since things aren't quite the way they used to be, I think back (fortunately because I'm old enough to do so) on some of the aforementioned things and try to pay them forward, especially to the younger generation who may be deprived of such things. I've come to realize that a lot of people nowadays don't know what good health looks like because they haven't seen it modeled for them. Fortunately, I grew up watching healthy strong role models, so I could look at them and say, "Oh, so that's what good health looks like." I had good examples to follow. We want to pay it forward because not everybody grew up knowing what healthy people look like.

Much joy can be found, I've noticed, in doing things the way nature intended for us to do them. One actually can feel healthy when one does manual labor and sweats. To put this trait into practice, think back to an instance or a time period when things were going well for you. Think about how happy you were when someone treated you with the I-got-you-covered attitude. It can be very gratifying to treat your neighbor the same way. When you think back to that good moment or period and you try to make someone else feel the way you did, you are paying it forward. It could be that you bought someone a ticket to a ball game because someone else did that for you years ago, and you were delighted. From a strong Christian perspective, we should be thinking of the good things that Christ did for people and try to replicate them. Jesus fed the hungry. He healed the sick. He showed compassion. He gave really good advice. He was a friend to people who needed a friend, and so on. As I study the life of Christ more and more, I think about how I can pay forward the kinds of good things He did for people.

When I was working as a volunteer in 2008 in Costa Rica, I was working on my last home for my time there. I soon noticed that the neighbor next to the house where I was working invited me over for a snack. She was an older lady trying to make a nice gesture. I noticed her family was poor, as they were using an old phone book as toilet paper. She even scrounged together enough money to buy me a little gift set of soap before I left. She saw the good I was doing by volunteering to help my fellow man, and decided to pay some good forward. Then the neighbor across the street had his house robbed while he was away. A couple of technicians came by to examine the situation and saw us volunteers working on the house across the street. They decided to do a good deed as well, and they volunteered to put a new door on the front of the house that was robbed. Again people saw good and decided to pay it forward in order to help out their fellow man.

This is what Jesus wants.

Remember, the weak will focus on all the neglect and dereliction that's going on among God's children and choose to participate in that sort of a lifestyle. How about if you be the strong Christian who decides to remember the good that once was and pay it forward to take care of your fellow man and to spread goodness?

Psalm 37:3 says, "Trust in the LORD, and do good; so shalt thou dwell in the land, and verily thou shalt be fed."

Chapter 80

A strong Christian sacrifices self-comfort to serve God

But thou, when thou fastest, anoint thine head, and wash thy face; That thou appear not unto men to fast, but unto thy Father which is in secret: and thy Father, which seeth in secret, shall reward thee openly. - Matthew 6:17,18

God has shown me throughout the years that there is strength in being willing to do without a lot of the things the world would have you believe you need. I remember the first time I went to Costa Rica in 2002. I fell in love with the country, but I was not yet ready to sacrifice my American comforts to live a Costa Rican lifestyle. There were fewer amenities there and I believed I wouldn't have had all that I'd need to get by there. Fast forward 14 years and my mindset is different now. I've come to realize that we don't need as much as we think we do in life, a lot of the time. It basically came down to a matter of me getting fed up with the American way of life. I had to get so fed up with what I was used to in order to appreciate the simple things in life. As a young child I'd poke fun at simplicity, but now I crave it. I'm now ready to live with less and do live with less. Sure I'm giving up a lot of experiences, but I'm learning a lot about people in the process, mainly how they seem to be controlled by what they think they need. I've learned that I don't need luxury items, and I have come to have gratitude for the simple things in life and to value relationships.

To serve God will mean giving up some or, perhaps, a lot of the comforts that one may have gotten used to. The application of this relinquishment actually shows some strength, for it shows one's willingness to deviate from the pull of the flesh. I've been told by someone who makes a lot of money and lives a luxurious lifestyle that it's about comfort, not status; I disagree. I look at the way he lives and feel that he could be comfortable with a lot less in his life. As a Christian I can see that he's not willing to carry his daily cross give up a lot of the luxurious comforts that go along with his type of lifestyle. Having lived with very little myself, I have come up with a pretty good idea of how little one actually needs to get by in this world on a regular basis.

When I arrived in Mexico in 2006, I had nothing but my luggage. Once there, I had to buy everything that I'd need or want including my transportation (bicycle), clothing, food, towels, soap, appliances, and so on. I then realized how little I needed. I was sacrificing some self-comfort to live a more God-centered lifestyle. What happens when we are given to a lifestyle wherein are hearts are tied to our material things? We get disheartened, mad, angry, vengeful, and so forth when those things are taken from us. That's why Jesus said for us not to store up treasures here on earth where thieves can break in and rob us of them. Store up treasures that thieves can't steal – the things inside of you such as knowledge and goodness. For me it took some years to get weaned off of things that prompted me to feel comfortable, but I came to realize that it can be done.

God doesn't want us tied down to a bunch of baggage. He wants us to travel lightly. Satan will try to have you chasing after those who seemingly are able to escape the consequences of living sinfully. He might have you thinking that if you can acquire a little more comfort, then you'll be content. The problem is that you'll already be in a mindset of "seeking more." So, once you have more, you'll seek even more, because of how good it feels to have more. Don't fall for it. Jesus traveled lightly. I'm sure He didn't stay in four-star hotels all along His journeys. He wasn't looking to get pampered; He was looking to save people from their sin and to set the captives free. He was looking to release people from their inner prisons where they were being held prisoner by their strongholds. Sometimes we will have to get comfortable with the uncomfortable to do the work of Jesus. Rest assured there is strength in it. I'm not saying to put your safety at risk. I'm saying to examine what you need versus what you think you need and go with the former. Having the strength to abstain from perceived comforts will carry you through uncomfortable moments. The more you can abstain from the comforts that control the weak-willed, the stronger you are. Be that strong Christian who sets that Christ-like example.

Chapter 81

A strong Christian recognizes areas in which he/she is still weak

Pride goeth before destruction, and an haughty spirit before a fall. - Proverbs 16:18

I love it when people are humble enough to admit when they are weak in an area. It actually takes strength to do this. As a child, I did not exhibit this strength. I wanted the world to think that I had lots of strength, but on the inside I suffered from self-doubt. It kept me from attempting a lot of things in life. As an adult, I've arrived at the place now where I am totally ready to recognize any areas in which I am still weak. For me, or for anyone for that matter, I find it easier to live out certain Christian traits than it is to live out others. This indicates that the flesh is still pulling at me hard in some areas. If you are still weak in an area, just admit it. People often are afraid to admit it because they don't want to be perceived as weak and/or vulnerable. A lot of times, I've noticed, people have a poor vocabulary. When they run out of words, they get an attitude in order to try to fake strength to hide their weakness. They do this instead of just admitting that they don't have the adequate vocabulary to express themselves. If I don't have the words to explain something, I simply say, "I don't have the words to explain this." People just might appreciate your honesty and the strength it takes to admit it than they will your "attitude."

I remember watching on the news several years ago a story about a Mexican man who got into an altercation with his brother. They were arguing and the man ended up killing his brother. When interviewed about it, the reporter asked him why he killed his brother. He responded, "Because I ran out of words." I understand the frustration one feels when one doesn't have sufficient vocabulary to express oneself. I didn't want to feel that frustration when speaking Spanish, so early on in my studies I decided that I'd study doggedly to learn as many words as I could. Now 20 plus years later, it's rare that I feel inadequate with my words. What I'm saying here is that it's alright to recognize and then to admit that you are weak in an area. Our pride oftentimes keeps us from recognizing and admitting our weaknesses. Once you've done your recognition and admission, make it a point to work on those weak areas to get strong. A lot of unwillingness to recognize our weakness has to do with our pride and ego. A lot of our fear regarding admission has to do with how we think people will perceive us if they know of our weakness. We are afraid we'll be seen as vulnerable, like an enemy in battle. Again we go back to the dangerous mindset that others have been equipped with superior judgment and are entitled to use it on us. Once again I remind you that your fellow man has not been equipped by God Almighty with superior judgment.

Be wary around people who claim to have it

all together and those who claim to have all the answers. They are typically very insecure people who are fronting so others will not find out about their weaknesses. I am attracted to those who regularly and nonchalantly admit their weaknesses. They are typically the more secure, honest, and trustworthy individuals. It's much better for everyone when an admission of weakness is made because then the weak person can go directly to focusing on adding strength to his/her life. Regarding depression, once I realized that it was self-imposed and not God-imposed, I saw that it was my weakness, not God's putting it on me. This helped me to abstain from further depression. Any time I feel pulled by the flesh to get depressed, I remind myself that it'd be my doing, not God's. I was weak in this area, for it was so easy for me to just put the blame on God. I recognized this area of weakness and did something about it. That's what we are to do as strong Christians. We are to recognize the areas in which we are still weak and do some introspection, some heart examination, to see why we are still weak in those areas. It ultimately always boils down to us wanting to serve some self-serving purpose rather than God. When we are weak in an area, we seek to satisfy the flesh, mainly because of pride, ego, and/or fear. Examine your own heart in this matter and get real with God. Recognize these things before Him and ask for His assistance in your areas of weakness. He should reveal to you what's been holding you back and how to fix it. The answer should lie in your willingness to serve Him and your desire to put away weakness in order to exhibit strength.

Jesus says in Mark 14:38, "Watch ye and pray, lest ye enter into temptation. The spirit truly is ready, but the flesh is weak."

Chapter 82

A strong Christian can handle the truth

And this is the condemnation, that light is come into the world, and men loved darkness rather than light, because their deeds were evil. - John 3:19

Currently my boss at my full-time job is not someone who likes to hear the truth when it's about him. I know from experience that I would be reprimanded if I were to tell him the truth about himself. I learned this mentality a long time ago. When I was in the second grade, I was supposed to ride the school bus home from school since I lived more than a mile from school. One day I was curious and wanted to see what it'd be like to walk home from school. I did walk home from school one day, and my mom was frantic with worry when I arrived home. She asked me repeatedly if I had walked home from school, and I repeatedly denied walking home from school. I had been taught somewhere along the way that I'd have the living stuffing beat out of me if I told the truth. Somewhere along the way I learned that lying was the way to stay safe. And so it is in our society oftentimes. People are all too often taught that the truth is bad for them and that lying will somehow get you ahead and keep you safe in life. Jesus doesn't quite look at it that way.

It's been said that the only people who have a problem with you telling the truth are those living a lie. There is truth to that statement. Have you ever noticed that the people who can handle the truth don't mind it when you tell the truth? The truth that they can handle, that is. Truth-handling seems to be a relative thing; some people can handle more than others. The fact is everybody can handle a little truth, but not everybody can handle a lot of truth. You want to be a strong Christian who can handle a lot of truth. There is strength in truth-handling, I've found. The weak tend to deny the truth and promote lies that proliferate evil and hide their inability to handle a certain truth. Satan is the father of lies. His goal is to distort God's truth so that it'll seem untruthful to you. For every godly truth that's out there, rest assured that Satan has countered it with a lie that will seem like truth to the untrained eye. Anybody who has ever sinned has been deceived into thinking that sin was good for them. Satan wants you to think sin is good for you, so that you won't end up doing God's work. Satan's main goal is to get your eyes off of the truth (Jesus) and onto anything of this world that will distract you from godly living.

The people that are still going around pushing lies are spiritually blind to what they are doing. They don't realize that the Truth will set them free. Living a lie because Satan has told you that you'll get ahead that way is not strength. Strength is being able to accept the truth that the weak won't accept. I used to push lies and had a tough time accepting a lot of truth. Then one day Jesus taught me that there is strength in truth-handling and that the truth was good for me. I can even remember back to my school days, in my child-like innocence, and telling the truth, and then looking at people strangely when they wanted to scold me or mock me for telling the truth. I was like, "But the truth will help you here! Why are you not agreeing with me!" There are devious intentions in the minds of those who seek to push lies, especially those who know what the truth is. If people know the truth, then why do they insist on pushing lies? It's because Satan still has them convinced that by lying, somehow they will get ahead and come out of a situation unscathed. Jesus doesn't want us to be deceitful. He never tried or did mislead anyone. He always told the truth. As strong Christians, we are likely to be hated or attacked for telling the truth. Look at the whistleblowers of scams and scandals who get harassed for exposing the lies that evil people tried to hide. People who lie or commit evil deeds don't like it when the truth is told because either they are exposed or they feel exposed. Sometimes people with a guilty conscience will attack you or get defensive if you simply tell a truth, not even necessarily about them.

Jesus told the truth and look what it got Him. He was crucified for it. The evil people of His day felt exposed and sought to shut Him up by killing Him. Jesus wasn't weak; His killers were. They couldn't handle the truth that Jesus spoke. Strong truth-handlers don't go around killing people for telling the truth. Eventually I did tell my mom the truth – that I had walked home from school – once she broke down and cried. The fact is I was raised by parents who had a problem with the truth, so that mentality was passed on to me. I wasn't brought up in a home with strong Christians. I was taught that truth-handling was OK ... to a degree. I was taught that truth-handling was acceptable as long as it didn't offend whomever I was telling it to.

As strong Christians, we aren't called to sugar coat the truth to protect the feelings of those who are incapable of handling it. We are called to tell the truth whether our audience can handle it or not. I'm sure Jesus didn't burn the midnight oil thinking of ways to craft His sermons so as not to offend anyone with a certain truth that he/she might not be able to handle. I'm sure Jesus just told the plain old truth and there were people who were offended and could not handle it. You don't want to be one of those weak people who can't handle it. You need to ask Jesus to reveal to you how and why the truth is good for you. The truth is meant to be only good for you. It isn't designed to ruin your life. There may be people who want to ruin your life once they find out a truth about you, but that's their inability/weakness regarding truth-handling. The truth may hurt for those who aren't yet able to handle it, but rest assured, once you realize that the truth is good for you (just like your vegetables), you'll see that the more truth you can handle, the stronger you'll be.

Chapter 83

A strong Christian is willing to pray for anyone

But I say unto you, Love your enemies, bless them that curse you, do good to them that hate you, and pray for them which despitefully use you, and persecute you; - Matthew 5:44

The above-mentioned verse may be for many the most difficult to live out in their lives. Man typically wants to do the opposite of what's mentioned in the verse. That's why Jesus had to tell people: so they'd know what strong living would involve. For man, it takes strength to love, pray for, do good to, and bless his enemies. Our focus for this chapter is on praying for anyone regardless of what they might have done to us. The biggest obstacles to us praying for those that attack us are envy, grudges, and ego. If we refuse to pray for someone, we are executing worldly judgment. We are taking offense. We haven't forgiven him/her. We are placing more value on what he/she did than on our ability to pray for him/her. We are giving control of our emotions to that person who offended or hurt us. We can be quick to forget that those that offend or hurt us are not operating from a position of superior strength. Strength does not hurt people; hurt people hurt people.

Why would Jesus ask you to do all those things to and for your enemies if doing so required weakness. Anything Jesus says for you to do requires strength. His goal is to strengthen you. Strengthening the Christian is spoken of and suggested many times throughout the Bible. Jesus wants to keep you from weakness. Praying for people, especially those who've hurt you or people you care about, is a sign of strength. It shows you have the strength not to be emotionally dominated by an attack from a hurting person. It often shows you know about real strength and that you are OK with the possibility of the person you are praying for becoming strong as a result of prayer, too.

As it insinuates in the verse, there will likely be those that will try to use you despitefully. I reiterate that those people aren't operating from a position of strength. They are hurt people. They are listening to their demons. People who follow Christ and godly wisdom don't go using people despitefully. Pray that they'd be delivered from their strongholds and their demons. Pray that they'd get the desire to acquire strength. Pray that their eyes would be opened to what they are doing. In order for breakthrough to occur, usually what is needed is for someone's spiritual eyes to be opened. There has to be a stronger desire to do good than to do evil. A lot of strong Christians have arrived at where they are because they saw the dead end in what they were doing and got tired of living in weak sinfulness. Many learned the hard way, usually because of their stubbornness, that hurting others was immature and weak. Now many of them don't wish to see others make the same mistakes they did, so they pray for those who are still enslaved by sinful living.

If you are attacked by your fellow man, tell him you will pray for him. You can even take it a step further by telling him you'll pray for the people who hurt him, as well. Most level-headed people will appreciate your gesture, for they are tired of hurting. Don't take it personally if people say no. You can always pray for people in private if necessary. It may behoove you to tell him that you were not trying to hurt him in the first place. Just like a dog who has been attacked repeatedly, hurt people often can get quite defensive and try to pass on their hurt. Do a little probing. Ask him if he minds if you pray for those who've hurt him. Tell him that after you pray for those who've hurt him, you'll then pray for him. You might mention to him how you overcame your own hurt because a strong Christian came along and prayed for you too, if that's the case. In any case, be the strong Christian who has no qualms about praying for someone. Remember, it's Satan who wants you to hold offenses against the person that needs prayer. Listen to God and pray for those He puts on your heart. It just might be the people who've hurt you.

Chapter 84

A strong Christian is willing to love anyone

And the second is like unto it, Thou shalt love thy neighbor as thyself. Matthew 22:39

I've actually loved an enemy before. It feels quite joyous to do so. For those given to unforgiveness, revenge, bitterness, hatred maliciousness, and so forth, this will be a hard trait to live out. Loving nice people is easy. The hard part is loving those which attack you; this is the part we'll focus on. We refuse to love those who attack us for the same reasons we refuse to pray for those who attack us. It does indeed take a good bit of strength to love difficult people. And regardless of what anyone says, it's OK to love people at a distance. It may keep you safe to do so, for some people may become even more enraged against you if they find out you loved them. Love is the one emotion which can overcome any and all evil. It can cure diseases. There is a chemical that God put into the body which is released when one truly loves another. The more reason you might have not to love someone you are loving, the stronger the dosage of this chemical will be when released in your body. This has healed sick people who loved others.

One of my favorite true stories I recall is about the loving man in the prisoner of war camp. Back during the war (I believe it was the Second World War), there were some prisoners of war in a camp being run by the enemy. The enemy soldiers treated the prisoners hatefully. Most of the prisoners in the camp adopted an attitude of hatred towards one another as a result. A spirit of hatred was rampant, but one man refused it. He remembered that it was hatred on the part of the enemy soldiers which killed all of his family, so he wanted no part of it. He decided he'd do his best to do nothing but love on those around him. Soon disease entered into the camp, and every soldier got sick ... but one. The man who loved his fellow man did not get the sicknesses and diseases that befell all others. He remained in good health. This was no accident. God designed the human body to keep healthy, provided man go about loving his fellow man. This is one of the awesome benefits of loving the unlovable. We also will be showing Christ-like strength when we love them.

God sees when we love our enemies, and He will reward us in due time. In 2011 I bought a pickup truck shortly after moving to my current location. I found it convenient to park it on the side of a driveway that I legally share with my next door neighbor. For some odd reason, it bothered him that the truck was parked where it was. One Saturday afternoon he decided to come over and bang on my door in a drunken state. I answered the door and he laid into me about moving my truck out of the driveway. He proceeded to cuss at me and threaten to do damage to the truck if I didn't move it within 24 hours. I decided to avoid conflict and moved the truck closer to my property. I knew he was suffering, did not know the peace of Christ, and had no one to really love him, except for maybe his live-in girlfriend. I recalled Proverbs 26:21,22 which say, "If thine enemy be hungry, give him bread to eat; and if he be thirsty, give him water to drink: For thou shalt heap coals of fire upon his head, and the LORD shall reward thee." I thought to myself, "He is a little on the skinny side, so he's probably hungry and thirsty." I went out and bought him a Christmas card and wrote inside of it, "Merry Christmas, neighbor!" I didn't sign it, but I did include a Subway gift card for $15, so he could satisfy his hunger and thirst.

A few months went by and I heard nothing from him. Then one day I found a tax stub in some papers I was organizing. It was the stub for my property taxes that I was supposed to have mailed in to the tax collector a month earlier. I knew I'd be late and penalized for late taxes, so I called the tax collector lady. I reached her voice mail and left a message admitting that I found the tax stub and wanted to rectify the situation as soon as possible. She called my voice mail a day or two later and said that I didn't owe anything, that some lady came in and paid my taxes for me. Since I had just moved to the area, I didn't know any ladies there ... except the one next door. Did she pay my taxes for me? I don't know. It might have been a God-sent angel for all I know that came in to pay my taxes. All I know is that God gives us a thumbs-up when we love His children, especially the difficult ones. Be the strong Christian who is willing to love anyone. You'll be following Jesus' example, and you'll be blessed in a godly way for it. Love others and love will come back to you someday somehow. Remember the weak hold sin against people and use that as an excuse not to love people. But you aren't trying to be weak. You are trying to be strong. The strong overlook sin and don't let that determine whether or not they will love someone. Real love does not depend on someone's amount of sin. The more you are willing to love the difficult, the stronger you will be.

In Luke 6:27 Jesus says, "But I say unto you which hear, Love your enemies, do good to them which hate you."

Chapter 85

A strong Christian exercises self-discipline to take care of the temple by way of the 5 divine facets of health insurance: C.A.R.E.D. (Cleanliness, Attitude, Rest, Exercise, Diet)

What? know ye not that your body is the temple of the Holy Ghost which is in you, which ye have of God, and ye are not your own? For ye are bought with a price: therefore glorify God in your body, and in your spirit, which are God's. - I Corinthians 6:19,20

Before the fall of man, there was no disease. All disease originates from sin, and sin originates from the desire to live dirtily. It may not be your own sin which caused your disease, but rather someone else's. Either way, it's a problem the world has to deal with. I like to focus on prevention. A lot of sickness and disease can be prevented by clean living. As strong Christians, we should strive to employ tactics of good hygiene and sanitary practices. We should wash our hands after touching questionable objects. We should bathe when dirty. We should avoid contact as well as possible with harmful substances such as insulation, dust, tobacco, mold, mildew, lead paint, fecal matter, mucus, carcasses, and anything else that could contaminate us. I'm not being germophobic or overly sensitive about this. I see sick people all the time, and those same people I see involved in unhygienic, unsanitary practices. They touch things that are clearly dirty and then put their hands in or near their mouths. I have a friend who one time was changing tires at an automotive shop and then suddenly grabbed for some fries with his bare hands and shoved them in his mouth, clearly thinking nothing of it. It might go without saying that the life expectancy of such a person is quite low.

Cleanliness is a big part of taking care of our God-given temple and we aren't to take it lightly. Keeping things clean is one of the biggest things we can do to stave off disease and illness. I myself have been sick an average of once a year throughout my life. My sickest time ever was when I was about twelve or thirteen and had a fever for a few days. The few times I've vomited in life can be attributed to lack of hand washing, both on my part and that of others. Anytime I eat, I always make a fervent effort beforehand at washing my hands as well as possible. It seems like some people don't mind getting sick. In any case, if people were more educated on the harmful bacteria that are actually out there, they might think twice about the dirty activities they get involved in.

Sexually transmitted diseases, I hear, are actually quite commonplace nowadays. Again, a dirty lifestyle will lead to such things. He who refuses to fornicate is unlikely to contract an STD. As for the mouth, he who eats clean is unlikely to contract one of the many diseases that afflict that willingly disobey God's plan for human food consumption. Sick days cost companies billions of dollars in lost productivity in the United States annually. To live cleanly, one must first have the desire to do so. To have that desire, one must first be educated that such living is even possible. The education is out there in the U.S. The problem is that man's sinful desire for dirty living is stronger than his desire to live cleanly. It's his free will, I'll admit, but, for many, the only way to get people on board with clean living is to convince them that clean living is more beneficial (and fun) for them. It really is more fun and beneficial. Sometimes all it takes is a good video to show the detrimental consequences of dirty living. At least that's enough for me. It will be easier for some than for others to adopt clean living practices. Just as with any other choice between healthy and sinful living, the strong will choose clean living, and the weak will choose dirty living. It's just that simple.

How is your attitude towards your temple? Do you regard it reverentially? Do you see it as the only vessel you'll have to carry you through your lifetime, one that should be taken care of well? You should. Your attitude plays a big role in determining your state of health a lot of the time. Negative emotions actually release chemicals that can weaken the body whereas positive emotions release chemicals that seek to preserve and/or restore good health. They say that laughter is the best medicine. I don't know how true that is, but it sure can make one feel really good in the moment. I've noticed that many people who tend to go through life weighed down by stress and negativity tend to age more quickly. I myself, so I've been told, tend to age slowly due to my clean and healthy habits and my can-do attitude that I approach life with.

Having conquered major obstacles and multiple crises throughout the years, I now look at a lot of the things that burden and weigh down others and laugh at them. I laugh not at the people but at the mentality they are approaching their problems with, mainly because I can recognize it because I've been there myself. I see my former self in their shoes. I can laugh because I've already overcome what they are currently struggling with, and I know how I can approach them in a loving way with advice for solving their dilemma. I find that those who get worked up over things are typically those who don't know how to handle those same things. I take joy in being the one who comes along in a Christ-like manner and calms them down with a workable solution to their issue.

I also feel that the part of me that refuses to grow old is also what is helping to keep me young and healthy. A lot of people buy into the idea that they must get old soon because "that's just what people do." I say, "Baloney." Genetics are a factor, but a lot of the time people choose a lifestyle of exponential decrepitude in which they age quickly because of willful temple neglect. I've noticed that the people who age the slowest typically are the ones with the best attitudes towards life. They tend to be resilient, bouncing back from depression quickly. They tend to be optimistic and are adamant about finding ways to get things done in life in a healthy manner. They tend not to dwell on how horrible things are, and they tend not to establish unhealthy relationships for themselves, which are often hard to get out of. They tend to be playful and frisky and choose their happiness rather than let others dictate it for them.

Healthy people know that proper rest is needed for optimum health. If things are weighing them down, they tend to write down the things and/or they pray and ask God to take care of whatever it is that's bothering them. If something is bothering you, chances are it's the Holy Spirit's way of saying that you need to pray about it. Once you are able to get to sleep, you should try to procure seven good hours of shut-eye. Studies have backed this up (including my own), and seven is also the biblical number of completion. Too much sleep and you can be tired all day. Too little sleep and you can be walking around like a zombie all day.

Get enthusiastic and passionate about your work. I remember reading somewhere years ago that emotional upheaval is the real cause of tiredness, not hard work. People who work passionately at something rarely get tired. Thomas Edison slept for about four hours a night and was wide awake during the day passionately and enthusiastically working on his inventions. He was not one given to emotional extremes. He was in harmony with nature and his body responded accordingly. Jesus got tired, but it was well after the average person would have gotten tired. Every time He healed someone, a little bit of energy left Him and went into the person that was healed. At the end of the day, He needed to rest like all humans do.

Understand that tiredness is not laziness. Tiredness is when one no longer has energy. Laziness is when one has the energy but doesn't feel like doing something. It's important for the strong Christian to understand the difference between the two, for you will be tempted to give up at some point. Knowing the difference between the two will help when it's time to examine your own heart. If it's laziness that's holding you back from doing God's work, then you have something to work on.

The Bible talks about its people taking a day's journey in several passages of Scripture. It's been estimated that a day's journey was roughly 22 miles or so. Maybe they got slowed down by all of their luggage; I don't know. Either way, the exercise did them good. The Bible also states that bodily exercise profits little, but back in biblical times, people didn't need to exercise really. Their lifestyles kept people in good shape. Nowadays most people need to exercise because, for one reason or another, they have gotten themselves into sedentary lifestyles which don't promote fitness. With all of the desk jobs and computer-assisted tasks that we rely on, people are more out of shape now than ever. I remember back in the seventies when it seemed like everyone and his mother were thin. If you notice, the further back in history you go, the skinnier people were. Rest assured that Satan has his hand in the obesity epidemic that's sweeping the globe nowadays.

People don't come out of the womb obese. They may carry some baby fat, but that goes away. People are bred into obese, sedentary lifestyles for one reason or another. God doesn't like this. Sin leads to obesity. He loves sinners and hates sin. He wants us to lived balanced lives, avoiding gluttony and greed. God wants us mobile. He wants us to move, both in body and in mind. We are to study to have healthier minds, and we are to use our God-given muscles to do His work. We were never meant to live lazily and let machines do our manual labor and our thinking for us. Many jobs have been lost because people have been replaced by robots. Years ago the average person could fix almost anything that got broken in his/her home. Nowadays the technology is so far-fetched that the average person has to pay a highly skilled technician exorbitant prices to get most of his/her things fixed.

Man, in his desire to be fashionably lazy, will seek out a heart attack by riding on his riding mower instead of pushing one like they did in the olden days. When he finally does have to do something by hand, he'll be so out of shape, that he'll either get out of breath or have that heart attack. He'll be shoveling snow or doing some manual labor to which he is not accustomed and then pain will set in where it was never meant to set in in the first place. The benefits of exercise are numerous, and I won't list them all here, but rest assured that proper exercise is vital to good health and being prepared to do the Lord's work. How can you take care of your fellow man if you are too out of shape yourself?

Your diet is equally important. The fact is I have never met a doctor who has prescribed junk food to one of his/her patients. They always prescribe God-made food such as fruits, vegetables, and nuts. The weak will have the tendency to commit suicide on the installment plan by eating man-made foods without the slightest regard for the foods that God put here for us. It should come as no surprise that the foods that make one the healthiest are the ones that come from nature. Natural is the way to go. Man will try to outdo God, as he does in pretty much every other area in life, by creating a palatable food that man will like. Man cannot outdo God in the nutrition department. God decided long ago what man would need and put the correct nutrients in the food He made for us.

Some people claim that all things have been made new, including God's meats. What I know is that the biochemical makeup of scavenger meats has not been made new, and man's digestive tract has not been made new. The unclean meats as described in the Old Testament are still unclean meats. Surely we can eat them and may be unlikely to die from one meal, but why eat anything that God says is bad for your health. Pork is probably the worst "offender" in this area. Pigs will eat anything: urine, feces, cancerous growths on other pigs, maggots, and so on. I've read testimonials of people who repeatedly ate pork and then got sick from it. Just like with any other harmful food, if it doesn't kill you right away, it will kill you slowly if you keep eating it. In the United States, many so-called foods are approved for human consumption simply because it's been determined that eating them one time won't kill people. Really? The fact is any man-made food eaten habitually will eventually put you in an early grave.

In Acts chapter 10 God showed Peter a vision of unclean animals and, in the vision, commanded him to kill and eat them. Peter told God he'd not do it, for he had never done such a thing. God was using the unclean animals in a symbolic way, because Peter would soon understand the analogy God was making, in anticipation of the coming of 3 certain men. In verse 28 Peter says, "...but God hath showed me that I should not call any man common or unclean." God wanted Peter to understand that the men were not unclean, but the animals. The animals still had the purpose of being scavengers and eating such animals nowadays still is not healthy for man. We should seek to ingest only temple-fortifying, God-honoring nutrients that come from the earth. Let's remember Genesis 1:29 which says, "And God said, Behold, I have given you every herb bearing seed, which is upon the face of all the earth, and every tree, in the which is the fruit of a tree yielding seed; to you it shall be for meat."

Chapter 86

A strong Christian has the humility to seeks counsel from those who are more knowledgeable

Only by pride cometh contention: but with the well-advised is wisdom. - Proverbs 13:10

I've come to enjoy seeking out those who've come before me in an effort to acquire knowledge from those who've experienced something I am going through or have yet to go through. Better safe than sorry they say. Well, we can avoid being sorry by seeking those who are either more knowledgeable or wiser than us. We need to put aside our egos and recognize that we weren't born having all the answers. Proverbs 22:17 says, "Bow down thine ear, and hear the words of the wise, and apply thine heart unto my knowledge."

Sometimes as young people who think we know it all, we tend to look at older people who have done nothing but make foolish mistakes with their lives. There is some truth to it, but everyone grows a degree wiser as he/she ages. I can recall being a young child who refused good advice even when I knew it was good advice simply because I knew it was coming from someone who was usually given to foolishness. Years later I'd mature and realize that even fools can spout out a little wisdom from time to time, and that it'd be OK if I listened to it.

Jesus spent time with His Father, so He acquired His Father's wisdom and knowledge. He didn't say, "No, Dad, I got this thing on my own. I don't need your advice!" Jesus had no ego problem. We sometimes do, though. Our pride is the biggest obstacle to our accepting counsel and knowledge from others. Sometimes we struggle with inferiority, so, to mask this, we try to act like we came into the world ready-made with "the answers." This is what the weak do. The strong Christian, however, chooses to remain humble and truthful. If he/she realizes counsel or knowledge is needed from someone else, it is sought from such a source. A fool will refuse to do this. Proverbs 1:7 says, "The fear of the LORD is the beginning of knowledge: but fools despise wisdom and instruction."

Proverbs 23:12 says, "Apply thine heart unto instruction, and thine ears to the words of knowledge." It might be an instructional video that you learn from or even someone younger than you. Be careful not to be the one who thinks he can't learn something from a younger person. Sometimes they have gone through special circumstances which have taught them things you may not have learned yet. Be the strong Christian who is willing to listen to those who are more knowledgeable, without regard to their sex, age, height, weight, or race. If you had all the answers, God would not have any need to instruct you in this lifetime. You are here on Earth to learn from others and to teach them what you have learned. Perhaps you can be the more knowledgeable person who counsels others.

Chapter 87

A strong Christian uses his/her strength for good, not for evil

Say not thou, I will recompense evil; but wait on the LORD, and he shall save thee. - Proverbs 20:22

God gives us strength so we can do good, but sometimes people use their **talents** for evil. Scientists will study the elements and arrange them in such a way to build a bomb that will harm people. Computer experts will become hackers to wreak havoc in cyberspace. Weightlifters and strongmen will overpower the weak to take advantage of them. All these types of activities are rooted in sin, in weakness. Strong people use their talents and strength for good, to help people. Nurses who know about nursing should help the sick. Nutritionists who know about nutrition should help those who don't know. Those skilled in mechanics should help those who are not skilled in it. We aren't called to be rogues, to deviate from doing good and to turn evil. Satan convinces many to do just that, though.

Jesus says in Matthew 12:35, "A good man out of the good treasure of the heart bringeth forth good things: and an evil man out of the evil treasure bringeth forth evil things." Many times we can tell if there is good treasure or evil treasure in someone's heart by what kind of things they bring. I'm talking about the person's behavior, the fruit that he/she produces. Is the person doing good or is the person doing evil? My earthly dad has high aptitude in mechanics. He's used that aptitude many times over the years to fix things for people. He has fixed bikes, automobiles, plumbing, and a multitude of other things that people use in life. He has strength in that area and uses it for good. I am skilled in linguistics, so I use that particular strength to tutor others who aren't as skilled, to resolve conflicts, to read and to learn, and to do a multitude of other things that bring good to the world. Using my strength in linguistics for evil would not be a sign of spiritual strength; it'd be a sign of spiritual weakness on my part.

Jesus says in Luke 6:43, "For a good tree bringeth not forth corrupt fruit; neither doth a corrupt tree bring forth good fruit." As strong Christians we are to bring forth only good fruit. The ignorant oftentimes like to pretend that they are coming forward with good intentions, and they often will assume that if no one calls them out on their evil fruit, that no one notices. Rest assured, the Christian with discernment will notice when evil is present. Oftentimes facial expressions give it away. There will be a diabolical sneer, a smirk or the like that indicates that the person is up to no good. The discerning person can compare the other person's behavior to that of Jesus. You might ask yourself, "Is what this person is doing practical?" Always look for the motive. Don't be afraid to ask people what their motives and/or intentions are. I usually ask people, "Where are you going with this?" or "what are you trying to accomplish here?" Some other good ones are: What are you up to?, What am I supposed to do with this information?, How are you helping the person/situation by doing what you are doing? The person that has evil intentions and something to hide may dissimulate and delay in responding. The person with good intentions usually will be quick and eager to respond.

Remember evil behaviors are usually learned from other evil people and are oftentimes employed by those who are spiritually sick. We aren't to repay evil with evil. We overcome evil with good (Romans 12:21). Be the strong Christian who overcomes evil with good and uses his/her strength to help people, to serve God's children. Work to create an environment where evil is drowned out. You can do this by overwhelming evil by bringing enough good to the situation. Get others on board. If others see how good can overcome evil, then they can join your cause to see it come to fruition.

Proverbs 17:13 says, "Whoso rewardeth evil for good, evil shall not depart from his house."

Chapter 88

A strong Christian seeks to give God all the glory

It is not good to eat much honey: so for men to search their own glory is not glory. - Proverbs 25:27

If we are brought up as people-pleasers and those living for the world's applause, we can fall into the habit of seeking self-glorification. We can feel powerful and superior when we get the glory for things. That's typically how the ungodly feel when they get the glory for something. The Holy Spirit will convict a Christian if he/she is tempted to soak up the glory for himself/herself. When there is glory to be given or attributed to someone, it should be to God. There are times when we need to own up to things and take the credit to resolve conflict or to avoid confusion, but the strong Christian should seek to give God all the glory, for everything we accomplish, we do it through His power.

Man can be greedy for fame and power and all the things that can accompany a glory-filled lifestyle. Jesus deserved the glory when He walked the Earth, but He didn't go about seeking it in a conceited way. He just did what He did, and people praised Him because, being God, He deserved it. The glory-seeker tends to be one who wants man's eyes focused on him/her, not on God. Having been brought up in Christian churches, I've always disliked being in the spotlight and participating in awards ceremonies. Something inside of me convicted me about me receiving the glory whenever I accomplished something seemingly great. When I was on sports teams, regardless of who the winner was, there always seemed to be some hooting-and-hollering glory boy tooting his own horn and rubbing the victory in the loser's face. There was a lack of humility there. There was no attribution to God for the victory.

Man's selfishness urges him to seek self-glorification. He can try to justify it by saying that his fellow man was put here to glorify him. When we take the glory for things, we tend to attribute our successes to our own efforts and fail to mention how God had a hand in them. Satan wants this. Satan knows that by you minimizing God's involvement in your life, He has succeeded in distancing you from God to a degree, which makes it less likely that you'll serve God because you've lost sight of the closeness of your relationship with God.

Remember, the weak still think their fellow man is equipped with superior judgment and are supposed to give man the glory. Let's give credit where it'd due. If someone praises you for an accomplishment, you might say, "Thank you and glory to God." The more you say this, the more you'll believe that's how it should be. The more you take the glory for yourself, the more puffed up your ego will be. We aren't called to have our egos puffed up. We are called to walk humbly and to make every effort to make sure God is the one who ultimately gets the glory for what happens in life. Be the strong Christian who resists the temptation to capture the glory, and give it cheerfully to God, for He deserves it.

Matthew 6:13 says, "And lead us not into temptation, but deliver us from evil: For thine is the kingdom, and the power, and the glory, forever. Amen."

Chapter 89

A strong Christian is willing to take up his/her cross daily

And he said to them all, If any man will come after me, let him deny himself, and take up his cross daily, and follow me. - Luke 9:23

What exactly does it mean to take up one's cross daily? It basically means that one is willing to endure the hardships that go along with a Christ-like lifestyle. It means one is willing to endure persecution for Christ's sake and not respond to the world's stimuli in a non-Christ-like manner. It means one is willing to be treated the way Christ was treated by His enemies. Physically carrying a cross is considered to be difficult. The cross in this reference analogizes the endurance of attacks on a Christ-like person with the carrying of a cross, like the one Jesus had to carry to His death. Taking up one's cross may suggest that one be willing to die for Christ's sake, too.

A lot of times when people first become Christians, they aren't ready to take up their cross. New converts sometimes want to follow Christ, thinking that doing so involves them simply praying to Christ for Him to zap their enemies and difficulties out of their lives. I recall a quote by Bruce Lee, the martial artist, where he said, "Don't pray for an easy life. Pray for the strength to endure a hard one." There is wisdom in his quote. You are more likely to notice the response to your prayer about enduring a hard life if you pray that prayer. I don't know of anyone who has claimed to have gotten an easy life by praying for one.

I see all the time people spending so much time, energy, and effort to avoid difficulties. I understand this mentality all too well, for I was like that. When I was in high school, I made an effort to take the easiest classes I could. I had little self-confidence, and I certainly wasn't yet ready to take on learning with enthusiasm. I just wanted to skate by and make it through school alive. I wasn't focused on learning in high school; I was focused on avoiding difficulty and trouble. I'd feel overwhelmed by "hard" subjects and bullies. I had been taught at home that I was always to depend on someone stronger than me to take care of my problems. I'd pay people to take care of my bullies and the difficulties that arose at that time. We often are taught to avoid conflict. Keeping out of certain conflicts can be a wise thing. There are times when it's best to mind one's own business. But, anytime two people are together, there will be a conflict in perspective at some point. Jesus' own disciples had conflicting mindsets when they were with Him. Jesus didn't run away; He addressed the issue head on. He got right to the heart of the matter. I had a heart problem in my formative years. I didn't want to confront difficulty head on. Fortunately, years went by, and God worked through me so that I'd gain the confidence and know-how to deal with life's difficulties.

If we look at the above-mentioned verse, we see "deny himself." Denying oneself has to do with putting one's ego and one's agenda aside for Christ's sake. We concoct "busy" schedules to avoid helping our fellow man, to avoid difficulties. Taking on life's difficulties and enduring them is what builds strength in you. I would not be where I am today if I had not endured my most difficult time -- the legal crisis of 2004. That one experience has strengthened me more than any other in my life. There was a determination inside of me not to be defeated. I could see the evil in the individual who sued me and that, therefore, there was no strength in him. He was a small, sickly, malnourished child who had been hurt and abused and was trying to pass on that hurt to me. As strong Christians, we should learn to address people's hurts. We needn't retaliate in a worldly manner. People want to rid themselves of their hurts, and oftentimes they try to do that by taking it out on us. Jesus addressed people's hurts, what was in people's hearts. Life's difficulties arise from what originates in people's hearts.

If all we do is run and avoid life's difficulties, people's hearts won't be mended and we won't grow in strength. Just like the sick person who wanders around town in continual sickness because every doctor's office he goes to refuses to let him in, people will continue to be spiritually sick if we don't address their spiritual sickness. There can be joy-filled strength that goes along with helping the spiritually sick. The weak will turn and run, whereas the strong will stay and persevere and increase in strength. You can be that strong Christian who puts aside your personal agenda to help your fellow man. Christ will give you the strength to endure your hardships if you are willing to endure them. It's a matter of putting aside comfort and being willing to grow in an area in which you currently are weak.

Jesus says in Luke 14:27, "And whosoever doth not bear his cross, and come after me, cannot be my disciple."

Chapter 90

A strong Christian avoids plate-loading

Come unto me, all ye that labor and are heavy laden, and I will give you rest. - Matthew 11:28

I grew up watching one-day people. They are the people who constantly claim that "one day" they will get to something. They will constantly load more and more onto their plate, claiming that one day those things might come in handy. They constantly are starting projects, so, therefore, they don't have time to finish the ones they start. They get overwhelmed by all the things in their life. They usually end up wasting a lot of time deciding on what to do next because they have so much to choose from. They care about their things so much that they spend lots of time cleaning them and caring for them. A lot of their things aren't things that are contributing to the furtherance of the Kingdom. I was this way in my younger years, and then I got really tired of that lifestyle. God spoke to me and said, "Let me lighten your load." He had me sell off or give away most of my superfluous things, things that I was not going to realistically use and weren't contributing to the furtherance of His Kingdom.

I felt so relieved, like a big weight had been lifted from my shoulders, kind of like I did when I was in college and dropped out of the Secondary Education program and just focused on the Spanish Professional track instead. A lot of the heavy laden that Jesus refers to in Matthew are those who are still pushing the world's agenda in an effort to get ahead via the world's way. It's not just physical baggage we are referring to here. People carry a lot of emotional baggage that is weighing them down. Simply put, people don't carry a Christ-like mentality in their daily walk, so they end up approaching their day with a worldly mentality, one that Satan has loaded up with all sorts of nonsense to make one feel tired. He knows that by making one tired, one won't have the energy, and often desire, to do Christ's work. People will care about and put so much emphasis on impractical, unimportant nonsense in this world that they don't make room for the practical important stuff. Addressing people's spiritual sickness, their addictions, their nutritional needs, their health, their education are things that are often neglected because people load up their plate with the world's methodology, thinking that's the best way.

As I've stated before, it's not physical labor that makes one tired; it's emotional upheaval. People get tired because of their perspective. I can go and lift weights all day in a room that's filled with other energy-filled athletes who are positive, upbeat, and encouraging and not feel tired at the end of the day. When positive energy is present, it's hard for one to get tired. When you take joy in exhibiting Christ-like strength, you rarely get tired. I can recall when I was put in a dairy department to work the overnight shift at a grocery store in 2005. I stocked yogurt every night and remember there being overstock. In other words, the guy who ordered the yogurt ordered too much. I would complain about this and vividly remember feeling physically tired as a result of my daily complaining. I physically felt tired from my complaining! Surely you can think back to a similar situation in your life when you felt tired because of your complaining about another person's shortcoming. Christ told me that my complaining was weighing me down. I felt a bit overwhelmed by my emotions because of my perspective about the situation in the dairy department.

All the time I see people who are worn down by life. Typically, they feel drained and have gone through life feeling "dragged around." In other words, they didn't approach life with a can-do, "getter-done" mentality. They just let life drag them along and along the way they picked up cuts, bruises, and wounds that left emotional scars. It doesn't have to be like this. This is when you really need to get alone with God and have a heart-to-heart. Pray and tell Him your priorities, your needs. Ask Him to reveal to you your real needs and your real priorities. People have a tendency to put passion and enthusiasm into the things that are highest on their priority list. Chances are, if you are heavy laden, you've been getting worked up about all the wrong things in all the wrong, unhealthy ways. All the time I see people getting worked up over nothing, over trivialities, over unimportant stuff. Then they go to bed but can't sleep because they are still trying to work that thing out in their mind. God can give you the rest you need. Reprioritize and learn some healthy Christ-like ways of dealing with the things on your plate. Remember we shouldn't try to be spiritual gluttons and add more to our plate than we can handle. God will give you what you can handle. If it seems like a lot, maybe it is, and know that He knows that you can handle it and that He wants to strengthen you. He will add more to your plate when He wants to see you increase, but you need to work on that which is on your plate currently. Remember, dessert is put on a separate plate. Just like your mom had you finish your main course before starting on your dessert, God will have you focus on your main priorities before He adds to your plate.

I don't usually get bogged down by excessive plate-loading nowadays. My priorities are in much better order now. I just take on what I know I can reasonably handle. If God puts something else on my plate, I just rest assured knowing that He has equipped me already with the strength to handle it. If you don't feel you have the strength yet for something God puts on your plate, ask God to show you the strength. Remember, we are the ones who overload our plates, not God. If you are feeling heavy laden in any way, introspect and ask yourself why you allowed it to happen and re-examine your priorities, and see how you got into the situation to begin with. All excessive plate-loading starts at home, with oneself. When you feel overloaded, get with God and ask Him to show you His heart regarding the matter and examine your own heart to see where you need to change.

Chapter 91

A strong Christian is content with God's provision

Not that I speak in respect of want: for I have learned, in whatsoever state I am, therewith to be content. - Philippians 4:11

Jesus says in Matthew 6:19-21, "Lay not up for yourselves treasures upon earth, where moth and rust doth corrupt, and where thieves break through and steal: But lay up for yourselves treasures in heaven, where neither moth nor rust doth corrupt, and where thieves do not break through nor steal: For where your treasure is, there will your heart be also." I sometimes wonder about the materialistic. With all the envy and the jealousy going around in today's world, I sometimes wonder about those who acquire material goods that they don't need in order to impress people who have no business approving of them to begin with. Most of the time, I find, when people find out you have something they want, they try to get their greedy hands on it. I remember about ten years ago I came into some money, and a couple of people found out about it. Well, those same couple of people soon hit me up for a loan. We need to understand that God will, in some way, provide all our needs and that we are to be content with His provision, for He doesn't leave us needy. Man might leave us needy, but God won't.

I can recall a few times in my life when I

actually stole something. I can attribute each theft to my own sinful heart. I wasn't content with God's provision. The thief basically says, "God won't provide." The thief has been fooled by Satan. God will provide. The problem is that man can be greedy. Man is oftentimes convinced that he needs something he actually doesn't. I have seen many times man get into trouble of some sort because he greedily acquired something he didn't need. God watches what we do with our finances and blesses us accordingly. If we act responsibly with a little, He may give us a little more. He wants us to use His provision to take care of His creations here on Earth. Most of the things man acquires that can gain rust or mildew are flesh-pleasing things. God wants us to acquire a different kind of treasure. He wants you and I to work on our character. Every time we do something for the Kingdom, we are becoming more Christ-like. There are a few people in this world that I consider to be treasures. That's because of the value they carry when serving their fellow man. They have the heart of a servant, something that is rare in today's society, it seems.

Jesus says in Luke 12:29-31, "And seek not ye what ye shall eat, or what ye shall drink, neither be ye of doubtful mind. For all these things do the nations of the world seek after: and your Father knoweth that ye have need of these things. But rather seek ye the kingdom of God; and all these things shall be added unto you." God wants us to seek kingdom-related things. He wants us to learn about the Kingdom and how to live like Jesus did. Those who seek to do the work of the Kingdom will have their needs met. As I stated earlier in the book, when I traveled around Costa Rica going to prayer meetings, I was fed there at the homes where the prayers were taking place. They didn't have to feed me; they just felt led to. Prayer is one of the greatest things we can do for the Kingdom. Learn how to pray and how to evangelize. Learn how to give testimonies and how to praise and worship God. Learn how to minister to the hurting and to heal the sick. The fact is, if you look at the things Jesus asks you to do, very little money, if any, is needed. Mainly what's needed is a willing heart. When you are ready and willing to serve, God will provide the means. We don't want to be ungrateful; we want to be content with what God provides, however little it may seem to be. As it states in the verse, God knows what you need, even before you do. He has ways of prepping people and situations behind the scenes so that you will be sufficiently equipped to do His work.

To do man's work, you'll need man's provision. To do God's work, you'll need His provision. Provision is the key word here; think of God as a "pro" with "vision." Be the strong Christian who is grateful and content for God's provision and trust that He knows what He's doing so that you can get His work done.

I Timothy 6:6 says, "But godliness with contentment is great gain."

Chapter 92

A strong Christian practices releasing ego to allow more room for truth and truthful instruction to enter

The fear of the LORD is the beginning of knowledge: but fools despise wisdom and instruction. - Proverbs 1:7

It is important to work on releasing our ego so we can allow truth and truthful instruction to enter our bodies and minds. The fool trusts in his ego and ends up with disastrous results. Take Matthew 7:24-27 for example. Jesus says, "Therefore whosoever heareth these sayings of mine, and doeth them, I will liken him unto a wise man, which built his house upon a rock: And the rain descended, and the floods came, and the winds blew, and beat upon that house; and it fell not: for it was founded upon a rock. And everyone that heareth these sayings of mine, and doeth them not, shall be likened unto a foolish man, which built his house upon the sand: And the rain descended, and the floods came, and the winds blew, and beat upon that house; and it fell: and great was the fall of it." The bigger they are, the harder they fall, as the saying goes. In other words, the greater someone's ego is, the greater the hurt they will suffer when they are hurt.

I can think back to many times when I chose to be led by my ego and subsequently ended up in some sort of trouble because of it. Sometimes

I had been given truthful instruction and advice on what to do (or what not to do), but I ignored it. Ego is the biggest blocker of truth that there is. It takes a humble and intelligent person to finally say, I can't do this my way; I need Jesus and His wisdom. I've noticed that I've been able to make great gains in the acquisition of wisdom and truth because I choose to have little to no ego when it comes to accepting the wisdom, knowledge, instruction, and truth of the Kingdom. All the time I see people needlessly suffering because they choose to run on ego instead of on godly truth. Many times I have tried to advise people by telling them the truth. They blew me off and went and did things their way; then they suffered and cried. I wanted to say, "I told you so." I'm sure people wanted to say that to me when I didn't listen to them when they tried to give me advice and truthful instruction. It takes strength to admit that you weren't born with all the answers. Man wants to be right. Oftentimes that's why he gossips. When he gossips, he tries to get a third party's confirmation that he's right. How about if we just focus on the truth with the knowledge that it will free us from untruthful living. What's untruthful living. It's when you live a life based on certain principles you want to be true, but actually aren't, because they fit a certain philosophy you are comfortable with.

I used to be one of those people who had a big problem with the truth. I wanted to go around believing and promoting the idea that I was born with "the answers." It took a lot of nasty falls for me to realize that I didn't have the answers I thought I did. Sometimes we just have to admit, "Hey, I was stupid, and I learned from it." It seems to be quite hard for a lot of people to admit that one statement, I've found. People with big egos don't like to admit that they could've been stupid. Well, guess what. We've all played the part of stupid person at some point. The sooner you can admit that, the sooner you can progress to greater truth acceptance and ego releasing. The way you grow in strength in this area is to accept whatever truth and truthful instruction you receive as they are. You set aside your ego and realize that strong people can accept and handle the truth. If something is not the truth, don't be afraid to say it's not. But, don't say it's not, if it really is, just because you can't handle it yet. Jesus makes the truth so that we can all handle it if we willingly set aside our egos. I can handle a lot more truth now than I could before, and I don't feel weak because of it. On the contrary. I feel stronger because of being able to handle the amount of truth that I can. I look forward to daily, regular truth and truthful instruction to enter me because I know I'll grow in strength and in knowledge as a result.

Jesus wants us to accept and allow His truth and His truthful instruction to enter us so we can be set free from living in lies. He knows that people suffer because they go around living lies. He doesn't want us to suffer, but the only way around suffering is to set aside our egos and allow truth in. You can be the strong Christian who does this and then comforts others who may be suffering because of some lie-driven lifestyle. Set the captives free by allowing the truth to transform your way of life and telling people how they too can be strong by letting in the truth that comes from Jesus.

Chapter 93

A strong Christian sees Jesus as the model for all human behavior

For he hath made him to be sin for us, who knew no sin; that we might be made the righteousness of God in him. - II Corinthians 5:21

People will say, "Show me who your friends are and I will show you who you are." We have a tendency to be like the people we hang around. Athletes act like athletes. Firemen act like firemen. Cops act like cops. Thugs act like thugs. Priests act like priests. Nuns act like nuns. These people act like others that they hang around. If this psychology holds true, doesn't it make sense to the strong Christian to hang around Jesus Christ if we want to be like Him? Jesus spent a lot of time with His Father. He prayed to Him, learned His vocabulary, His mannerisms etc. Jesus walked and talked like His Father did because He spent a lot of time with Him. If we are to imitate Jesus to the max, then we need to spend a lot of time with Him. If He is to be our model for walking and talking, shouldn't we study and practice His mannerisms and speech?

I grew up watching TV shows wherein one man would go on special missions to accomplish some great good. He'd rescue somebody or defeat a bad guy. I saw these characters as models for human behavior. Even though I grew up from a young age as a Christian, the world had taught and convinced me that Jesus' behavior was weak. As a young person, I didn't want to follow weak people. I saw Jesus as a nice, friendly yet mushy guy. Rest assured Jesus is not weak. He's the strongest person who ever lived, at least emotionally speaking. He prayed hard before His Crucifixion. Most of us would probably cry and beg our killers to spare our life if we were being taken to our death on a cross. And then there are the nails. He willingly subjected himself to that pain and suffering out of love. Jesus said that no one has greater love than he who is willing to lay down his life for his friends. Jesus showed this kind of love and then some, for He died for all, including the worst person you may think of (whomever that may be). Hopefully we won't have to die for people, but it is the model that Jesus set for us in such a case.

Everything He did we are to imitate. The way He spoke to people, the emotions that went along with His responses, the types of questions He asked, the way He carried Himself on a daily basis, the frequency and earnestness of His prayers, the compassion He had for the lost and the hurting etc. If we don't see Him as the model for some type of human behavior, we are basically saying that we know better than Jesus how to do something. Believe me, you don't know better than Jesus how to do something. Egos need to be set aside, and humility needs to have a place in our daily behavior patterns.

Once we realize the strength that there is in doing things the Jesus way, we can experience the joy that goes along with such behavior. When we suffer, usually it is our ego that suffers. That's why it is so important to set aside the ego. When we are operating from a position of truth-acceptance, we keep in mind that, regardless of what happens to us, we are the ones who are operating in strength. Those who aren't yet strong enough to handle the truth and still try to make us suffer, aren't operating from a position of strength. When you are approached by such people, it may be a good idea to first address their hurt. That's what Jesus did. He didn't beat around the bush with people. He went right to the heart of matters. He asked questions that pointed to hearts, intentions, and motives. He came here to heal the hurting. You can be the strong Christian who imitates Jesus by addressing people's hurts.

Whenever I'm verbally attacked by someone, I ask, "Who hurt you that you would treat me this way?" The spirit of truth will be with you when you ask this, and it's quite possible that the person will get overwhelmed by it and start to get emotional. I realize that these people's hurt usually didn't start right when they interacted with me. A lot of times you just might remind someone of another person in his/her past who hurt him/her, and now he/she is taking it out on you. Don't fight fire with fire. Address the hurt like Jesus did. Oftentimes people will calm down when you show sincere concern for their well-being. Jesus always showed concern for people's well-being. Be that strong Christian who does the same. Make a fervent effort at imitating Jesus' behavior on a daily basis in all areas of your life.

Chapter 94

A strong Christian abstains from idolizing or deifying any human other than Jesus

Thou shalt have no other gods before me. - Exodus 20:3

I can recall looking up to certain actors and bodybuilders when I was younger and dreaming about being just like them. Most of them were very healthy individuals in some way. I got interested in lifting weights by watching men like Lou Ferrigno and Arnold Schwarzenegger on TV. I wanted to run fast like Steve Austin. I wanted to have the powers of the characters I saw on TV. I idolized many of my childhood heroes. People create idols for themselves because they don't find comfort in following Jesus. They look for some alternative because, for those who are not strong, the Christian way of life is not exciting. I understand this mentality all too well. As young people without healthy mentors, we wander around trying to fit in and seek out those who seemingly have "the answers." We look for answers about how to live life the best way we can, and we latch on to those who will accept us and take us under their wing.

I can remember as a fifteen-year-old befriending a gay guy in his thirties just because he paid attention to me. He helped with bicycle repairs and offered friendly advice. I looked up to him for that alone. This is a mild example.

How about young girls who would cry and scream their heads off when the singer Michael Jackson would walk by? I remember such fanaticism back in the 80's. The red carpet is rolled out for "human deities" and those whose eyes are not on Jesus bow down and vainly follow them. Admiring people for their Jesus-like qualities is fine. The problem is when people idolize and blindly follow another human, imitating every nuance of their lives to the best of their ability. It's kind of like when I bought my first Trans-Am and wanted to fix it up so I could live out my very own Knight Rider experience. I idolized such an experience, even if it were short-lived. I deified the guy driving the Knight Rider car. In my mind, he could do no wrong. When we look at others in such a way, we can be quick to forget that they are sinners too. They make mistakes and fall short of God's glory. No matter how awesome or superb you may think someone is, he/she is not God. The weak forget this often.

Anytime I am tempted to celebritize or deify another person, I remind myself that he/she is a sinner, that he/she can't save me, that he/she has committed his/her fair share of mistakes in life. When we look to deify someone, we are essentially setting ourselves up to envy someone whom we were never meant to envy or to imitate to begin with. The only one we can safely imitate is Jesus. If people exhibit Jesus in their behavior, then that's fine; we can copy that. We just need to make sure we don't elevate people above us and put them on some pedestal.

When I'm at work, I don't put the bosses on a pedestal. I keep in mind their authority, but I also keep in mind that we are all children of God, and God doesn't play favorites. He's no respecter of persons, and I shouldn't be one either. I keep things equitable by speaking to people like they are on my level. We aren't to elevate or to put down anyone. We are to treat others as brothers and sisters.

Be the strong Christian who looks at people as children whom God loves. He didn't put anyone of us here to be above others. We are all on equal ground, regardless of the pedestal that others have created for their idols. People can and will come up with all sorts of fancy names for dignitaries such as President, Chancellor, and King, but only Jesus is worthy of such a title. The strong and humble will remember this.

Colossians 2:8 says, "Beware lest any man spoil you through philosophy and vain deceit, after the tradition of men, after the rudiments of the world, and not after Christ."

Chapter 95

A strong Christian refrains from producing filthy, destructive speech

But now ye also put off all these; anger, wrath, malice, blasphemy, filthy communication out of your mouth. - Colossians 3:8

Usually, cussing is our verbal way of conveying strong emotion. We let our emotions get the best of us, and we feel like we are losing control. We feel like we need to outdo someone else's emotional output to show that we are in control or that we have the advantage in a situation. When we cuss, we show that we feel strongly about something. We insert expletives to indicate that something/someone is really good/bad. The person who uses such filthy speech usually has a mindset given to worldly judgment, usually is not even-tempered, and usually does not put much faith in God's handling of situations.

Sometimes we can produce filthy speech as a defense mechanism. For some it's a way of faking strength. The fact is our words have power. Jesus made people come back to life with His words. He commanded demons to come out of people with His words. He used words to build people up. The weak in this world will use words to try to destroy people. All sorts of slander, blasphemy, rumors, gossip, revealing of secrets, lies, deception, dishonesty etc. have ruined the lives of many people. A lie perpetrated by my accuser in 2004 could have ruined my life. Just a few destructive words could have destroyed me and my future. Well, I have won that battle. I am stronger now than ever before because of that crisis. But, a lot of people go into depression and never come out of it. Families are torn apart. Jobs are lost. Relationships are broken. Bank accounts are emptied. Many negative and horrible things can and do happen just due to destructive speech. When you speak filthy, destructive speech against your fellow man, you are not showing love, and you are not exhibiting the I-got-you-covered attitude. You are essentially saying that you don't care about your fellow man or what negative thing might happen to him. God frowns upon this. It was this negative attitude that went against Jesus during His betrayal.

The weak person who produces filthy, destructive speech isn't one who typically goes around looking to build his/her fellow man up. That person, if he/she gossips to you about someone else, will most likely gossip about you to another person, too. Satan has convinced those people that they will feel powerful if they can trash talk their fellow man to a third party and get an agreement. Oftentimes, this occurrence is perpetuated and a rumor is passed around and soon, a victim is attacked and/or bullied. The people who agree to keep the rumor in circulation will hold whatever the trash talk was about against the person, that is, the target. Jesus would never approve of ganging up on someone. Whenever I hear such trash talk directed at me about a third party who is or is not present, I ask the talker, "What do you want me to do with this knowledge? Am I supposed to form a negative opinion now about the third party and jump on the judgment bandwagon the way you have?" I go right to the heart of the matter, as Jesus would. I ask, "How are you helping the situation by gossiping to me about that person? How much time have you spent thinking of a solution to so-and-so's problem, and how soon do you plan on approaching that person with a sincere offer to help him/her in a Christ-like way?" I may even go as far as saying, "I don't want to imagine the kind of trash talk you are probably speaking against me behind my back." As a strong Christian you need to cut that thing off at the root. The root is the evil in the heart of the trash talker.

A strong Christian will keep after filthy, destructive communication, knowing that there are only evil motives behind it. Be that strong Christian who stands up to talk that seeks to destroy people and look only for ways to build people up with truth-filled words of encouragement.

Chapter 96

A strong Christian resists succumbing to worldly pleasures

He that loveth pleasure shall be a poor man: he that loveth wine and oil shall not be rich. - Proverbs 21:17

This may, indeed, be one of the hardest traits to live out for many people. We are all guilty to some degree of succumbing to worldly pleasures. I've done it myself thousands of times. As strong Christians, we will be tempted on a daily basis. We will always have that battle of the Holy Spirit versus flesh-pleasing activities and indulgences. Which one will we follow? The one you take more seriously is the one you will follow. It often will depend, because of our weak flesh, on our current state of mind, or mood, in a given moment. You might be hungry for some food on a Tuesday and justify eating a whole pizza or a whole tub of chocolate pudding (been there, done that) because your diet doesn't start til next Monday. Either way, just know that resistance to worldly pleasures will always be your strong move. The weak will succumb. They haven't disciplined themselves enough yet not to succumb. It's not just a matter of knowing better. If it were, all you'd have to do is just tell everybody to stay away and convince them that doing so is good for them, and then you'd have nothing to worry about. Life isn't that simple unfortunately.

This is why we need to be in prayer on a regular basis: to pray for the strength to resist succumbing to worldly pleasures. I can assure you that every time I succumbed to a worldly pleasure, I didn't pray that day, at least not for strength. I could go and write a book just on the dangers of succumbing to worldly pleasures. All sorts of trouble and diseases we can acquire by succumbing to worldly pleasures. How about the guy who visits a prostitute and ends up getting a sexually transmitted disease? How about the farmer who gets cancer because he ate pork chops religiously for years? How about the broke guy who lost all his money on gambling? These people exist. Proverbs is correct when it states that "He that loveth pleasure shall be a poor man." Why? Because the lovers of pleasure tend to spend their time and money on it. They tend not to invest wisely. God sees this and lets people fall victim to their sins. Pray for the strength to resist succumbing on a daily basis. You'll be glad you did. The more you do this, the craftier Satan has to be to try to tempt you to succumb. This will happen. Be aware of it. Most people who succumb aren't even aware that Satan is the one tempting them. Let's not be lulled into a false sense of security by thinking that, if we prayed once for strength to resist, then we will be alright from then on. I have come a long way in my strength increase, but even I need to pray about getting into the right mindset wherein I remember my strength, I keep my eyes on the prize, I remember my identity, and I long to see Satan lose in his attempt to tempt me. Remember, God does not tempt man.

If you walk as a strong Christian and avoid worldly pleasures, others will see your example. You may just be the one who inspires another (maybe your child) to follow your example. Jesus did not succumb to flesh-pleasing pleasures. Surely His flesh was satisfied with food and drink, but those things did not have a hold on Him. The key here is not to let the pleasures of this world control you. If you feel compelled to keep coming back to a pleasure, it controls you. It's funny, in an ironic sense, how the world seems to have made the vices of alcohol and tobacco just cheap enough that even the poorest of people seem to be able to afford them. Rest assured Satan is behind that. Anyway, people given to those things often think that they are in control, that they can quit anytime. I see those same people returning time and time again to their vices. Just as a dog returns to his vomit, a fool will return to his folly. Only in this case, the fools are being controlled by their addictions. The flesh is too weak to say no. The person, not knowing the Holy Spirit personally, doesn't know how to say no. The person doesn't know how to refuse Satan's offer of "just one more time." This is why we need to come along as the strong Christians in the lives of the weak and show them the way. Show them strength and encourage them so they can realize that they can be strong too. Oftentimes it's mainly a matter of convincing someone that real strength lies in resistance, refusal, and refuting - refuting the lie that Satan tries to convince you of regarding a worldly pleasure. You need to refuse His offer and resist his temptation. As a strong Christian, you will want to remember the three r's: resist, refuse, refute. Start your day with prayer and ask for strength. With strength you will have what you need to employ the three r's and come out successfully when approached with the temptation to succumb to worldly pleasures.

Chapter 97

A strong Christian competes only with himself/herself

It is an honor for a man to cease from strife: but every fool will be meddling. - Proverbs 20:3

As a strong Christian, I have no sinful desire to feel superior to my fellow man. I was not called by God Almighty to compete with my fellow man so that I can show my dominance or make him feel inferior. I desire only to improve myself daily and compete only with my former self. Those with inferiority/superiority complexes look to compete with their fellow man to satisfy their egos. Competing with your fellow man only sets you up for further feelings you weren't called to have regarding your relationship to your fellow man. If you lose in competition, what happens? Oftentimes people will feel hatred, jealousy, envy, vengeful, angry, inferior, embarrassed and so on. If you win in competition, you might feel superior and then justified at looking down your nose at your opponent. Those who seek to win against an opponent don't typically look to build up their opponent. Football coaches and players spend inordinate amounts of times studying opposing players to figure out their weaknesses so they know how to beat them in competition. Soccer fans have been known to go wild and humiliate opposing fans. They have burned buildings, turned over cars, and caused much damage to public and private property. All this because of the sinful competitive spirit that resides in man.

I'm not saying a little friendly ball playing is bad, but it's when evil enters the heart of an opponent to make the other guy/team feel defeated or inferior that it becomes problematic. I've studied bodybuilding competitions since the 1980's. I love the sport of bodybuilding, but God revealed to me that many bodybuilders suffer from approval addiction. They think that their fellow man was put here on Earth to judge them, and they seek that judgment. They want to hear that they are better than the other bodybuilders on the competition stage. Their spirits cry out, "Approve, approve, approve!" Oftentimes there will be a big disappointment in the heart of those who lose the competition. Some athletes have been known to commit suicide as a result of losing in competition. Their egos could not handle such a whopping loss. Here is an idea: You can avoid setting yourself up for a disappointing loss by not competing with others in the first place. When you compete with yourself, you have only yourself to blame if you lose. You don't have to take it out on anyone else. If you win against yourself, the victory is quite sweet. You needn't boast; just give the glory to God for your success.

I remember last year bench pressing twenty pounds more than I did when I left high school. I had left high school twenty years earlier. I was competing with my former self. I wanted to lift more than I did then. When I finally achieved success, I didn't boast about it to anyone. I didn't publicize my achievement at the time. I simply thanked God for empowering me to become stronger than I was before. That felt very gratifying. I had no one to put down, no one to make feel inferior. Beating your old self in an area of life feels good. Maybe you can read now whereas before you couldn't. Maybe you are evangelizing to people now whereas before you didn't have the words. We aren't called to satisfy our egos by competing with our fellow man. Oftentimes competitors will even resort to cheating to beat their competition. That's even more proof of the evil that's in the heart of some competitors. People that compete with themselves don't typically have a reason to cheat. Beating yourself in competition the honest way shows an honest heart. Jesus wants us to have an honest heart.

We aren't called to prove to our fellow man that we are better than him by beating him in competition. We are called to help him improve himself. We are called to improve ourselves. Oftentimes evil can be removed from situations by removing the competitive spirit that is present. I often say, "Where there is no sin, there is no drama." You can be the strong Christian who removes the drama by removing the sinful competitive spirit that may be present in a situation. If you notice this spirit, call it out. Ask those who seem to have this spirit about it. Again, we are aiming to get at the heart of a matter. Don't be afraid to be the strong Christian who speaks up and calls out this spirit if it is present. You might just prevent an unwarranted conflict from happening.

Proverbs 10:12 says, "Hatred stirreth up strifes: but love covereth all sins."

Chapter 98

A strong Christian practices moderation instead of overindulgence

For the drunkard and the glutton shall come to poverty: and drowsiness shall clothe a man with rags. - Proverbs 23:21

It has taken a long time for me to get where I am with my moderation. I grew up watching my mom overindulge in the things of this world, and she paid the price for it. I sought to overindulge as well. My physique began to change in an unflattering way as a result of my obsession with food. Like many, I fell into gluttony, greed, and neglecting my fellow man. I felt the world owed me that which I desired to have. I loved pleasure more than I did caring for my neighbor. I was convinced you couldn't have too much of a good thing. We overindulge because of how satisfying it feels to the flesh. Sometimes we feel we missed out on something when we were younger, so we overcompensate by overindulging in things we don't need.

Jesus says in Luke 21:34, "And take heed to yourselves, lest at anytime your hearts be overcharged with surfeiting, and drunkenness, and cares of this life, and so that day come upon you unawares." Jesus knew the dangers of overindulgence. It's kind of like the thief who steals because he feels God won't provide enough, except the overindulgent person goes overboard by being greedy. They might trust that God will provide enough, but he/she wants more than that, and doesn't necessarily steal to get it. The overindulgent person seeks pure flesh-pleasing. They don't have anywhere near the strength level that's needed to fast. If obesity and all the accompanying diseases weren't enough, the fact that you take more than enough should indicate your desire for your neighbor to have less. It's like taking 2/3 of an ice cream sandwich and giving the remaining 1/3 to your neighbor when he needs just as much food as you do. This attitude typically accompanies the greedy, gluttonous person. Selfishness is at the root of that thing.

It takes great self-control, discipline, and strength to refrain from overindulging in the things that please you the most. It could be sex, food, drink, drugs or anything else that seems or does have a hold on you. Overindulgence is typically a stronghold which people need to break free from. I ended up with hives several years back because of my overindulging in salty foods. My lower lip would swell up to three times its normal size when I ate something salty. I paid over $1,000 in doctor bills to get to the bottom of the issue, since I didn't originally know what was causing my hives. Overindulgence harms our health. It shows how little self-control we have. A lot of Christian strength is indicated by our ability or willingness to control ourselves. Once I began to eat healthily and in moderation on a daily basis with no junk food, I found that my body soon wasn't craving the junk it had craved before. I didn't need to eat very much to feel full. My physique started looking healthier again. I still get minute cravings from time to time, but they subside quickly once I begin to satisfy those cravings for man-made food. I'm practicing moderation in all areas of my life now: food, time spent, exercise, reading, sleep etc. and I feel much more healthy as a result.

You can grow in this area of Christian strength too. You need to reprioritize how much time you're spending on things and how much of a consumer you are of the pleasures in your life. Balance is the key, as they say. Remember, the weak who overindulge typically allot little time for God and much time for flesh-pleasing. The strong Christian seeks balance. It takes strength to refrain from those things which you think will satisfy the flesh to the max. Be the strong Christian who seeks to show God you are serious about refraining from overindulgence. His resources are to be used for His purposes, not for pleasing the flesh more than is necessary.

Chapter 99

A strong Christian remembers where he/she came from

And they came with haste, and found Mary, and Joseph, and the babe lying in a manger. - Luke 2:16

Let us not forget our humble beginnings. Joseph and Mary were a young couple without a lot of money. Jesus was not born in a golden delivery room. He didn't come here to be flashy or showy. Whenever man is vaunted, he essentially takes God down from on high. Man who doesn't have a proper perspective of God will often try to make himself a god. He often seeks to be the one envied, the one who gets the glory. He will put on appearances and do all that he can to epitomize the superficial lifestyle. He will walk around with his chest puffed out, his head held high, and looking down his nose at his fellow man, especially the people who aren't on board with the superficial lifestyle. He seeks to impress his fellow man and to receive approval, admiration, and envy for his accomplishments, purportedly all his own. He is proud to be a self-made man. He chooses to forget that someone once chose to clean his behind and change his diapers.

It would seem rather karmic how supposedly great athletes fall victim to debilitating illness and diseases, especially the ones who refuse to be humble, the ones who choose to boast of their "greatness." Just yesterday I met a former pro bodybuilder who suffered from a stroke and now is in a wheelchair full-time. He chose to be great in his day, while damning God aloud. He had chosen to live for man's applause, not for God's cause. He had chosen to ignore the fact that God gave him all of his gifts and talents and the people who raised him. God was being dishonored in the man's life. Now that he is in his golden years, he takes things a little more slowly. I'd like to think he has come to realize that it was God who brought him this far, although I have yet to notice him acknowledge God publicly. Either way, we should all remember that one day every knee will do obeisance before Jesus and we shall acknowledge Him as Savior.

We should live our lives like people who seem to constantly keep in mind that we remember our humble beginnings. So many live as though they've totally forgotten where they came from. They do so because, typically, they want others to focus on them so they get the glory, not God. It's like they are crying out, "Notice me, me, me, me! I did it all on my own; all this greatness I achieved on my own because I was born great!" This is what the weak do. The strong will remember where they came from and will live like they remember this. Jesus did not live boastfully. He spoke assertively and authoritatively and walked boldly, but remained humble the whole time. We can do this too. The key is not to walk and talk with an air of superiority. We should remain even-keeled, acting neither inferior nor superior. Remember, there is no weakness in meekness and humility; there is only strength. Those who don't have strength will try to fake it by getting an attitude and "acting" strong. Those of us with discernment will pick up on this. The strong will avoid acting; we will actually live out the strength. True strength will be had by those who choose to remember where they came from (from humble, diaper-changing experiences), not by those who go around pretending they've always been strong and that their strength is self-made. Be the one who actually chooses real strength which comes from God.

Chapter 100

A strong Christian refuses to get offended by the ignorant

Great peace have they which love thy law: and nothing shall offend them. - Psalm 119:165

Recently on Christian radio, I heard a preacher urging us listeners to be offended if someone calls us a racial slur; I disagree. The offended value what the offender says above what God says about us. If what God says is true and what the offender says is not, then why are we going to give value to something that is untrue? Why are we going to listen to someone who clearly chooses to lie about us to us? Why are we going to allow an offender to control our emotions by us getting worked up over a foolish, untrue comment? I'm not; are you? We shouldn't be offended by anything, including foolish comments made by the ignorant. All the time I see people getting worked up by foolish comments made by foolish, ignorant people in order to stir up negativity in the intended audience. This is such a waste of time. By us valuing such comments, we are essentially suggesting to those watching that they should do the same, that they should value untrue statements as if they were true. Satan has a way of controlling the weak through their emotions. He likes to agitate situations by having God's people get worked up over foolish comments.

Jesus says in Matthew 11:6, "And blessed is

he, whosoever shall not be offended in me." He also said in Matthew 18:7, "Woe unto the world because of offenses! for it must needs be that offenses come; but woe to that man by whom the offense cometh!" We aren't to go around trying to offend people, but we aren't to sugar-coat things, either, in order to protect the feelings of those who can't handle the truth. Jesus never sugar-coated anything. In fact, I like it when people say to me, "You offend me with those words." Really what I'm hearing is, "I can't believe you would have the audacity to tell me a truth that I can't handle." Their getting offended, in essence, serves as confirmation to me that I was indeed telling them the truth. Satan likes to whisper in people's ears, "Tell them you are offended so that they will feel guilty about what they said to you." Satan does this to shut up truth-telling Christians all the time. If the person you are talking to gets offended, you know he/she is not yet a strong, truth-handling Christian. He/she might be a Christian, but he/she still is in that "offended" mindset. This will be another example of your discernment in action if you pick up on this when dealing with such people.

Do you suffer from Christian diabetes? Christian diabetes is that seemingly wonderful feeling the unlearned Christian gets when he/she has been exposed to an overabundance of sugar-coated preaching that comes from a preacher who tailors his/her message to agree with the digestibility of his/her congregation, so as not to offend anyone in it. The Christian diabetic tends to swallow hook, line, and sinker every word that comes out of his/her preacher's mouth, failing to take into account that those words were carefully crafted to protect the fragile feelings of all those within earshot. Such preachers do exist, and I have been around them and heard their messages. I once had one tell me that his congregation would stone him if he told them too much truth. We, as strong Christians, are to use discernment at all times, even in church. We aren't to blindly accept everything a preacher says, just because he/she is called a man/woman of God. Let the Spirit of Truth speak to you. If in doubt, research the matter for yourself. I can recall hearing one message one Sunday from a pastor of mine which dealt with Jesus' death. Two days later I heard another well-known preacher on the radio preach a message in contradiction to my pastor's message. Well, logically they can't both be right. At least one must be wrong!

Remember, the ignorant person doesn't think that he/she is ignorant. Some people will willfully mislead you, and they think they know better when, actually, they don't. Some preachers will sugar-coat their sermons so as not to offend people because, they know, if people get offended they will likely not give an offering and/or return to that church. It happens all the time. I say preach the truth anyway. The weak will bow down to the god of money for fear of offending. The strong will not walk in fear of offending, nor will they get offended by anything or anyone. Be that strong Christian who refuses to get offended by the ignorant. Remember, those who know better do better, and those who don't do better, are so because they don't know any better.

I Corinthians 2:8 says, "Which none of the princes of this world knew: for had they known it, they would not have crucified the Lord of glory."

Chapter 101

A strong Christian walks daily with a positive outlook, not a negative one

And whatsoever ye do in word or deed, do all in the name of the Lord Jesus, giving thanks to God, and the Father by him. - Colossians 3:17

I'm sure Jesus saw many disheartening sights in His day: demon-possessed people, sick people, hurting people, hatred etc., but I'm also sure He didn't get discouraged or overwhelmed by what He saw. I'm sure He didn't say, "Well, this really sucks. Look at all the crap I have to deal with here on this mudball called Earth." Jesus had answers. As the Great Physician He came here to address the needs of the sick and the hurt. I'm sure that, with Him wanting to be people's friend, He approached people with a smile, an upbeat attitude, and a positive demeanor.

Those that walk in darkness tend to have a negative daily outlook. Have you ever noticed how a lot of public, sin-filled places tend to be darkened? Strip clubs tend to be dark. Bars tend to be dark. Muggers tend to attack in dark alleys. Liars will tend to hide their eyes with dark glasses. The Grim Reaper is dressed in all black etc. Jesus is dressed in white. He said in John 8:12, "I am the light of the world: he that followeth me shall not walk in darkness, but shall have the light of life." Church buildings wherein the truth is preached regularly tend to be well-lit. Those places of sin such as bars tend to be dimly lit because the owner is making an effort to minimize the exposure of the shameful sin that takes place there. The place will be lit just enough so that people can walk without tripping, but not so much that their accompanying sin is given "too much" limelight. There is no freedom or joy to be had in walking in darkness. Often the people who frequent those places are looking for others with whom to share their misery. The weak will walk with a negative mindset, going around ignorantly devoid of a Christ-like mindset.

The positive strong Christian, however, will go around knowing that Christ has the ability to set the captives free. The captives are the negative people. The positive people don't always have everything go their way, but they do walk in the assurance that Christ has the answer to whatever problem they might face. It's understandable why negative people are the way they are. When you have nothing but worldly ideology to cling to, you can get discouraged quickly. You get free by getting the truth. You must set aside your ego and allow the truth in. Once you have the truth, you are equipped to walk with a positive outlook. When Christ is your leader, there is no problem that He doesn't have an answer to. Satan lies to people and tells them that there is no solution to their problems. So, oftentimes, they go to alcohol or some other affordable vice which gives them a sense of control over their situation. The vices that people turn to actually work to destroy people's health, and Satan knows this. Satan will use whatever distraction he can to keep you from seeing that Jesus has the answers to your problems. People will seek refuge in all sorts of health-destroying behaviors, which is actually a form of rebellion against God. Satan will be laughing when he sees people engaged in such behaviors.

Be the strong Christian who laughs at Satan when he tries to convince you that Jesus doesn't have the answers. In fact, I love it when Satan speaks to me in this way because I have learned to recognize his voice, so I end up laughing at him for being foolish in his attempt to convince me that his way is better than Jesus' way. This laughter brings health to me, and I end up telling Satan off as well. It may take a while for you to get to this point because doing so requires a lot of discernment when it comes to hearing God's voice versus Satan's voice.

Give thanks to God for giving you another chance to increase your strength whenever a new challenge comes along. He will enable you to handle whatever He allows in your life. It's OK to have a little self-doubt in your life; it's normal. You don't, however, want to suffer from self-doubt. Suffering from it entails it impeding you from doing normal everyday activities such as backing into a parking space that is 17-feet wide when your car is only 5-feet wide. Yes, I know someone like this. He who thinks negatively will tend not to foresee potential, godly solutions to life's problems. He who thinks positively will tend to entertain the possible godly solutions that Christ can provide to life's problems.

Romans 8:31 says, "What shall we then say to these things? If God be for us, who can be against us?"

Chapter 102

A strong Christian works diligently and wholeheartedly at whatever task is before him/her

And whatsoever ye do, do it heartily, as to the Lord, and not unto men; - Colossians 3:23

Some people will spend their entire lives searching for the "easy" way out. Satan has convinced them that manual labor is the enemy and that passing the buck is the way to go. Everyday I see people sloughing off their work onto the next guy because they still believe that lie that Satan told them. The fruits of your labor cannot be overstated. Whatever you sow, you shall reap. If you apply mediocre effort, you will get mediocre results. God is not in the mediocrity business. Everything He does, He does well. He mapped out the DNA of everything in our world during Creation. Diligence indicates an attitude of continual effort to accomplish a certain task. Wholehearted effort involves giving something your all. This is how we are to approach our tasks in life. Jesus never healed anyone halfway.

Do to something halfway is to imply an attitude of laziness and not caring, or neglect. Doing things wholeheartedly lets our light shine and lets others observing know that we are following God's lead. It lets others know we see the value and reward in doing things in such a way. I can recall the summer I started studying

Spanish doggedly. I didn't have many materials: just a tiny dictionary. It was all I had, but I remember studying it nightly when I lay in bed to learn new words. On Saturday nights when everyone else was out partying and getting drunk, I'd be in my room studying, knowing that there'd be a payoff for all my hard work someday. I remember how frustrating it was not knowing words, so I was determined to learn as many words as I could to minimize or eliminate the need to constantly look up words I didn't know. Eventually I'd make alphabetical lists of adverbs and other parts of speech that I could study. Soon I had entire packets with hundreds of words for each part of speech. Then I bought an idioms book and studied it regularly on my work breaks for about ten years straight. I'd practice using the words and idioms I had learned with the Spanish-speaking workers at the stores where I worked. I went on to live in Mexico, the Dominican Republic, and Costa Rica, all of which afforded me the opportunity to practice my conversational skills with native speakers and to acquire their idiomatic phrases. It's been over twenty years since I first started studying Spanish, and now I don't fear holding a normal conversation with a native speaker. I know some native Spanish-speakers who've been in the U.S. for twenty years and still struggle to hold a basic conversation with an American. It's because they haven't worked diligently and wholeheartedly at their task.

In our society I see people suffering the consequences of a gluttonous, half-hearted lifestyle all the time. People needlessly suffer from all sorts of diseases that afflict the sedentary. Obese, God-dishonoring people are everywhere. There are a few that live diligently, and their results are made manifest. A lot of times you can see their results in their physiques. I can often tell who's been diligent and who hasn't just by the kind of physique they bring to the table. An imbalance can often be quickly noted. A person will be neglectful in one area, but diligent in another. It's like the studious bookworm who is full of book knowledge due to academic diligence, yet is obese because physical diligence has been neglected. We need to be careful to guard against imbalance. I've met a few rare obese people who were hard workers but remained obese because they went all day without food and then stuffed themselves before bedtime. Therefore, their physiques and health suffered even though they were working hard and diligently all day. We need to be diligent about having balance in our lives, too.

Remember, what we do we are to do for His glory. Our light is to shine before men so that we may serve as an example of godliness. Read Proverbs. It has many verses which deal with the pitfalls of laziness and the gluttonous lifestyle. The weak will go around promoting laziness and passing the buck, thinking that the next guy will have more time to deal with the thing they don't want to deal with. The strong pay attention to details and do things thoroughly, knowing the positive, godly results that will follow. The strong tend to have a mindset bent on success and know that hard work is the only honest way to achieve success. It's not about comparing the perceived size of our success to others that matters; it's the fact that we know how to achieve success that will take us far and get us some real results. The lazy man will reap what he sows. There's no way around it. Half-hearted effort will get you half-hearted results.

Proverbs 28:19 says, "He that tilleth his land shall have plenty of bread: but he that followeth after vain persons shall have poverty enough."

Chapter 103

A strong Christian seeks to eliminate any and all non-edifying stuff from his/her life

And he said unto them, Take heed, and beware of covetousness: for a man's life consisteth not in the abundance of the things which he possesseth. - Luke 12:15

Years ago when I was going through my legal crisis, it dawned on me that relationships with people are what matter most in this lifetime. God said in Genesis 2:18 that it's not good for man to be alone. It's up to us to focus on the important stuff in life. Relationships matter. Things that seek to promote the furtherance of His Kingdom matter. Building people up matters. It really is survival of the fittest. Those who are the least educated and least healthy tend to perish first. That's why it's so important to focus only on the stuff that matters most in life. So, we need to take a look at our inventory and do an evaluation to see which things need to be eliminated.

I remembered Jesus talking about not building up treasures for ourselves here on Earth. I can see why not. I can think back and see how much time, energy, and money was wasted on fruitless things in my life. I would spend hours at the arcade when I was in middle school. With my pattern recognition ability, I was able to beat the video games I played easily, but soon came to realize that there was no real fruit in beating video games. I then got into regular weightlifting the summer after 8th grade and took an instant liking to it. I saw the fruit in physical fitness. I would ride the mile and a half or so to the gym almost every day that summer and lift for hours. I had eliminated something non-edifying from my life and replaced it with something edifying. The Holy Spirit spoke to me and said, "There is value in this (physical fitness, dedication etc.)."

Years later I would apply that same philosophy towards my material things. During my legal crisis, I was in rebellion against God. I held a grudge against Him and sought comfort in food, movies, chocolate candies, music, baseball cards, and whatever other flesh-pleasing things I could acquire. I spent well over a thousand dollars on Roberto Clemente baseball cards. I convinced myself that if I had the entire collection of his cards, that my life would be complete. I acquired about half the cards I wanted over a five-year period and, by that point, was convinced by God that I needed to get rid of my baseball card collection. I sold every last card, I'm sure for much less than I paid for it. What good did those cards do me? All I could really do with them is put them on a shelf in my room, stare at them, and say, "Wow, how pretty these cards are!" There was no edifying value to them in my life. They did nothing to further His Kingdom or to build me up. I did end up reading a couple of biographies on the life of Roberto Clemente and learned some lessons from those readings. That had value. That served to edify me to a degree.

I absolutely dreaded that lonely feeling that I got when I was surrounded by lifeless things. I was lacking love in my life. I imagined myself in a hospital death bed, all alone with no visitors, focusing on my illness and how all the material things I had accumulated in my life did not matter. This is hypothetical, of course, but it served as a vision of what could happen if I went down the wrong road in life. I would not want to end up regretting not having spent time with loved ones because I was too busy seeking financial success or seeking pleasure. What I've noticed is that a lot of where you get in life has to do with whom you know, or, better yet, who knows you. So, it makes sense to spend our time working on our relationships and putting out a positive vibe when we deal with people. Most of my decisions to do things in life come from my interactions with people, not from my imaginings during my alone time.

If you notice, when people have a lot of material things that don't serve to edify, those things get a lot of attention oftentimes. Trophies are cleaned and accolades are dusted off. We waste time on preserving the things of this world. Jesus wants us to eliminate all those things and follow Him. To do His work, we can't be preoccupied with the fruitless things of this world. If I'm set on going out to heal people one day, I can't be fixated on returning home as soon as possible to clean house because I will have company over tomorrow. Cleaning house shouldn't take too long if we don't have much to clean! Remember, the weak will cling to the fruitless things of this world. The strong, however, will seek out that which edifies and furthers His kingdom. If the things you have have no eternal value and aren't useful in edifying God's people, then they need to go. Check your sentiment. Most things are kept for sentimental reasons. Sometimes this is OK as long as a godly use is attached to the keeping of such things. If not, then God's will will need to supercede your emotional attachment to those things. He who has his priorities in proper alignment will usually be the most ready to serve God when he is called to do so. Be that strong Christian with only edifying things in his/her arsenal, ready to serve at a moment's notice.

Jesus says in Luke 14:33, "So, likewise, whosoever he be of you that forsaketh not all that he hath, he cannot be my disciple."

Chapter 104

A strong Christian looks to fortify his/her vocabulary with exhortative words and statements

And with many other words did he testify and exhort, saying, Save yourselves from this untoward generation. - Acts 2:40

"Tell me who your friends are, and I will tell you who you are." That's a famous saying we here from time to time regarding our identities. The fact is we tend to talk like the people we hang around. Growing up I spoke standard American English, but, around the age of 13, I began to adopt the verbal peculiarities of a family who had West Virginian roots. I still maintain them even though it's been years since I've spoken to the family. Similarly, Jesus talked like His Father talked because He spent a lot of time with Him. Jesus adopted His mannerisms, His vocabulary, and other traits. He spoke authoritatively and assertively because that's how His Father, the One He spent much time with, spoke. He possessed a fortified arsenal of vocabulary to be used successfully in life's situations.

What kind of people are you hanging around? Are they people who are full of positive reinforcement, constructive criticism, and practical knowledge or are they full of something else? Are you choosing a nourishing environment which enables you to thrive, flourish, and prosper? Do the people around you customarily speak words of exhortation in order to build up their fellow man? Are you around go-getters who abound in diligence to achieve success? Do you habitually study and make a fervent effort at retaining usable new words? Do you consult a thesaurus to acquire synonyms to help reinforce and reiterate your explanations for forthcoming oral presentations and/or soliloquies? Do you practice formulating declarative statements so you don't come across as wishy-washy? Do the people around you seem like they strive for healthy communication? Are they habitually gossiping to you about a third party to get you to jump on the judgment bandwagon and form a negative opinion about the third party? Just some food for thought here.

When Jesus asked questions, He typically asked questions that pointed to the truth, people's hearts, and people's motives. Instead of fighting fire with fire when dealing with a hurt person, He focused on the hurt and its origin. That's what we are to do as strong Christians. We aren't to get defensive and try to outanger the hurt person. I will compassionately and sympathetically ask a hurt person who gets an attitude with me, "What have they done to you? A lot of times hurt people want to know that someone cares about their hurt. You can be the strong Christian who comes along and addresses the hurt to get at the heart of the matter. Find out what happened. Ask them who lied to them. Ask them who chose to treat them in an ungodly way in order to cause pain and suffering. Ask them who didn't want them to grow up and walk in Christian strength. The fact is most hurt people are only one caring question away from breaking down and opening up to share their hurt with you. Be the strong Christian who is willing to go the distance to come up with and ask the questions that are necessary to reach the hurt people.

The Bible is replete with verses that promote encouragement. At work I deal with people who unwittingly try to encourage me to participate in harmful gossip. I discourage them by focusing on their motives. I ask them, "What am I supposed to do with this information now? Am I supposed to form a negative opinion about the third party so we can all gang up and try to thwart their chances of becoming a strong and mighty Christian?" Usually the gossips will have little or no verbal response to this type of questioning that points at their hearts.

Satan, knowing human nature, will make a dogged attempt at taking advantage of those with poor vocabulary and poor communication skills. He saw the way Jesus spoke while here on Earth and will do his utmost to keep us from talking like Him. Just as the child molester takes advantage of his/her victim's verbal ineptitude when it comes to discussing abuse, Satan has his tactics to keep the Christian from speaking in a godly way during moments of duress. Satan knows our primal instincts can tend to supercede our calm nature when we are attacked. Have you noticed how some people just start swinging at one another when emotions run high? They don't have the calmness that's needed to organize their thoughts and present them rationally. They let their fists do the talking. Oftentimes the less educated a person is, the more likely it is he/she will take to the physical instead of to the verbal when emotionally charged. There's a good chance they don't possess a vocabulary that is highly devoid of cuss words, so that primal worldly attitude rises up and comes out of their mouth. Oftentimes people lack the descriptors that are needed when telling our stories to a third party. This lack of vocabulary can make all the difference in nabbing a bad guy. That's why it is so important to learn to describe truthfully the things in your world. Learn vocabulary that uplifts and exhorts, and that describes body language and facial expressions. Learn onomatopoeia. Study your tenses and use them formulaically. For example, when God gave the Ten Commandments, He used the future tense. He said, "Thou shalt..." In other words, "from here on out" is what He meant. When I was working at a grocery store the other week, a kind woman asked me if I needed help in lifting a heavy blue pallet. I assured her, "I will lift it; I have that strength." In the first part I used the future tense to declare what I would do and to indicate the lack of doubt on my part. In the second part, I used the present tense to confirm to her a God-given trait I'd be currently using.

Examine sometime the vocabulary of the

weak. You shall know them by their fruit. They will tend to gossip, to lie, to speak negatively in general, to be pessimistic, to walk with their head down, to be self-deprecating, to be insulting, to be wishy-washy or unsteady in speech and action, to show little or no desire for self-improvement, to show no desire to lend a hand to their fellow man. You can be the strong Christian who fortifies your vocabulary with exhortative words and statements bent on uplifting others and yourself. Surround yourself with other positive and loving people that will encourage your growth. You will likely notice a boomerang effect: the exhortation and love you send out will come back to you.

Chapter 105

A strong Christian seeks to implement a plan upon recognizing an opportunity for progress

Commit thy works unto the LORD, and thy thoughts shall be established. - Proverbs 16:3

The gifts and other things God puts in your path you are to use to devise good. On the TV show MacGyver, the main character devised a plan to save the day using whatever materials he had in front of him in a given moment. Similarly, we are to be Christian MacGyvers, so to speak -- by using God-provided resources to get the job done. The job will involve making some sort of progress in the furtherance of His Kingdom. For this chapter, I will use the example of vocabulary implementation as my illustration.

Oftentimes we just need the right vocabulary and to use it well to accomplish our mission. Many people we come across are not strong Christians, so we will have to be their mentor. Most people do not grow up seeing strong Christianity in action, so they don't know what it looks like. The same way people don't grow up with healthy role models, people won't imitate what they don't see. It'll be up to us to model strong Christianity for them. If you see someone devoid of godly vocabulary when they describe their life, help them by providing some good words so that they can have a well-supplied word bank on which to call. In English we have the good fortune of being able to create some awesome hyphenated words which work to attribute our blessings to God. For example, instead of saying "My God-damned leg hurts," say "My God-blessed leg hurts." If we can speak of God cursedly, then we can speak of Him blessedly too. Instead of saying that I have to walk ten miles drudgingly, I say "I will use my God-given legs to walk ten miles to do His work." I will say that I'll lay my God-given hands on the sick. I'll say that I'll eat only God-supplied food. I'll say that I'll go on God-blessed missions. I'll say that I'll use my God-healed body to do more of His work. I'll say that I'll use my God-given tongue to praise His precious and mighty name. Do you get the picture now? I saw an opportunity to use vocabulary in a God-honoring way. I implemented a plan to make progress in my Christian talk which will ultimately affect my Christian walk.

When people lack healthy role models and mentors, they are basically being robbed of the opportunity to see how healthy people do things. I used to wander around society wondering why people were so unhealthy. Then the Holy Spirit reminded me that those people probably didn't have healthy role models to look up to when they were growing up. They didn't have the chance to look at a healthy person and say, "Oh, so that's how healthy people live. That's how that healthy living thing is done." If we go around modeling strong Christianity, people will have an opportunity to look at us and say just that about strong Christianity. They can say,

"Oh, so that's what strong Christianity looks like. I think I might like that." Something to that effect they might say. A lot of the healthy habits I have today I adopted from people who modeled them before me. I saw healthy role models while I was growing up, so I imitated them because I liked what I saw. I liked how it made me feel to live the healthy lifestyle. People often look for what I call "the hidden clause." The hidden clause is a perceived, non-existent ability to escape the consequences of sinful living and thereby make out joyfully. The most frequented place in the Scriptures where people try to find this clause is at Romans 6:14 and 15. People look for verse 6:14a, as if it existed and contained a clause which licenses us to sin all that we want because we are covered by God's grace. Rest assured, God doesn't give free passes on sin. You reap what you sow. 1 Corinthians 10:31 advises us: "Whether therefore ye eat, or drink, or whatsoever ye do, do all to the glory of God."

As the weak tend to lack the I-got-you-covered attitude, they may notice opportunities for progress, but are unlikely to implement a plan upon recognition. I wish I could say that most people are all about self-improvement, but many are not. Most people tend to be about self-indulgence. The strong will tend to set aside self-indulgences to make room for progress which furthers His Kingdom. It could be anything under the Sun that has to do with helping out mankind, including ourselves, to make progress. The fact that you take the initiative to even make a plan shows a servant's heart. God likes and wants servants' hearts. Be the strong Christian who devises a plan for progress, who models strength to others, that they may be inspired and have an example to follow. Remember, Jesus made Himself available to carry out godly plans, one example of which is denoted in John 5:30: "I can of mine own self do nothing: as I hear, I judge: and my judgment is just; because I seek not mine own will, but the will of the Father which hath sent me."

Proverbs 14:22 says, "Do they not err that devise evil? but mercy and truth shall be to them that devise good."

Chapter 106

A strong Christian seeks to acquire more knowledge about the world God created for him/her

And God made two great lights; the greater light to rule the day, and the lesser light to rule the night: he made the stars also. - Genesis 1:16

As we study the Bible, we learn that God created this world for us to use in God-glorifying ways. Wouldn't it be a good idea to ask for His leading in using the world around us for His purposes? Well, sometimes we lack knowledge in certain areas and need to be led by those who know more about those areas. For example, let's say I don't know much about God-made foods, and I want to learn more about them. What do I do? I consult someone who knows about them, probably a nutritionist, perhaps a farmer. When I want to learn about the weather, I contact a meteorologist. When I want to learn more about physics, I consult a physics teacher and/or a physics textbook. God put us here, not so we'd be ignorant, but that we'd seek to acquire more knowledge about the world He created for us.

The world is here for our enjoyment. There are many natural wonders such as Niagara Falls, the Grand Canyon, forests, caverns, marine life, the creatures of the land, of the sea, and of the air. There are polar bears and snow. If you look around, there is a purpose in everything on

Earth which points back to the Creator of it all. Scientists tend to study God's creatures to see what they are good for. Dogs, for example, can be used to help the sick, the blind, the lonely, the weak, and the hurting. Horses can be used for transportation, Oxen can be used in farming. God used a big fish to keep Jonah safe in the Bible. In Costa Rica volcanic heat is used to heat water naturally at a hot springs resort. During the winter, some people can use God-sent snow to get in a good calorie-burning sweat through diligent shoveling efforts, which helps one's health. God sends us some vitamin D through His Sun. He provides some oxygen through His trees.

Soon I'd like to begin studying, with great fervor, physics and chemistry. I failed to take advantage of these subjects when I was in public school, so now I'd like to take advantage of learning about those topics, so I can enjoy seeing God's hand in them and so that I can maybe utilize them in a God-honoring way in the future. This is what God wants. He wants us to learn about the world He created for us so we'll use it in God-honoring, God-glorifying, kingdom-furthering ways.

You may notice how miserable people tend to be when they get involved with only man-made things. People that live in the city tend to be more stressed out than people who live in the country. I live in a semi-rural setting with few neighbors, but when I want some relaxing time in nature with God, I go to a park that is nearby that has some woods by it. I go to the center of the woods and sit on a bench or just walk amongst the trees and soak up whatever God wants to pour into me that day. I will talk to Him as well. I let Him know of my concerns, my prayer requests, my gratitude for the things in this world that He provided. I thank Him for my blessings, and my curiosity wheels start turning if I see something He created that I'm not knowledgeable in yet. It's good and healthy for us to get back to nature. Nature tends to have a calming effect on us. God designed it this way. God-created things in nature emanate peaceful vibes to which we can be attuned if we seek a harmonious relationship with those things. It's kind of like how the aloe plant has curative effects. Nature was designed to benefit us. Satan knows this and has been successful at getting man to avert his gaze and to focus on man-made things instead of God-made things. Satan will prey on human frailties and knows that the sick will tend to focus on their sickness and not on godly missions. Satan wants to rob you of your health, the thing you count on most to get you through this life. That's why it is so important to get back to nature and learn about God-created things so we can stay on track to do godly work in healthy bodies.

Don't be an ignorant weakling who walks around aimlessly devoid of how this world can work in our favor. God designed this world for our well-being, knowing that healthy people can serve Him best. Be the strong Christian who seeks more knowledge about this God-created

world so you can use it to your advantage in
God-honoring, kingdom-furthering ways.

Chapter 107

A strong Christian seeks self-improvement on a continual, daily basis

My son, despise not the chastening of the LORD; neither be weary of his correction: For whom the LORD loveth he correcteth; even as a father the son in whom he delighteth. - Proverbs 3:11,12

Man's ego is the biggest hindrance to his seeking of self-improvement. I have worked with many a fool who, at a young age, thought that they had nothing more to learn in life. Wise old men tend to say that the older they get, the more they realize they don't know stuff. There is wisdom indeed in that statement. The older people get, the more they tend to realize that they are still ignorant in an area of knowledge. The weak are the egotistical ones who purport to have all of life figured out. There is, I suppose, a typical ego problem that accompanies many young people. Oftentimes we have that mindset of superiority wherein we want to feel superior in knowledge in an area, so we proclaim ourselves to be experts after learning a little about something. Some people will think that they have something down pat and that they know it all. I have learned that no matter how knowledgeable I am in an area, there is always something I don't know about it. The mindset of those who seek to boast of their superiority in an area is, in essence, a fear of inferiority. Man fears being seen as weak, so he tries to fake strength in an area. It is actually a sign of weakness to do this. Christian strength involves letting go of one's ego and recognizing the need for improvement.

The strong Christian, realizing he/she is not a know-it-all, seeks self-improvement on a continual, daily basis. I emphasize "daily" because we are to take things one day at a time and not get worried about the future, since our future is in God's hands. Even though I may be considered an expert in Spanish grammar, there are still areas in which I may have some doubt. So, I study those areas even more to gain strength and confidence in them. In Proverbs we are advised to learn wisdom. This is a big part of self-improvement. Self-improvement has to do with acquiring more knowledge and truth so that we can be further enabled to do His work. How can we preach the Gospel if we don't study and learn it? How can we walk in Christian strength if we don't learn about it? The whole point of this book is for you to seek out knowledge about Christian strength so you can implement a strong Christian walk in your daily life. If you are exhibiting Christian strength traits today that you did not exhibit yesterday, because you didn't know of them, for example, then that is an example that you have self-improved.

Self-improvement is not about promoting yourself as a celebrity who has it all together. It's about making yourself healthier, stronger, more diligent, more knowledgeable, and better prepared to do His work. Benefits are to be had with self-improvement. They say education is expensive, but ignorance is really expensive. I can recall years ago foreseeing two different possible futures for myself: one of myself being impoverished, struggling to get by in the inner city on low wages and paying high rent; the other of myself being well-educated living on the outskirts paying minimal mortgage payments. I chose the latter. I find that the more I improve myself, the better equipped I am to handle what life throws at me. I often see uneducated inner-city people struggling to do things their way, often because they don't know any other way. I saw that trap when I was younger and wanted nothing to do with it. I chose not to subscribe to a lifestyle I was not meant to have. I chose knowledge over status in order to avoid a lot of the pitfalls that befall those that are sold on unnecessary, God-dishonoring lifestyles.

I enjoy being around the elderly sometimes because I can often count on them to provide me with some wisdom, if I don't already have it, about some area of life. Those people can help you with your self-improvement. They can also do the reverse, so be careful. Enjoy correction when it is merited. You will only benefit by doing so. Be the strong Christian who sets aside ego to partake in daily, continual learning and self-improvement activities. Evidence of your strength in this area will be tied to the amount of diligence you apply in the improvement department. Lack of strength, as is found in weaklings, is evidenced by their slothfulness and egotism in this department. Remember, we self-improve for our edification and so that we can serve Him better!

Chapter 108

A strong Christian sees sin as problematic and seeks to eliminate it

She said, No man, Lord. And Jesus said unto her, Neither do I condemn thee: go, and sin no more. - John 8:11

In this lifetime we possess free will. Each day we either try to sin or we try not to sin. There is no accidental sin. All sins committed are willfully committed. A person may not realize he/she has sinned, but, nonetheless, a sin has still been committed whether one realizes it or not. The choice is ours. That's why Jesus told the lady "sin no more," because He knew that she had the power not to sin; it'd be her choice. And so it is with us today: either you see sin as acceptable or you see it as problematic. The weak and spiritually blind see it as acceptable whereas the strong and spiritually discerning see it as problematic. The more sighted you are in your spiritual walk, the more you'll see how sin ruins people's lives.

Some people think that God's grace is a license to sin; it is not. I went to a church in Maryland for five years where it was taught that you can go around sinning all you want because you are covered by God's grace. God may not strike you dead with immediacy with a lightning rod, but, rest assured, the consequences for sin have been built into the laws that govern the universe. Have you ever noticed how many individuals who engage in homosexual behavior end up with AIDS, or how those who engage in the gluttonous lifestyle typically end up with all sorts of bowel-related and/or heart diseases? God doesn't play favorites and doesn't give free passes just because you promise Him you will sin "just one more time." Many people don't want to take sin seriously. That's why the world is in such turmoil today. Any problem on Earth today can be traced back to sin. Any sinful activity that man engages in can be traced back to one of the dangerous mindsets of man, some of which I have mentioned in this book. Sin is allowed to proliferate and multiply more so because of man's unwillingness to take it seriously than because of any other cause. Satan has people lulled and thinking that a little sin isn't so bad. Jesus took sin very seriously. That's why He lived an entire sinless life. That's why He died for the sins of the world. Because sins are serious matter. Rest assured that God doesn't play games. He does, however, incorporate the benefits of healthy, God-honorable living into the laws of the universe. People that choose the healthy lifestyle and are disease-free aren't that way by accident. Man's biochemistry was designed by God Almighty to agree with healthy living habits. There is nothing healthy about sin...ever.

The weakness of the flesh keeps man as a slave to sin. Perhaps no more is that evident in the United States than in the fruitless pursuit of the American Dream. The American Dream is actually a true nightmare. I've studied it much and used to pursue it myself until my eyes were opened to the fruitlessness and futility of it. It's something that is often elusive, like the proverbial carrot on a stick which Satan dangles in front of a hungry person. Our hunger should be for a godly lifestyle. In this country I see needless suffering all the time because people are futilely pursuing the American Dream. What exactly is the American Dream? I'd define it as an unnecessary, flesh-pleasing lifestyle sold by Satan to people willing to enslave themselves apart from God in order to acquire, possess, utilize, and show off to one's neighbor the things which are Jones-family-approved and leave man with a God-sized hole in his life at the end of the day. Oftentimes the American Dream will require that its pursuers bow down to the ungodly and be willing to succumb to the gods of sin in order to keep that Dream pursuit going. The Dream pursuers do so because they know that if they refuse, they will lose their job (as in my case at the supermarket) and/or they will end up in jail. And we all know that those in jail have been precluded from Dream acquisition activities. Man's fear of being kept from Dream pursuit or acquisition activities is the one thing that most deters him from living a godly lifestyle. It's the one thing that most tells him not to carry his cross daily. The psychology of it is rather simple: Follow the crowd, keep your mouth shut, stay trouble-free = be able to pursue the dream; Follow Jesus, speak the truth, take a firm stand for Christ = be likely to go to jail.

I decided a long time ago I didn't want to be

pushed around like some spineless deadbeat who refused to take a stand for Christ. God showed me repeatedly how the pursuit of the Dream was fruitless. God proved to me that the Jesus lifestyle was where real happiness and freedom were to be had. The Jesus lifestyle is fulfilling and won't leave you hungering for more, as opposed to the Dream lifestyle. If I ever start to lose sight of my identity in the Kingdom, I start singing a song that goes something like this, "I am no longer a slave to sin; I am a child of God." There is something about singing those words that resonates in me and brings peace to my soul. I think it's because I am singing the truth. Whenever I sing a song that is untrue, the Spirit of God lets me know it is untrue. There won't be harmony between my soul and the lyrics in such a case.

We are meant to live simple lifestyles. I've noticed that the more man relies on his fellow man and the material things of this world, the less he tends to depend on God. Satan is backing the mentality of those who mainly seek out the things of this world to fulfill their needs. That's why God wants us to be educated, so we depend mainly on Him and are less likely to bow down for our needs to those with an evil agenda. The weak are those who typically say, "Well, I can't help but sin daily." Really? Just because you are surrounded by sinners doesn't mean you have to act like them. The strong will take a stand and promote abstinence. The strong will exercise their right not to sin. Study the sins mentioned in the Bible. Learn what they mean and study how Jesus behaved. The DNA of Jesus kept Him from being able to sin. Our DNA is a bit different. However, we can make a conscious effort not to sin. Sooner or later all men will see the fruitlessness of sin. The choice is ours. Will you choose to follow the crowd and sin like it can't be helped, or will you fervently make an effort at seeking to avoid it? It can be done. I've done it. It comes down to a matter of strength. If you don't think you have the strength to keep from sinning in an area, pray for it. God will give it to you for sure. It's up to you to use the strength, though. Be the strong Christian who sees sin as problematic and admirably utilizes strength to avoid it in order to honor God.

I Thessalonians 5:22 says, "Abstain from all appearance of evil."

Chapter 109

A strong Christian keeps on keeping on when betrayed

Jesus said unto him, Verily I say unto thee, That this night, before the cock crow, thou shalt deny me thrice. - Matthew 26:34

I've basically lost count of all the people who've made empty promises about helping me to fix up my property. I think it's somewhere in the thirties. Over the last five years one person after another gave me their word that they'd be there for me to work for pay at my home. People swore up and down and promised me repeatedly that they'd help. Most were no-call-no-shows. Each time I was left with that immediate feeling of overwhelming dread, knowing I'd have to go it alone. I realize now that God was working on my character as well as teaching me about the character of others in my society. I became more diligent as a result and did not hold grudges against those who were not yet at my level of health, strength, and diligence. I essentially was betrayed by those who told me I could trust them. Church people, fathers, tradesmen, professionals, business owners and the like all failed to keep their word and, moreover, failed to tell me that they weren't going to keep their word. Jesus was betrayed as well.

In Luke 14:18 Jesus says, "And they all with one consent began to make excuse. The first said unto him, I have bought a piece of ground, and I must needs go and see it: I pray thee have me excused." It should come as no surprise, given people's poor communication skills nowadays, that most people who promise to keep their word with you will fail to do so. God allows us to experience the heartbreak that goes with betrayal so that we learn to depend on Him more and less on man. Some say Jesus was betrayed by just Judas; others say that He was betrayed by all 12 of His disciples. Either way, Jesus did not get depressed and hold a grudge against His betrayer(s). He knew it was coming and was prepared to keep on to fulfill the Word no matter what. If someone betrays me, I realize he/she did it out of ignorance. That person clearly doesn't take seriously loyalty to Jesus and the Word of God. When people failed to show up to help me at my house, the flesh in me wanted to get angry with God for not sending the people, but the Spirit spoke to me and told me that God was actually protecting me. He showed me that I would've wasted a good deal of His money on those people had they shown up. As I stated before, He was showing me the character of those people, and He was preparing my heart to find the joy in diligence and in manual labor. Knowing that I was willing to show up to work when no one else was was satisfying. I could tell I was growing in strength and that my diligence was increasing. I could see how awful it is to betray someone, which deters me from being a betrayer.

I can recall an incident in which I was

betrayed by a co-worker in the late 90's when I was working the overnight shift at a grocery store. I remember hearing him tell another co-worker that they'd conspire to get rid of me. They tried to mistreat me so I would quit; it didn't work. In the end, they ended up quitting and moving on while I hung in there for three more years before moving on to other grocery stores. I didn't give up or give in. I didn't cave. I kept on keeping on, using my strength to endure hardships in the workplace. I was determined not to be a quitter or play the role of weak and quiet victim. Along Jesus' journeys, He had haters. He had many followers, but, as is the case with anyone who goes around telling the truth, He also had His share of evildoers who wanted to shut him up. He kept on preaching anyway until He was finally convicted of blasphemy. As strong Christians, we aren't to cave in due to threats and haters. We are to keep on doing the Lord's work, not fearing what man can do to us. Satan uses the fear of man to dissuade Christians from speaking and acting boldly for Christ's sake.

Remember, the weak will typically do things like shut up, bow down, give up, get depressed, and get apathetic when betrayed. The strong, however, will keep on keeping on, doing God's work undeterred, knowing that they may stand alone and that God will never betray them. The strong remember that God will continue to be their great Provider regardless of how man treats them.

Chapter 110

A strong Christian seeks to make the most out of every day by being active

Go to the ant, thou sluggard; consider her ways, and be wise: - Proverbs 6:6

Growing up, the world had taught me that manual labor is the enemy. Like many people, I had bought into that lie. Manual labor is not your enemy; laziness is. Fortunately, I learned early on the truth about this. Some people never do learn this truth and spend their whole lives seeking to avoid manual labor, physical exertion, and other things that require effort such as thinking and lifting a finger. I see this all the time. I can tell how people feel about manual labor or physical activity by how reticent or willing they are to engage in it. Do they cringe, cower, or back away in the face of a task that would require physical effort on their part, or do their eyes light up like a Christmas tree because they are feeling eager to get started? I'd fit in the latter group; most would fit in the former. Since the early days of man, Satan has lied to man about manual labor and has convinced him to try to avoid it, because he knows that it is actually a good, God-honoring thing. People do tend to think it's a good thing...as long as someone else is doing it. All the time I see the pass-the-buck attitude regarding manual labor. Either people try to avoid it altogether or they do just the bare minimum to get the results they want. Even in the gym, people start lifting weights and then quit early because they were hoping it 'd be easier. Once I learned that manual labor is my friend, and not my enemy, doors of opportunity started to open up for me.

Both of my current jobs I do, one full-time and one part-time, require a good deal of manual labor. That's what I like about them. They keep me healthy and productive in a God-honoring way as I use my God-given temple diligently. The more active I am, the more results I get. The more I sweat, the healthier I become. I've noticed I have gotten quite a bit of results in life as far as owning homes, vehicles, books, a healthy body, and having good finances because of my commitment to being active every day. If our potential lifespan is limited to 120 years here on Earth, then the clock is ticking, so to speak. Jesus wants us to enjoy life and use our gifts to the fullest during our time here. I've noticed that the people who spend their lives always trying to avoid activity, get few results. They tend to live in poverty and typically live a sedentary, junk-food-filled lifestyle in which they always look to do the bare minimum to stay above the pain line. What's the pain line? It's that imaginary line that people draw for themselves to divide pain from pain-free existence. Many inactive people look to live just barely above the pain line, taking pain medications whenever they dip below the line. Such foolishness can be avoided by living a results-oriented, active, diligent lifestyle. This is what God wants. Back in biblical days, people walked extensively like it was no big thing. A day's journey or three days' journey was not uncommon in the Scriptures among those who did God's work. We are to use our God-given muscles in God-honoring ways such as firemen who rescue people to get God's work done in this world. In doing so, we please God, we serve His people, we increase such an attitude, and we get healthier as a result. As the saying goes "take care of the bod, and the bod will take care of you."

Being active involves not just the physical but the academic too. We are to read God's word actively and then we are to apply it to our lives. We are to live it out and to preach it to others. Recently at work, because of some backbiting and negativity on my co-workers' part, I've been applying some biblical knowledge and modeling healthy conversation for those not in the know. People often don't exhibit healthy verbal communication because it hasn't been modeled for them. As strong Christians we are to model it for them. We are to show and explain the benefits of diligence. Co-workers have begun to ask me for my advice because they see that I am getting results with the way I do things. They seek my assistance when they see that they are less skilled than me in an area. People would consult Jesus because they knew He had answers they didn't have. If this happens to you in your Christian walk, then you are probably doing something right.

The active strong Christian lifestyle is one

that entails doing God-honoring and God-serving activities that get results for the Kingdom. They say an idle mind is the devil's workshop. There can be truth to this. You never want to get to the place where you say, "I am bored." The strong Christian always looks for some Kingdom-related activity to participate in. If you find you have nothing to do, pray for someone. Spend time thanking God for something or someone. Plan out some activities that will further His work. Plan a hike and then go on it. Go to the gym and lift weights and do cardio. Many of the ideas for this book God infused in me while I was doing cardio in the gym. Lifting weights is not useless. Sometimes it's the only exercise some people can get, especially office workers. The benefits of exercise are innumerable. Lifting weights and/or working out makes you better at the things you like to do such as playing sports. It's important to keep that blood flowing, for an unfit person tends to be less willing to apply effort in Kingdom-furthering activities. I see this a lot.

Remember, the weak will go around believing and pushing that lie that manual labor is the enemy and that physical activity should be avoided. The strong will get spiritually aroused, so to speak, when they see an opportunity to use their God-given muscles to do His work. They will be eager and excited about breaking a sweat. Statistics show that people typically don't appreciate their health until it's gone. God takes it seriously and so should you. Don't be a statistic. Be the strong Christian who looks and is joyous about living an active lifestyle in a God-honoring way.

Proverbs 13:4 says, "The soul of the sluggard desireth, and hath nothing: but the soul of the diligent shall be made fat."

Chapter 111

A strong Christian refuses to play the role of cripple

I can do all things through Christ which strengtheneth me. - Philippians 4:13

About a year ago I was working out at another gym and continually saw an older gentleman named Terry working out day after day. I couldn't help but notice he had a spinal deformity and used poles to walk with. His one leg was shorter than the other. He was about sixty years of age I guess. He didn't appear to have an award-winning physique. I began to admire him for his daily attitude of perseverance, especially since the gym was usually empty when he was there. I struck up a conversation with him one day in the locker room and asked him, "What do you have that makes it so that you need to walk with those poles?" He said, "I have cerebral palsy, and I'm not giving up on God." I said to him encouragingly, "You're already beating everyone who is at home sitting on the couch!" Terry's body was crippled, but his mind was not. Crippled people aren't the problem. It's the able-bodied people who go around acting crippled that are the problem.

Regardless of how much or how little we possess in this world, we are to use all that we have to serve God til our dying day. Instead of blaming God, due to a jealous heart, for what we don't have, how about if we use that energy to do something for His Kingdom. I recall seeing a video about a woman who was born with no legs and was adopted by parents who had one unbreakable rule for her: she was never to say "I can't." The little girl with no legs kept the rule and found ways to get things done. She went on to become an athlete, participating in softball, basketball, and become a world-class tumbler on the trampoline. She was inspiring and, perhaps unknowingly, serving the King in a God-honoring way. Nowadays whenever I hear someone say "I can't," my immediate question to him/her is "Who told you you couldn't?" I go right to the heart. I go right to the lie and say things and ask questions that lead to the truth. It doesn't matter if I can only lift 225 pounds on the bench press in the flesh. If God wants me to bench press 500 pounds, I believe He will give me the strength to do so. Whatever God wants you to do, He will enable you to do it, no matter how daunting it may seem. Just as David took down Goliath, God can and will use His "Kingdom magic" in your life in due time.

As able-bodied strong Christians, we are to use what we have to serve Him until the end of our days. Just because where you live is not glitzy and what you do is not glamorous doesn't mean your efforts are meaningless. People didn't appreciate what Jesus did either. People doubted he was who He said He was. He went on undeterred, doing His Father's work. People with the crippled mindset typically suffer from self-doubt and spend their days coming up with every excuse under the Sun as to why they can't do something, why something won't work for them, and the perceived fruitlessness in potential labor. They fail to focus on how and why things *will* work. They tend to suffer from defeatism, which tells them that they won't be successful no matter what. The fact is, as long as you're trying, you're achieving some degree of success. The only failure is the person who won't try. The mentally crippled are those who've bought into that lie that manual labor is the enemy. They haven't been convinced by a healthy role model that God can and will enable them to do His work, with the emphasis being on "His work." They haven't had mentors coaching them along the way, feeding them truth-filled words of encouragement. Satan has convinced them that they need to try to just skate by, applying as little effort as possible in life and leaving the "real work" to the capable. As God's children, we are all capable of doing something for His Kingdom. Sometimes we need a little nudging, especially when we've spent so many years buying into the lies that Satan has told us in an effort to separate us from Kingdom-furthering activities.

Don't be the weakling who constantly cries out, "I'm crippled. I can't do anything!" Be the strong Christian who possesses and exemplifies a getter-done, can-do attitude. This is what makes God smile: a servant who serves Him joyfully. Be the strong Christian who follows Jesus' example in all areas of your life. It's easier said than done, I know, but remember, the more you are willing to do the Jesus thing, the stronger you will be. Now go out and do the Jesus thing!